D1502616

Creating Contact, Choosing Relationship

Richard C. Page
Daniel N. Berkow

Creating Contact, Choosing Relationship

The Dynamics of Unstructured Group Therapy

Jossey-Bass Publishers · San Francisco

Substantial discounts on bulk quantities of Jossey-Bass books
are available to corporations, professional associations, and other
organizations. For details and discount information, contact the
special sales department at Jossey-Bass Inc., Publishers.
(415) 433-1740; Fax (415) 433-0499.

For sales outside the United States, contact Maxwell Macmillan
International Publishing Group, 866 Third Avenue, New York,
New York 10022.

Manufactured in the United States of America. Nearly all Jossey-Bass
books and jackets are printed on recycled paper that contains at least
50 percent recycled waste, including 10 percent postconsumer waste.
Many of our materials are also printed with vegetable-based ink; during
the printing process these inks emit fewer volatile organic compounds
(VOCs) than petroleum-based inks. VOCs contribute to the formation of
smog.

Library of Congress Cataloging-in-Publication Data

Page, Richard C., date.
    Creating contact, choosing relationship : the dynamics of
unstructured group therapy / Richard C. Page, Daniel N. Berkow.
       p.   cm.—(The Jossey-Bass social and behavioral science
series)
    Includes bibliographical references and index.
    ISBN 1-55542-654-9
    1. Group psychotherapy.   2. Interpersonal relations.
3. Communication in small groups.   4. Small groups.   5. Group
psychotherapy—Philosophy.   I. Berkow, Daniel N., date.
II. Title.   III. Title: Unstructured group therapy.   IV. Series.
RC488.P 34   1994
616.89'152—dc20
                                        93-48625
                                          CIP

FIRST EDITION
HB Printing   10 9 8 7 6 5 4 3 2 1   *Code 9448*

The Jossey-Bass
Social and Behavioral Science Series

Contents

Rationale for a Theory of Unstructured Group
Therapy • The Nature of Unstructured Therapy in
Group Settings • An Ontology of Relationship
Within Awareness • The Process of Unstructured
Group Therapy • Patterns of Relationship
• Existential Values and Therapeutic Process
• Creation of Meaning by Individuals and Groups
• Individuality and Interdependence
• Interdependence of Individual and Group
Gestalts • Relationship Dynamics and Structured
Therapy Groups • Relationship Dynamics and the
Larger Society

Preface

The field of group therapy has been affected by a trend in the literature toward structured interactions. Generally, this trend has defined strategies for managing certain communication skills within specific kinds of structured groups. Advantages to learning about these strategies include the minimization of anxiety for therapist and participants and the ability to define predictable interventions and outcomes. However, experienced group therapists are likely to recognize that a good deal of uncertainty is created by the influence of a multitude of factors that interact constantly within group process. Each person brings a unique history to the group, and each can create a new direction for interactions at any given moment of a group's process. Therefore, a good deal of this process is likely to involve unstructured interactions—that is, those that have not been predetermined by a theme and that have not been specifically predicted by interventions of the group's leader.

As a group process develops over time, members are likely to feel less dependent on a leader to provide structure or direction and are more likely to interact spontaneously. Additionally, therapists in any number of settings are likely to find beneficial results from providing opportunities for members to learn from each other through the deepening intimacy that occurs when themes and modes of response are neither predetermined nor structured by the therapist. *Creating Contact, Choosing Relationship* has been written to address the dynamics and learning that occur through relatively unstructured processes of interaction. Although these relationship processes do not have a predetermined form, they are structured by the participants themselves in ways that are influenced by the continuous effect of group members upon each other.

  Creating Contact, Choosing Relationship describes a comprehensive and integrative perspective about the nature of human contact in group settings that do not use structures to predetermine the content and outcome of interactions. This integrative perspective has herein been applied to the communication processes and relationships that are developed between group participants. We have described how this healing process operates and how participants can benefit from engaging in interactions that are not structured.

Audience

This book will be useful for practitioners or students who intend to organize or conduct unstructured therapy groups. Readers will find that theory and technique have been blended in a manner that emphasizes individual and collective enhancement of awareness and direction in relationships. The individual has been treated as potentially creative and self-directing. The person has been described as simultaneously unique and universal, as self-creating and created through participation in relationship. Making a personal identity has been viewed as a paradoxical process that unites the collective and the individual. Meaning is simultaneously created through interpersonal interactions and perceptual processes within persons. "I" and "we" are mutually involved in a cocreative process that develops human identities, lives, and meanings. Therapy groups can use unstructured interactions as the basis for exploring this cocreation and for developing new meanings that enhance growth and direction.

This text stresses that awareness is a key factor in therapeutic interactions. Readers will learn how awareness forms the basis for responsible participation in an atmosphere of freedom. Throughout, this book stresses the importance of awareness for leaders and members, particularly those aspects of awareness that form and improve relationships. It delineates the universal themes of love, power, and justice as relationship processes that form the heart and soul of group therapy. These themes form an inclusive frame of reference that can be applied by any of a number of practitioners in a variety of possible settings. Therefore, psychologists, counselors, social workers, occupational therapists, nurses, and other mental health personnel who work in group contexts will find useful theoretical and practical information in this text. Readers will see that specific forms and patterns of communication have been linked to the interpersonal themes that allow relationships to develop in a group.

In addition to professionals who organize and conduct therapeutic groups, students of therapy will benefit from the learning presented herein. Students will find that this material challenges them to combine various ways of thinking about their ability to experience growth and healing. Affective, cognitive, social, and ethical dimensions of being are brought together. Students can use this text as a basis for understanding how their own growth and development of awareness within relationships interact with their practice of therapy in a group setting. They and other readers will be encouraged to develop a comprehensive theoretical framework that includes their own experiences in relationships with others and their personal systems of values.

General readers will find this material rewarding if they are interested in the integration of psychological and philosophical aspects of life and growth. They can consider the concepts presented in this text in relation to their own understanding of personality as a blend of individual and communal aspects of being. Additionally, the general reader will discover that human growth can be understood as a process of constructing meaning that unites existential, social, and psychological aspects of awareness. Readers can use this material to reflect on how they have constructed their own life meanings through participation in various groups and relationships. They will also be assisted to examine how their awareness of themselves as individuals has been formed through relationship processes and how incomplete relational processes are brought into present interactions with others in social and cultural contexts.

We have used an existential focus as a basis for examining interactions between persons and within the group as a whole. An ontological emphasis is used to understand human functioning. We place importance on the human endeavor to create and develop meaning within a process of being, one that has individual and interpersonal aspects. Substantive components of this ontological focus have been derived from Paul Tillich's explanation of the dynamics of love, power, and justice. Martin Buber's philosophy of "I-thou" relations, as well as gestalt and person-centered theories, has been used to develop a rationale for using group therapy to assist the growth of individuals. Group phases have been explained in terms of underlying themes that reflect degrees of interpersonal relatedness and awareness. Practicing therapists will find that the themes discussed in this text will assist them to interpret ongoing interactions in the context of relationships that form between individuals and within the group as a whole. Group leaders will learn how to bring these ideas to members' awareness. They will also learn how timing and awareness play a significant role in leadership skills. Students and laypersons, as well as practitioners, can use this text to help them recognize themes such as love, power, and self-actualization in self and others.

Overview of the Contents

Chapter One introduces readers to central concepts and topics covered in the text. It proposes a rationale for integrating existing theory and provides a context uniting personal and collective goals for health and well-being.

Chapter Two offers a discussion of two essential process goals: work on personal problems and the development of interpersonal learning. It describes the use of feedback to enhance authenticity, as well as the kinds of personal and interpersonal binds that can be created through the use of denial. It presents the concept of the group as an interpersonal field, with awareness viewed as the context for developing I-thou relatedness.

Chapter Three presents an integrative framework for conceptualizing self-actualization. Self psychology and existential perspectives help describe how the self functions to expand or limit opportunities for growth and healing on personal and collective levels of being.

Chapter Four defines and elaborates the key constructs of awareness, freedom, and responsibility. These are treated as a gestalt since these three aspects of human being affect each other and define, limit, or enhance one another's functioning. Awareness is the basis of an interpersonal field that can increase the development of meaning or distort the human potential to make meaning through exploration and dialogue. Splits in awareness distort perceptions of responsibility, whereas integration of awareness allows responsibility to be grounded in experience.

Chapter Five provides a similarly gestalt-oriented interpretation of love, power, and justice. Various aspects of love are explored, including self-love, agape, eros, and *epithymia*. We have shown how the functioning of love and power can be integrated or split; it can create relationship patterns that enhance communion or perpetuate estrangement. The challenge of creative justice is presented as the basis for opening interpersonal communication and forms of interaction. These interactions are developed in a manner that does not predetermine responses or outcomes.

Chapter Six presents a phase-oriented discussion of the development of relatedness in groups. Each of the following five phases are explored in depth: preliminary socialization, ambivalence toward authority, exploration and self-revelation, patterns of mutual relationship, and ending. This discussion of group process brings together constructs presented in earlier chapters (for example, self-actualization, awareness, freedom, responsibility, love, power, and justice).

Chapter Seven describes how members in a healing group become increasingly responsible for cocreating the interactions that assist exploration and growth. The chapter examines ontological infusion—that is, the ways that members can orient communication toward awareness of meaning within the process of being with one another. As this process develops, meaning is constructed and awareness can then link personal being with interbeing and mutual enhancement of self-actualization. The Taoist skill of *wu-wei*, or nondoing, can be used by group members to allow individuals to lead without imposing or manipulating. *Wu-wei* does not mean inactivity but represents a fearless and nondefensive entry into the interpersonal life of a group. The chapter also explores the links between mutuality, creative justice, and ethical forms of relationship.

Chapter Eight provides an analysis of group therapy theory as described in the text, ethical implications, and applications of theory to practice. It discusses potential conflicts of values between practitioners and institutions and elaborates political, social, and cultural aspects of implementation of theory.

Case examples have been used in several chapters to illustrate the major principles that are discussed in *Creating Contact, Choosing Relationship*. To preserve client confidentiality, we have disguised the identities of all clients and the settings in which they were in unstructured groups.

This text has attempted to provide an innovative, ethically oriented framework for group counseling. This framework is designed to account for interactions that are influenced on an ongoing basis by changing personal and interpersonal dynamics. Although the outcomes of such interactions are not known in advance, they are coherent and understandable. Readers can assess growth and healing by using the constructs provided in this text; practitioners can gain awareness of how individuals and groups can enhance or undermine the development of relatedness and responsibility. We respect the creativity and uniqueness of individuals and particular groups in the theoretical system we have provided. We respect and honor capacities for self-definition and self-direction. Therefore, this book is not designed to provide recipes for successful therapy; instead, it offers an analysis of the dynamics of therapeutic groups that attempts to use modes of communication and the gestalt of love, power, and justice to explain interpersonal healing in human groups.

March 1994

Richard C. Page
Athens, Georgia

Daniel N. Berkow
Manhattan, Kansas

The Authors

Richard C. Page is a professor of counselor education and counseling psychology at the University of Georgia, Athens. He received his B.A. degree (1966) from Denison University in history, his M.R.C. degree (1971) from the University of Florida in rehabilitation counseling, and his Ph.D. degree (1976) from the University of Florida in counselor education. He is a member of the American Association for Marriage and Family Therapy, the American Counseling Association, and the American Psychological Association. He was awarded a Fulbright Scholarship in 1988–89 and taught at the Department of Applied Psychology, University College Cork, Cork, Ireland.

Page's main research activities have been in group counseling and therapy, drug and alcohol treatment, and multicultural counseling and therapy. He has done extensive research on the effectiveness of unstructured therapy groups with drug and alcohol abusers, high school students, university students, physically and emotionally disabled individuals, and persons who live in other countries. More than sixty of his articles—at least twenty on the effects of unstructured therapy groups on different client populations—have appeared in professional journals, including *International Journal of the Addictions, Journal for Specialists in Group Work,* and *Journal for Counseling and Development.*

He has also worked extensively with illicit drug abusers: he set up the first therapeutic community to be established in a prison setting for female inmates with drug abuse problems in the state of Florida, and he worked for three years as a counseling psychologist at a therapeutic community for illicit drug abusers in Atlanta, Georgia. He is a former editor of the *Journal of Addictions and Offender Counseling.* Page is currently a faculty member of the counseling psychology and community counseling programs at the University of Georgia.

Daniel N. Berkow is a therapist for the University Counseling Services at Kansas State University in Manhattan, Kansas. He received his B.S. degree (1984) from Colorado State University in occupational therapy, his M.A. degree (1989) from the University of Georgia in guidance and counseling, and his Ph.D. degree (expected 1994) from the University of Georgia in counseling psychology. He is a member of the American Psychological Association.

Berkow has had three years of work experience in a community mental health center and has conducted unstructured therapy groups with a variety of populations. He has published articles in the professional journals *Counseling and Values, Journal of Multicultural Counseling and Development,* and *Small Group Behavior.* He has research interests in qualitative research methods and assessment of the effects of counseling and therapy.

Creating Contact,
Choosing Relationship

Chapter One

Introduction:
Structures Within
Unstructured Group Therapy

The term *unstructured group therapy* seems to have gained popular acceptance because these groups appear to lack formal structure and systematic organization. Why then write a formally and systematically organized work about this kind of activity? One answer is that if we examine what occurs in unstructured therapy groups, we find that there is indeed an organization to the proceedings. This organization is not imposed by authority and may not be initially apparent. However, a great deal of the therapeutic value of these groups results from an intrinsic human structuring ability; this affects interactions if there is an environment that makes possible the expression of this ability.

Amoebas and rivers may initially appear shapeless and lacking in formal organization. However, if a person investigates these phenomena with care, a definite organization appears. We become aware of it as we learn to observe the role that amoebas play in a large whole, in an ecology of living beings. A river also plays an important role in an environmental ecology. In the same way, we can learn to observe how interactions in an unstructured group

1

relate to a larger whole, an organization formed by the lives and relationships of participants. The apparent looseness and freedom that characterize interactions in an unstructured group form a basis for communications that have specific purposes and meanings. These link specific interactions with each member's ongoing experience and pattern of relationship and with the pattern of interactions that is formed by the group as a whole. What initially appears to be an unstructured form of relationship, if examined with care, thus reveals itself to be an organized and meaningful activity.

The interactions that occur in unstructured group therapy can be considered aspects of an organized form of activity—namely, the activity of human relationship. Unstructured group therapy therefore reflects the structures that human beings give to their interactions. Unstructured therapy attempts to respect the intrinsic structures involved in human communication *without* imposing external structure upon members' communications. Some external organization is always involved in therapy groups—for example, the temporal limits of the group and the physical setting in which interactions take place. However, every attempt is made to optimize the atmosphere of freedom that allows members to create their own process and to discover the intrinsic structures and patterns that affect their communications.

Rationale for a Theory of Unstructured Group Therapy

This book has grown from the authors' attempts to clarify how best to understand and conceptualize the inherent organization involved in human relationships insofar as that organization affects the process of therapy. We had both observed the powerful healing process that can be released through interpersonal communication in a group setting. Yet we found that existing theories of group process had not really met our needs for understanding various aspects of the therapeutic process. Some that we felt had not been adequately addressed in previous theories included adequate descriptions of the interpersonal tensions and connections that members create as they interact in a group, analysis of the modes of communication that affect therapeutic process, and the rationale for members' frequent use of their group to deal with past relationships as they work on present relationships.

We have attempted to address behavior, affect, and cognition within a perspective that views the person as potentially whole and unsegmented. This perspective can be considered a holistic view. The person is seen as functioning most effectively when thinking, feeling, and acting are integrated and are mutually influencing. No one aspect of people needs to control the other aspects if there is harmony in their interactions. People become what they do, *and* their doing reflects what they intend to become. The integration of various aspects of being occurs through creating a whole that is more than the sum of its parts. Personhood can be considered human awareness in developing experiential meanings—that is, meanings anchored in living perceptions and feelings. Experiential meaning arises within the action of an encounter and is not imposed from an external source. Therapy therefore encourages persons to create and experience meaning within the actions of these encounters.

The key aspects of communication and relationship that influence therapeutic process must be understood and integrated to form a coherent theory of group therapy. These key aspects are, of course, defined in part through subjective experiences and perceptions of human behavior in groups and other relationships. We have observed that treating individuals as potentially responsible beings who are essentially free to make choices leads to the most effective results in therapy. Freedom needs to be assumed to be a reality in a theory of group therapy based on the actual perceptual dynamics that lead to constructive change. (The reality of freedom does not negate the fact that people are conditioned by past relationships and are limited by various physical factors and conditions.)

Human freedom is essentially the freedom to choose awareness or to avoid it. The choice to be aware leads to the recognition of responsibility; the avoidance of awareness leads to irresponsibility. Thus, in our view, the experience of freedom and the recognition of responsibility are inevitably linked, both in theory and in its application to therapeutic interactions. The movement of individuals toward healing and growth always involves awareness and cannot occur if individuals choose to avoid freedom and responsibility. The activity of being aware in organizing perceptions is the basis of the dynamics through which interactions are structured in an unstructured therapy process.

The Nature of Unstructured Therapy in Group Settings

The self can be understood as an interactive whole that forms and is formed by relationship (O'Hara, 1984). The self is created through contact and relationship and also makes contact and chooses relationship. The self does not exist separately from relationships, and relationships are a manifestation of the nature of the self. The self is an "I" that is simultaneously a "we." It is formed through dialogue and interaction (Friedman, 1992). Even the most rugged of rugged individualists would have no identity apart from the social and cultural relationships through which the individualist identity was formed. Of course, many other forms of individuality are possible apart from the type that tends to deny the value of "we-ness." Unstructured group therapy is an ideal setting for learning how "I" and "we" are aspects of one process of being and becoming. Although valuing "I-ness" may seem to preclude valuing "we-ness," unstructured group therapy can often promote what Arnett (1989) has termed "the dialogic reality that much of life rests in our creative search for the unity of opposites of seemingly separate camps" (p. 58). The apparently opposite vectors of force created by I-ness and we-ness are reconciled if unstructured processes in human groups lead to the establishment of healing and creative dialogue.

In unstructured therapy, leaders of groups tend to assist members in struggling with their own uncertainty about how to communicate clearly, find answers or directions, and relate to others. Unstructured group therapy becomes structured through participants' choices of modes of communication, attention to specific themes, and movement toward certain roles in relationships. An unstructured format allows participants to confront how their own choices have affected the forms of communication employed in interactions, the topics of concern upon which they focus, and their use of roles. Participants in these groups can potentially learn a great deal about who they are being and becoming with others because they draw upon their own sense of themselves and on their own established patterns of interaction as they confront the ambiguity and uncertainty of unstructured situations.

Initiation, modification, and termination of structures through mutual influence and assumption of responsibility are the process through which group members create their therapy. In this process, a leader's not providing direction is not necessarily a good thing and being directive is not necessarily a bad one. However, there is great importance that the leader maintain awareness and an open and accepting attitude toward members. To set up rules that certain forms of interaction are good or bad would undermine the group's sense of freedom and members' mutual responsibility for forming group process.

An Ontology of Relationship Within Awareness

An analysis of the leader's communications in terms of their being directive and nondirective is not sufficient to understand how healing groups operate. It would be possible to examine members' interactions using their cognitions and concepts; yet such an analysis would minimize the effects that members' feeling states and nonverbal communications have on one another. Members mutually influence not only cognitions and perceptions but also the basic process of being with others. It is, of course, difficult to define and analyze aspects of a construct that is as global as a "process of being." This construct is abstract and only partially within the realm of empirically based science (it is also involved in such realms as art, literature, religion, and philosophy). A person's process of being involves aspects that are immediate and nonverbal as well as those mediated by cognition and perception. Nonetheless, we felt that it was necessary to base our observations on such a global and abstract construct because we needed to address the immediate and nonverbal aspects of relationship as well as those that are cognitively mediated.

A basic "map" for conceptualizing the process of being and forming relationships that proved to be of great value for an analysis of therapeutic groups was that provided by Paul Tillich (1954) in his book *Love, Power, and Justice*. Tillich was an influential existential philosopher and theologian whose works, such as *The New Being* (1955), had an impact on twentieth-century philosophy and theology. Tillich's interest in psychotherapy and the concepts presented in his book *The Courage to Be* (1952) have influenced psychological theorists such as May and Yalom (1984).

Love, power, and justice are elements of the process of being that have relevance in a variety of cultures and contexts. These elements can be seen to be active (in different proportions and with varying degrees of integration) in any human relationship. We decided to use love, power, and justice as *ontological* (the attempt to comprehend the meaning and process of being) categories to discuss the intrinsic dynamics of relationship and communication—that is, those that exist within any process of relationship and communication. Although we can validly address the *epistemological* (the attempt to comprehend how we know and the limits of our ability to know) aspects to comprehend dynamics of love, power, and justice, the ontological aspects struck us as being of equal importance. In this text, *being* includes interpersonal relationship, the relationship of persons to nature, and that of individuals to the potential depth of their own process of being.

The core ontological elements of love, power, and justice are useful as constructs that can help explain how individuals' world views are integrated with a process of relationship, and vice versa. In principle, the integration of love, power, and justice indicates how group members can operate without interfering with one another. If love, power, and justice are operating in disharmony in a group, its members are likely to interfere with one another's integrity, possibly by being judgmental or by selectively disengaging. If power is emphasized in a manner that infringes on love, participants may create norms that encourage autonomy without respecting needs for support. If love is emphasized in a manner that encroaches on power, norms may be created that encourage interpersonal closeness without honoring needs for independence. Justice can be encouraged in a manner that undermines needs for love, power, or both, depending on the norms that are formed to regulate the expression of interpersonal desires and demands. Yet if the ontological elements are integrated, participants in a relationship will see themselves as able to enhance others' experience of growth and well-being, to accept differences creatively, and to understand the feelings of others.

Disharmony between love, power, and justice within an individual's perceptual field can lead to barriers in awareness such as denial, repression, and compartmentalization. If the ontological elements are united, an individual's perceptual field will function as an integrated whole, and all aspects of experience will be accessible to awareness. Thus, an individual's willingness to be aware can influence patterns of love, power, and justice in a way that increases integration in perception and relationship. Similarly, if an integrated dynamic of love, power, and justice is present in a group or relationship, participants are encouraged to accept and exercise their potential to be aware. We have attempted to conceptualize the core ontological elements in a manner that allows us to (1) account for the role that awareness and self-actualization play in the integration of love, power, and justice and (2) account for those relationship dynamics that we have subjectively experienced to be most effectively therapeutic. We did not want to treat our subjective experience of therapy in isolation, and we have made efforts to draw connections between our own observations and relevant theory and research in this field.

We have constructed a theory that can account for a process wherein individuals build groups at the same time that these enhance members' individuality. Although individuals construct relationships, they cannot become individuals without participating in relationships. Relationships make individuals as much as individuals make relationships. We have met with a common misconception among clinicians that for persons to work on themselves as individuals, they need to seek individual counseling; group participation is conceptualized as merely a means to enhance social skills. On the contrary, however, we have found that participation in a group allows members to address two central process goals that have the potential to enhance individuality. These are (1) engagement in communication that provides feedback about individuals' concerns and problems and (2) greater awareness of self through learning that occurs in the development of interpersonal relationships.

Although we value the therapeutic power of individual therapy, we do not believe that group therapy has any less potential power for increasing individuals' awareness and expression of uniqueness. Philosophically stated, this belief in the power of a group to enhance individuality is based on the principle that through the universal the particular comes to be and through the particular the universal exists. In psychological terms, through the collective the individual comes to be, and through the individual the collective has its existence—ideas that we will discuss later.

The Process of Unstructured Group Therapy

Unstructured group therapy can be defined as an organized human activity in which individuals meet with the intention to share their resources for mutual growth and healing without imposing a preconceived structure on the process, dynamics, and outcome. Unstructured group therapy is an organized human activity and, as such, is an intentional activity. The structure of these groups is the result of collective responsibility, is fluid rather than static, and is subject to change when individuals in the group decide to redirect their focus of attention.

This kind of group, during the initial stages of its development, may be anxiety provoking. The process of unstructured therapy therefore needs to encourage members to use their anxiety and uncertainty as a means to enhance awareness. Anxiety and uncertainty represent opportunities for decision making and for the recognition of responsibility. The cohesion of such groups must develop from within through actual relatedness, as there is no external authority dictating a theme or goal. If members feel free to express feelings of anxiety, this communication has the potential to build cohesion.

As implied earlier, the essential theoretical position supporting unstructured group therapy is that responsibility is a central factor in psychological health and well-being. Opportunities for members to have choices and to make decisions about interactions, relationships, and the direction of the group are viewed as environmental conditions that allow experiential learning. The leader of such groups is responsible for helping to create an atmosphere that is conducive to members' acceptance of an unstructured situation that provides such opportunities.

The construct of responsibility is obviously important to an understanding of how unstructured groups can facilitate growth, health, and worthwhile relationships. *Responsibility* can be defined behaviorally, cognitively, socially, legally, morally, or on an individual basis. All of these levels of interpretation imply the existence of a person who is an agent, who can be aware of consequences, and who can be viewed as a being who makes choices. Responsibility implies that, to some extent, the person is a creator of his or her perceptions rather than being a passive recipient of them. A person may be responsible for interpreting a situation in a particular manner, for setting certain goals, for acting in a specific manner, or for maintaining a system of values that affects interactions.

A group situation is an especially relevant setting for individuals to confront how their values and attitudes affect their relation to others. Some individuals may suffer from an inability to recognize themselves as responsible agents involved in a relational process with others. An unstructured therapy group can provide them with feedback and opportunities to observe themselves in this process. By developing responsible relationships in a therapy situation, an individual can gain experiential learning that can be generalized to situations outside the group, thus increasing adaptability and enhancing the individual's sense of engagement. Other individuals may already experience themselves as responsible beings but may believe that an unstructured therapy setting can enhance self-awareness and can challenge their creativity and openness. They may wish to participate in an unstructured therapy group that is organized as a vehicle for exploring styles of relationship or as an occasion for experiential learning and personal growth.

There are some factors that affect the suitability of unstructured group therapy for individuals. This form of therapy may not be appropriate for those who have specific behavioral goals that they wish to work on, who experience excessive anxiety in groups or in unstructured situations, or who have difficulty focusing in this kind of environment. Usually, such persons will choose another form of therapy when they have been advised of the nature and demands of an unstructured situation. It is desirable that unstructured therapy groups be attended on a voluntary basis. If individuals have the opportunity to make an informed choice about participation, this choice in itself supports their ability to recognize themselves as responsible beings.

Members who exhibit compulsive attention seeking, who show frequent outbursts of hostility, or who are dealing with an imminent crisis can be disruptive to a group. Unstructured groups are, however, well suited for helping such members receive constructive feedback that might not be available in an individual therapy setting. Therefore, it would be a limitation to view the goal of unstructured therapy as gaining cohesion by excluding potentially disruptive members. There may, of course, be situational or institutional factors that affect the composition of the group, and leaders may sometimes limit membership to those persons who are less likely to provoke personal anxiety.

Members of an ongoing group who become destructive toward other participants or to the process can usually be handled by other members. It is rare that a member becomes so disruptive that expulsion becomes necessary. Typically, such incidents can be helpful to the development of mutually determined norms for participation. How the members respond to such circumstances can indicate their willingness to recognize responsibility for the direction of the group. These events can be part of the group's coming to terms with fears of deviant modes of expression and behavior. Sometimes apparently disruptive behavior can be a prelude to discussions of feelings that are difficult for members to express or to "own."

It is most consistent with the theory of unstructured group therapy to view clients as individuals who suffer from problems in living, rather than to view particular clients as unsuitable because of a diagnosis or some other label. The purpose of an unstructured group is to allow members to determine their own values and norms. It would be inconsistent with this purpose to have predetermined ways of judging the value of members. The theoretical views of existential-humanistic therapists such as Maslow (1962), Perls (1969), Rogers (1961), and Szasz (1961) support our assumption that all human beings are potentially valuable participants in the human community. This assumption indicates the potential viability of unstructured therapy groups with heterogeneous populations.

Because we focus on the interactions through which individual and collective decisions form a process of being, we do not concern ourselves with questions about the essential nature of human beings. Thus, human problems are not viewed as evidence of a negative essential nature or as proof that the environment has distorted an essentially positive human nature. Problems are seen as opportunities to increase awareness by learning about the nature of interactions and choices that are involved in problems. Psychological problems often reflect difficulties that people have in dealing with conflict in relationships, barriers in awareness, and anxiety concerning the recognition of responsibility. These kinds of problems, no matter how severe, are (at least theoretically) capable of being improved. Psychological problems may be intertwined with genetics, the environment, and neurology, but cannot be completely attributed to their effects. Psychological problems essentially stem from conscious and unconscious decisions that have led a person to diminish his or her own potential awareness.

Clients who benefit from unstructured therapy view themselves as having at least one, and typically all, of the following characteristics. (1) They believe they would be likely to respond positively to an opportunity for interactional learning. (2) They see themselves as having life problems that can be explored in a relational context. (3) They would like to increase their perception that intimacy with others is possible. (4) They want to experience a sense of involvement with others or to have an experience of communing with others. (5) They believe they would benefit from being in a supportive and democratic group atmosphere. (6) They would like a chance to give and to receive honest feedback or would like to learn to do so. Individuals who are informed about the process goals of group therapy may decide that individual therapy is more suited to their needs. A combination of group therapy and individual therapy is sometimes highly beneficial for individuals who are capable of working on their concerns in a setting where they share attention as well as in one where they are continually in the center of attention.

Patterns of Relationship

The concerns of unstructured therapy are in many ways analogous to those of a democratic society. Freedom is presumed to be a psychological reality and a valid social principle. The unstructured therapeutic group encourages the acceptance and enjoyment of diversity; these groups promote a form of learning that acknowledges persons' divergent abilities, values, and subjective experiences. Unstructured group therapy seeks to create an atmosphere of freedom where individuals can explore their ability to trust others and to communicate clearly. Participants are encouraged to be aware that all people can have intrinsic value. This value could be termed the value of personhood if that is understood to mean that individuals are capable of being aware and able to play a part in the pattern of relationships through which they exist.

A basic theme of this book is that our *patterns* in relationships have an impact on our lives and on those of others. These patterns can be discussed in terms of the interaction of love, power, and justice in relationships. Previous patterns of love, power, and justice can represent unfinished business from families of origin, peer groups, or other intimate relationships. Members often recognize and wish to confront the patterns of relationship that they have previously established, especially if they experience a dynamic in the group that is different from that of their past relationships.

Successful unstructured group therapy is often assisted by the leader's (and other members') willingness to proceed without relying heavily on preconceived strategies or expectations. If a group leader enters the therapeutic situation with an attitude of openness and with a willingness to share authority and control, he or she will be more free to be aware of the special dynamics that unfold. A group leader intent on controlling or directing the process can miss aspects of interactions that do not fit his or her preconceived goals. The qualities of unique individuals that emerge within specific interactions are the proper focus for unstructured group therapy. This emphasis differentiates unstructured therapy groups from those that attempt to achieve specific outcomes regardless of the unique qualities of the participants.

Writers have at times differentiated the concerns of counseling from those of psychotherapy. This text, however, does not distinguish between group counseling and psychotherapy, preferring to address a ground that is common to both of these fields. This common ground is the context and process of group relationships and their impact on the process of each member's self-actualization.

For our purposes, *self-actualization* can be thought of as a process through which a person becomes simultaneously more independent and more aware of and involved in relationships. Because we view self-actualization to be of interest to both counseling and psychotherapy, we have used the generic term *group therapy* to describe the activity wherein people meet collectively to further their own healing and growth. Self-actualization can occur in personal growth, counseling, or psychotherapeutic groups.

The term *leader* has been used to designate the individual who conducts therapeutic groups. This usage should not be misconstrued as an indication that group therapy simply consists of a leader and his or her followers. Rather, the initial responsibility for organizing and introducing the group, as well as for determining basic ground rules (such as confidentiality, the duration of the group, and limits for emotional and physical coercion), involves a leadership role. The individual who performs this role inevitably is perceived by members, at least initially, as the group's "leader." He or she thus has a specific significance in the development of a group. It is difficult to understand the developing pattern of relationships in a therapeutic group if the activities that differentiate the part of the leader are not considered. A successful group evolves through developing a decreasing sense of psychological distance between the leader and members and a lessening of the perceived power differential between the leader and other participants.

Existential Values and Therapeutic Process

Therapy cannot be meaningfully considered as free of values, or as limited to encounters with concretely observable behavior. Persons' feelings, perceptions, and values interact to produce change throughout the life of individuals and that of a group. Some aspects of change can be meaningfully considered the result of observable overt behaviors. However, a great deal of the impact that members have upon one another results from nuances of verbal and nonverbal communication that are experienced on emotional and intuitive levels of awareness. The leader of unstructured therapy groups can function most effectively if he or she can be aware of how a group atmosphere develops an almost tangible quality of harmony or discord. To the degree that ontological elements are functioning as a balanced and integrated process, a therapeutic environment is being created.

One of the authors had an experience during a sixteen-hour-long marathon group conducted with illicit drug abusers that taught him how members' feelings, perceptions, and values interact to influence a group's atmosphere. The marathon was being held in a residential drug treatment center with men who had been released from prison to receive treatment. This author, a counseling psychologist, acted as a consultant to this program; the other group leader was not a staff member of the program, but a volunteer who had worked with the author in many other groups.

The residents had been in groups in this drug treatment center prior to participating in this marathon; they typically took part in what were called Synanon-Transactional Analysis groups every week. These were highly confrontive and emphasized forcing the residents to change attitudes and behaviors. Peer pressure and negative labels were used as a means to change attitudes. By contrast, the leaders who were conducting the marathon placed much more emphasis on helping residents to become self-aware and to examine and change their own attitudes and behaviors.

In the first eight hours of the marathon, the members avoided examining anything personal and refused to provide feedback that was specific and focused. During the break, the leaders talked privately and agreed that they felt disappointed by what had happened in this group up until this time. After the break was over, however, and the interaction started again, the atmosphere was completely different. The members gave one another specific feedback in a concerned way and were also willing to express their feelings about the problems that they faced.

This change appeared to the leaders to be dramatic and illustrated the ways that the values and perceptions of the leaders and members combined to produce a change in atmosphere that was therapeutically significant. The group environment changed during this marathon primarily because of the nonverbal interactions that occurred during the first eight hours. Both the leaders and the members indicated that the group had been personally meaningful once it was finished. Members gained sufficient trust to allow for direct expressions of their awareness of each other. The result was a new alignment of love and power in the group. Members then became free to work toward a form of justice that allowed them to give to and receive from each other.

An existential value system underlies our view of the person as a being who is continually formed through a process of encounter and relationship. We have portrayed the person as an active agent involved in a life process that allows for the expression of both creative and destructive capabilities. Creativity becomes ever more apparent as we are able to comprehend peoples' unique phenomenological realities, the worlds that they construct through the activities of perception and association. These worlds reveal various meanings and perceptions of beauty or threat as individuals respond to their encounters with others. Although persons are able to create, they are also able to be receptive and responsive. They not only make meaning actively but their ability to be open and passive allows them to receive impressions and meanings from nature and from others. If members engage and are open to one another, their interactions can help them to balance their abilities to be interpersonally active and passive; they can learn how to use these interactions to enhance the process of relationship.

The participants in unstructured therapy groups can be considered as potentially whole beings. This potential allows a person to be considered without unnecessarily splitting the physical from the psychological process, the cognitive from the affective process, or the "rational" aspects of awareness from the "irrational" ones. An ontological analysis is not antirational, but it *is* an attempt to understand persons as they exist prior to the application of categories that fragment what can be a whole experience. A person's sense of meaning is originally a preeminently experiential sense of reality. Experientially unified meaning can be split by various polarities that develop as conceptual thinking is used to set one aspect of experience against another (for example, controlling self and controlled self, ideal self and real self, love and hate, good thoughts and bad thoughts, or good feelings and bad feelings). Polarities impede self-actualization if the person is not able to realize that he or she is simultaneously the creator and container of these polarities. The ability to engage in relationships is diminished if people project unwanted aspects of polarities onto others (Perls, Hefferline & Goodman, 1951/1980). For this reason, we have attempted to minimize the application of polarizing conceptual categories to our understanding of group members' experiences.

Creation of Meaning by Individuals and Groups

Individuals can creatively bring together the polarities of which they are aware into new forms of being and expression (Perls, 1973). The person is capable of living as a creative being because actualization has creative potentials. Thus, the person does *not* create a separate sense of meaning out of an existential void, contrary to the writings of such theorists as Becker (1973), Sartre (1956), and Yalom (1980). Forming personal meaning within a meaningless void would turn out to be self-defeating even if it were possible.

The person makes meaning through actively participating in interactions, and by actively receiving or rejecting what is given in these. He or she thus becomes aware of meanings that are "created" and "given" through the process of being. These meanings are experiential wholes that connect a person, through an ongoing subjective experience, with others, with nature, and with the process of being. The person can choose to invest energy and awareness in what occurs in encounters with others, and this choice leads to the discovery of new meanings. The person therefore lives in an experiential universe of meaning rather than in a meaningless universe. Theorists who have written about the relationship between individual experience and a universal meaningful process include Buber (1970); Fromm, Suzuki, and De Martino (1960); Jung (1958); Maslow (1962); Rogers (1961); and Tillich (1954). These theorists portray persons as unique creators of meaning who may have to move through meaninglessness to come to terms with an inherent meaning within the process of living, one that is not personally created. The meaning within life and experience that is *not* personally formed is of potentially greater depth than one that is.

The proposition that all meaning is not created individually is an important concept for a theory of group therapy. This concept paves the way for an understanding of the group itself as a healing force. The power of the group as a whole does not come about at the expense of members' individuality. In fact, this power is diminished if members create norms that require a sacrifice of individuality for the sake of group belongingness. The power of a therapeutic group is at its maximum potential when norms encourage and accept full individuality and when the group itself can assist individuals to create meanings from within their unique experience of encounters.

The group can be considered as a gestalt—that is, as a whole that is more than simply the sum of its parts. Similarly, throughout this book, we consider love, power, and justice as a gestalt. When these elements function in an integrated manner, they take on a unique quality of wholeness that is also more than the sum of parts. This wholeness can affect an individual, a relationship, or a group. Perls, Hefferline, and Goodman (1951/1980) write, "Meaningful wholes exist throughout nature. . . . they are meaningful in the sense that the whole explains the parts; they are purposive in that a tendency can be shown in the parts to complete the wholes" (p. 302). This gestalt orientation helps form our frame of reference toward human groups and toward the function of the ontological elements.

The tendency to form meaningful wholes from within experience is a basic quality of human awareness. There may be an equivalent tendency in nature to create meaningful organizations within the movement of energy. At any rate, we have viewed persons as aware beings who can choose to form a more comprehensive and whole experience by coming into contact with and integrating aspects of experience that are uncomfortable or threatening. People can also choose to retreat from increased awareness. The movement toward awareness is enhanced by a willingness to accept freedom as a reality and an openness to the movement of present encounter. Environments that restrict personal freedoms are ones that tend to generate impositions on the movement of awareness. Psychological maneuvers to avoid awareness by constricting and distorting contact in the present or by unnecessarily focusing energy on the past or future also restrict freedom and awareness. Given a willingness to be open and a free environment, awareness tends to increase intensity and extensity. The more members and the leader are willing to encourage freedom for exploring feelings and perceptions, for maintaining authenticity in communication, the more healing and growth are fostered.

If preconceived directions or artificial limitations on persons' explorations of self and others are imposed, a constrained atmosphere results. Members of a restrictive or group environment are likely to experience greater difficulty in making the necessary choices to move toward personal and interpersonal integration (McClure, 1990). In an unfree environment, members may be rewarded for moving toward a prescribed form of wholeness that is an imposed and artificial solution to personal problems. This form of wholeness is a barrier to the wholeness that persons can create within their own perceptions of ongoing experience.

Individuality and Interdependence

People who meet in a free environment for the purpose of promoting their own growth often use their group as an opportunity for experimentation with new interpersonal behaviors and new ways of perceiving experience. They give and receive honest feedback about their feelings and observations as they become willing to trust others and the group environment. If a group promotes authentic communication, members learn about their individuality—how they perceive themselves and how others see them. They learn how their choices affect their relationships with others and how they either accept or avoid responsibility for various aspects of their life process. Although a group setting can provide an excellent atmosphere for learning what it means to be an individual, this environment can also promote an awareness of interdependence. Members learn about the value of interdependence as they discover that the therapeutic process in a group is a collaborative one.

The individual in a group setting tends to become aware that he or she is not in actuality a self-enclosed unit but rather exists in reciprocal interaction with a human environment (Agazarian, 1992). Individual responsibility for awareness and interaction does not contradict the reality of mutual responsibility in this regard. The individual member in a therapeutic group tends to become aware of the importance of mutuality in relationships. If members experience a "wall" between themselves and others, this is likely to become increasingly more permeable as trust and openness are established. Authentic individuality is increasingly realized as interpersonal walls are penetrated and allow for mutual influence (Polster & Polster, 1973).

An individual's option to choose to withdraw from a relationship or from a group always needs to be respected. Otherwise, the potential for authentic relatedness based on choice becomes diminished. If interdependence is to be established on genuineness and choice, then independence must not be sacrificed for the sake of cohesion. As a person's unique and independent movement toward wholeness unfolds within the group process, that individual simultaneously connects with specific others and with the larger group. The individual movement toward wholeness and integration is simultaneously a personal concern and a collective one. The conceptual framework that we have presented for organizing and conducting unstructured therapy groups is based on the understanding that individuals are simultaneously unique and universal.

Unstructured groups provide evidence of the potentially mutually enhancing relationship between individuality and collectivity as members themselves assume responsibility for determining their group's direction. This assumption of responsibility leads to the recognition of a shared purpose that allows members to perceive themselves as functioning together; this recognition also leads individual members to see that their personal contributions affect the establishment of an atmosphere of freedom and trust.

Individuality grows from an understanding of distinctness. People learn how they are different from others and how others are different from each other. This understanding can grow only through relationship and interaction. The interactive process that is necessary to form individuality is an essentially universal human process. Human growth and self-actualization occur through a creative synthesis of the polarity of self and other. A self develops from contact with others, and the distinctness of others is increasingly recognized and accepted as the self becomes strong and healthy. The self has no existence without others, and others are defined in relationship to the self. If self-actualization is a process that is simultaneously individual and universal, there should be great potential for a group setting to enhance self-actualization. There can be no such thing as self-actualization that is a project of an isolated and separate "I". Self-actualization can only be a process that involves persons with persons and persons with nature. This process is evidenced through creativity, awareness, and contact. The self that is actualized is not a thing, not a concept, and not a possession. The self is awareness within life process, awareness that is able to establish a mutual exchange of energy through communication and relationship.

Members can interact in ways that encourage alertness to individuality and universality or they can avoid such interactions. They can enhance their consciousness of individuality by acknowledging and accepting differences in participants' perspectives and experiences. Members can become more alive to universality as they discover some common ground in their life experiences and as they recognize a common purpose and a shared process for which they need each other's cooperation and involvement. They may avoid acknowledging differences if they find them threatening. Members can retreat from recognizing differences by focusing only on similarities in beliefs and experiences and by not disclosing their prejudices or presumptions about those who are different. Members generally avoid awareness of universality if they are afraid of losing their individuality to the group and if they maintain a rigid perception of their group as a place where they are likely to be coerced by others into particular forms of behavior or belief.

The group members generally benefit from the learning that exploration of conflicts within and between persons can provide. Moving toward wholeness does not mean denial of differences or conflicts, although this denial can be used as a defense against anxiety (Agazarian, 1992). Participants can create a growth-promoting group culture without requiring that everyone like each other. However, if members experience a bond of affection and concern, they are more likely to be able to assist each other's healing and growth. A person who feels too isolated or estranged in a group is unlikely to benefit, but bonds of communication with even one other member can sometimes have a deeply therapeutic impact. A successfully therapeutic group allows members to become more able to recognize their responsibility for dealing with their own perceptions of reality and also permits members to use their experience of differences and similarities to expand their learning about themselves and others.

Members may find that there are one or two other participants with whom they achieve a feeling of intimacy, whereas they may feel that some others are distant or hostile. Group leaders or other members may not be able to predict when and how intimacy will arise. However, it is more likely in an environment that promotes freedom, openness, and honesty. The use of structured exercises to promote closeness may diminish the experience of freedom and authenticity that is most conducive to intimacy. Unstructured groups have the advantage of providing an atmosphere where uncontrived intimacy can potentially be experienced. Intimacy develops as members can enjoy differences. Successfully therapeutic groups provide an atmosphere wherein members can identify with the experiences and feelings of others without losing their perception of their own and others' uniqueness.

Educational or structured forms of therapy may also be helpful for some clients who wish to understand how to develop worthwhile relationships, how to express needs assertively, how to communicate empathically, and so on. Yet an unstructured setting has the unique potential of allowing ontological dynamics to be confronted in a direct and open manner; it can permit examination of these dynamics within ongoing interactions because there is no set agenda to which members must adhere. Persons are free to develop their own forms and structures for examining themselves and their relationship dynamics. They are free to establish intimacy or to move away from connections with others.

If experiences of intimacy do occur, participants are likely to fully own responsibility for them. They are less likely to misperceive that an educator or a leader providing structure is "really" responsible for any feelings of closeness. Individuality is enhanced in unstructured groups because members are encouraged to recognize they are creating the patterns of their interactions. Participants can also benefit from discovering a universal aspect to their experience that was not the result of a teaching that was simply handed to them.

Interdependence of Individual and Group Gestalts

One of the dilemmas of many theorists who have previously developed philosophies of group therapy was to explain how individual growth can occur in a group setting. It seems paradoxical that people can become stronger individuals because of group experiences. Some personality theorists, including Freud (1948), expressed extreme skepticism about the overall beneficial effects of most groups on personality development and value formation. It will be emphasized throughout this book that individuals can benefit from (or be hurt by) their group involvement and that they in turn can influence the type and quality of the atmosphere that evolves. This kind of mutual influence can best be addressed by conceptualizing group activities in terms of gestalts or integrated configurations of meaning.

We believe that individual and group development are interrelated and that the ingredients central to the formation of a helpful atmosphere in a therapy group affect individual development; in turn, individual growth influences the creation of a therapeutic group atmosphere. The development of groups and individuals who make up these groups cannot be discussed in a meaningful way in isolation from one another. We have explained the bipolar function of groups on an individual basis (focused on awareness, freedom, and responsibility) and an interactive basis (focused on love, power, and justice). We have discussed the importance of awareness along with its concomitants, freedom and responsibility, and shown how these function as a gestalt to influence the values and self-actualization of an individual.

We have also emphasized that the interactive elements of love, power, and justice affect the atmosphere and relationships that form in a therapy group. Thus, we believe that love, power, and justice exist as a gestalt or dynamic in a therapy group and influence its development. We further view these two gestalts as interrelated. Their mutual influence occurs during any human interaction. For this reason, awareness, freedom, responsibility, love, power, justice, and self-actualization are all relevant constructs that need to be discussed when an ontological theory of group therapy is developed. These constructs explain the gestalt function of group activities as each individual interacts with others and with the group as a whole.

Relationship Dynamics and Structured Therapy Groups

Structured counseling groups can be more appropriate in certain situations than unstructured ones. When members have only a short time to participate (eight weeks or fewer), then it is often helpful for a leader to facilitate a structured group (by using exercises or by having a defined focus). Sometimes members have specific reasons for joining a counseling group, such as learning job-seeking skills, that make a structured group appropriate. Even in structured groups, however, it is wise for the group facilitator to focus on the relationship dynamics that affect what is being learned. These dynamics can interfere with what is being taught or can facilitate learning.

One question that readers might ask is how the dynamics of an unstructured therapy group compare with those of structured groups. For instance, if the leader uses exercises to facilitate the group process, how does this affect the relationship dynamics of a group? If a group is set up to achieve certain goals, such as teaching the participants assertiveness or job skills, do the same dynamics occur that operate in an unstructured therapy group? The answer to these questions is that the same relationship dynamics that affect the atmosphere and interpersonal learning that occurs in unstructured therapy groups also affect the dynamics of structured groups (groups that use exercises or intend to teach members life skills).

Even in a counseling group established around a particular theme or objective, the ways that the members respond to what is taught depends to a large degree on the relationship dynamics that occur in these groups. If a group leader helps members to feel accepted and respected, then they will be more likely to respond in an open and positive way to what is being taught in the group. People who feel affirmed as persons in a learning situation are more able to take full advantage of what is being taught and to realize their full potential as learners. Additionally, they are more likely to find creative ways to apply their learning to their individual life circumstances. It is important to remember that both structured and un-

structured groups can help members to develop more healthy relationship styles and to become stronger individuals. These objectives
are more likely to be realized in any group setting when love, power,
and justice operate as a unified gestalt.

Relationship Dynamics and the Larger Society

The dynamics of members' interactions in a group reflect their dynamics in other social groups. Thus, the theoretical issues that are
explored herein are relevant not only for practitioners of group
therapy but also for any one who is attempting to understand how
patterns of relationship affect human growth and development. Ontological dynamics apply to all relationships because they all involve some assertion of power, some desire for connection, and some
form of justice that mediates the effect of one participant on
another. Any relationship will be created through mutual awareness and will be affected by how participants recognize and define
their responsibility toward themselves and the others involved.
Readers are therefore likely to find that the dynamics that have been
discussed in terms of members' interactions in a therapy group
apply to other interactions as well.

Because unstructured therapy groups allow members to confront universal aspects of being with others, there can be applications for unstructured groups in a variety of settings. Specific
settings and populations can create unique challenges for practitioners. Each setting and culture gives different forms to the activities of love, power, and justice. Individuality and interdependence
are defined variously in different cultures and subcultures. Yet the
creative dynamic that evolves from the relationship of the individual to the group and of the group to the individual takes place in
every culture. The dynamics of ontological integration can be considered universal in nature and integrated on both individual and
collective levels of perception.

The dynamics of relationship can be considered from a range
of perspectives: individual, family, group and community, cultural,
and global. These levels are different perspectives related to a gestalt
that can be considered universal in nature, reflecting the reality that
the whole is more than the sum of parts. There is no one true

perspective about the dynamics of being and human relationship; nevertheless, the more that it can include the diverse forms of relationship that people create, the more useful that perspective will be for conducting groups that can involve members with different backgrounds, personal perspectives, and cultural conditioning. A comprehensive and integrated view of reality that allows flexibility is probably more useful for conducting therapy groups than a narrow view based on knowledge of the "truth."

We invite readers to explore their own dynamics of love, power, and justice while reading this book. Readers can relate these forces to their own experience of becoming an individual and their own learning about how interdependence plays a part in that process. One can extend an understanding of one's own process of relationship to include the processes of others whom one has observed in families and groups. Each individual represents an intertwining of the personal and universal aspects of love, power, and justice. Each individual is affected by past relationships, family interactions, and cultural patterns that have conditioned thought and feeling. Each individual is capable of confronting his or her own pattern of being and able to relate this learning to interactions with others and with groups. We therefore invite the reader to consider not only how ontological dynamics affect the course of therapeutic groups but also how they affect the construction of their own lives and lives of significant others, relationships in which they are involved, and social systems in which they participate. Therapists who conduct individual or group therapy can only become more effective as they learn to be aware of the dynamics that influence individuals and social systems in a universal sense, as well as the specific dynamics arising from particular events and life histories.

Chapter Two

The Importance of Process Goals

Analysis of the dynamics that affect group process can lead to a recognition that complexity and ambiguity are characteristic of many of the communications between participants. Members sometimes communicate on different levels simultaneously—for example, on a direct level, on a symbolic or metaphorical level, and on a nonverbal level. Complexities that occur in communications between members can be simplified by defining certain core concerns, focal points that form a common center around which multiple levels of communication occur. We can make the task of conceptualizing unstructured group therapy easier by relating various forms of interpersonal communication to the basic focal points of therapeutic process. We have referred to these focal points as process goals because they form directions for meaningful explorations of experience.

Two Goals Within Group Process

Process goals are not end products that a group strives to achieve or create. Rather, they serve as anchors within a group's process that allow members to invest energy in their group and to experience it as more than a collection of separate individuals. These goals focus energy within the group and within the present, rather than outside the group's spatial and temporal context. We have defined two basic process goals that can be observed consistently to anchor the process of therapeutic groups. These goals arise naturally (and almost inevitably) within the process of unstructured group therapy.

The basic process goals are (1) the development of a climate that promotes disclosure of individual concerns and that is supportive of members who work on personal problems and (2) the emergence of meaningful interpersonal learning focused on present relationships between members. We can define process goals rather easily, but understanding the emotions and communications that develop around them is often far from simple. Participants may struggle to appreciate how one another's unique personal perspectives, values, and assumptions are affecting their work on problems and their interpersonal learning. However, it is generally when members simply accept one another's differences that the most effective progress on process goals occurs.

Group members, including the leader, are likely to benefit from clarifying their personal assumptions and values. Understanding the effects of one's own personal history is also helpful, especially insofar as it affects one's awareness of others. If members assist each other in clarifying personal values and the effects of personal history, they can gain mutual understanding that assists their movement toward constructive work together. A member's values and history play a part in expectations and hopes and help determine what each participant believes would be meaningful or therapeutic in interacting with others.

A group is most likely to facilitate therapeutic directions within ongoing interactions if members collectively both perceive the value of addressing process goals and accept responsibility for moving toward them. Members can have a constructive impact on their group's process if they disclose thoughts and feelings that demonstrate an awareness of others as persons and an awareness of self as a participant involved with others. These kinds of disclosures help to create a climate wherein it becomes possible to explore problems and acknowledge present relationships as real.

The two process goals tend to arise within group process as members acknowledge involvement with one another. However, members can form resistances toward the process goals as these begin to become apparent. Resistance can be evidenced by retreating from problems that are disclosed, minimizing the significance of problems, and minimizing or avoiding meaningful interpersonal contact. Resistance is sometimes expressed as an unwillingness to invest one's individuality in a group's process, as a lack of respect for the personhood of others, or as avoidance of responsibility for determining directions for growth. These kinds of resistant interactions can create a group climate that reflects interpersonal defensiveness and restricts open communication (Agazarian, 1992). Group members cannot be forced to deal with resistance, since attempts to force awareness usually increase it. If, however, members work through the anxieties involved in resistance, they may choose to make their group a place where it is safe to discuss problems openly and to acknowledge interpersonal relatedness as meaningful.

Members' perceptions of the role of the group leader are often based on their assumptions that the leader has theoretical and experiential knowledge that will help facilitate movement toward these two goals. Members often assume, or would like to assume, that the leader is a person who can promote a group atmosphere wherein members can be comfortable in sharing problems. Participants often view their group leader as a person who they believe can assist them in learning from present relationships.

A leader's effectiveness in addressing the process goals is enhanced by the development of sensitivity to a variety of communication styles and personal needs and problems. If a leader lacks this sensitivity, he or she may encourage group members to avoid dealing with their different ways of communicating; the members may adopt the leader's norms for defining the nature of valid problems for discussion and valid styles for interpersonal relationship. Members may then covertly or overtly strive for approval, recognition, and attention in a manner that undermines genuine communication and honest expression of feeling. Those who most closely approximate the norms of the leader may then dominate group interactions. If members feel that goals are being imposed on them, they may "revolt" at some point in the group's process or they may terminate their involvement. Therapeutic use of the two process goals can also be diminished if the leader or other members seek harmony at the expense of individual differences. Members may then avoid expressing disagreement, may ignore uncomfortable feelings, or may become detached observers who avoid expression of divergent views to maintain acceptance.

Members may not always perceive themselves as being in a group to learn about responsibility in communication and interaction. Participants may also not see themselves as being in a group to discuss personal problems and concerns or to learn about interpersonal relationship processes. Some members may simply want to experience being with others or may arrive with little awareness of how such groups can contribute to integration and growth. Participants may be unsure about what problems (if any) they want to discuss and may be quite uncertain about how (and whether) to form relationships with other members. If their group's process begins to be perceived as trustworthy by these members, they are likely to decide how they can disclose concerns and how they can form relationships with others. An atmosphere of trust tends to facilitate the emergence of the process goals even if members are naive about the process of therapy and do not know what to expect.

Members who have expectations based on previous group experiences will come to recognize that their current group presents unique dynamics that affect the disclosure of concerns and the development of relationships. The present group will never have exactly the same dynamics as other groups. Comparisons with previous experiences or unrealistic expectations based on other groups' dynamics can be used to avoid dealing with the process goals within the context of a present group (Leszcz, 1992; Yalom, 1975). Similarly, unfavorable comparisons of present relationships with past ones can have the effect of suppressing current opportunities for communication. Each group is a unique event, and therapeutic interactions occur as members are able to express themselves as unique individuals and to accept other members in the same way.

The process goals that we have defined tend to arise within an existential framework as members address ultimate concerns. For example, it is possible that focusing on anxiety about freedom or death would involve disclosure of personal problems. If they are willing to disclose anxiety about freedom or death, members often relate these experiences to difficulties that occur in making choices, maintaining personal goals, or achieving a sense of identity. Freedom and death may be underlying themes that are not discussed overtly. Additionally, anxiety related to freedom and death can be associated with specific career concerns, relationship dilemmas, or negative self-concepts. Confrontations with freedom or death are thus themes that intertwine with various personal concerns and problems. Similarly, confrontation with anxiety related to meaninglessness or isolation often occurs as members discuss ongoing relationships, either within their group or outside their group. For example, participants might discuss how feelings of meaninglessness affect their relationships with significant others or with those at work. Members may disclose how perceptions of isolation affect their interactions with others within or outside their group.

The importance of the two process goals in unstructured group therapy is not limited to any particular theory. For example, the study of psychoanalytic groups, existential groups, and person-centered groups leads to the conclusion that the two basic process goals are addressed in each theory. Psychoanalytic groups move toward an atmosphere where members are comfortable discussing problems and current relationships by encouraging *free association* (Wolf & Schwartz, 1962). Free association is a process of the uncensored sharing of thoughts and feelings in a nonjudgemental environment. Existential therapy groups move toward the process goals by emphasizing self-awareness and responsibility issues for participants (Corey, 1990). Person-centered groups are based on the philosophy that participants can be trusted to know how they can best use their group to enhance their own self-actualization (Rogers, 1970). The process goals can be identified as aspects of self-actualization if we note that as people learn to live fully and effectively (as they self-actualize), they learn how to develop worthwhile relationships with others and how to confront problems creatively and constructively.

Therapists often align themselves with schools of therapy according to their congruence with a particular relationship style. Within the context provided by a theoretical frame of reference, individual group leaders will define an orientation toward interpersonal learning. Leaders also develop a personal style that helps facilitate an atmosphere wherein members can feel comfortable to work on personal problems, difficulties, or unfinished business. Developing an awareness of process goals contributes to our understanding of how leaders and members develop interactions in a group setting in a therapeutic or nontherapeutic manner. An effective group leader respects and encourages individuals' intrinsic motivation toward therapeutic use of their group. This leader does not attempt to instill motivation through an authoritarian stance. Such a stance tends to foster resistance and to generate an environment of dependency or mistrust.

Members of various types of unstructured therapy groups (person-centered, existential, and psychoanalytic) often choose to use their time together to develop relationships and to discuss concerns and problems. We assume that if a group develops an open and therapeutic atmosphere, members are likely to choose to move toward the process goals. These goals are not the property of any particular theory but emerge within group process as members define for themselves how to use their time together constructively.

The Principle of Inclusivity in Unstructured Therapy Groups

A leader who organizes a therapeutic group often has the option of selecting members who are either relatively heterogeneous or homogeneous (according to various more or less overt characteristics). A group leader who believes that creativity is important may well believe that heterogeneous membership is desirable. Members' ability to relate creatively and empathically is likely to be stimulated and challenged in a heterogeneous group. The capability to accept divergent views and experiences of problems is also likely to be challenged if membership is heterogeneous. If people are excluded because they do not fit a certain profile, a leader may be organizing a group according to principles that inhibit the development of creativity and lessen opportunities for members to learn to accept diversity.

Of course, communication can be facilitated if members initially "speak the same language." Moreover, groups are often organized around a shared problem, such as drug addiction or issues of loss. Members may also have certain similarities in world views. Yet they are likely to discover that there are important differences in their perspectives. An atmosphere of freedom is a central factor that affects members' opportunities to learn about aspects of experience that are divergent from norms that have been adopted by members outside or inside the group.

One reason that groups are often developed around specific initial concerns is practicality—that is, certain settings are often oriented toward specific concerns. Another reason is that anxiety about meeting with strangers can be diminished if participants believe that others in their group will be like them. A policy that encourages diversity in views and backgrounds of members may heighten the initial anxiety of an unstructured situation. However, members of such groups often discover that they learn a great deal about who they are and how they are with people simply by being with others who initially seem different. In particular, members are often impressed by universals that they encounter in such a situation. People who are uncomfortable with individual differences may not choose to attend a heterogeneous group. However, if participants choose to attend in spite of anxiety about the inclusion of others with divergent problems or social status, they are likely to find that they can accept these differences and can grow from "exercising" their ability to be accepting.

Members of therapy groups that are homogeneous in such categories as social status and cultural background and that isolate themselves from conflicting feedback from others behave like other social or political groups. Such groups are likely unquestioningly to accept mutually shared prejudices and defenses, may develop a kind of "groupthink" based on common assumptions, may deny awareness of events that do not fit prejudices, and may develop a sense of identity based on their "exclusive" group characteristics (see Janis, 1982). Members may develop a rationale for maintaining one pattern of relating to others in their group and another pattern for relating to people outside of it. However, all the aforementioned problems that can occur in homogeneous groups are only likely to arise if they are encouraged by the leader. If that person initiates a "flight from freedom" in a homogeneous group, members can be induced to adopt norms that assist each other to avoid anxiety. Group leaders may also encourage members to adopt restrictive norms to maintain a position of prestige. By contrast, if a group's leader is comfortable with open discussion and the exploration of experience, members are likely to move through an initial tendency to want to be the same as others to an increased awareness of each others' unique concerns and individual perspectives.

One potential benefit of an unstructured group is the opportunity to help participants to develop a less exclusive and more open approach toward interpersonal relationships. Of course, people should not be pressured into attending if their awareness of difference leads to unacceptable anxiety; but as individuals are able to accept varied aspects of other people's experience, they not only develop an attitude of openness to others but may also develop an acceptance of divergent aspects of their own experience. Members who become open to other participants do not *necessarily* become more open toward their own experience, but they often realize that valuing the first thing implies value in the other. Typically, a member must explore his or her own feelings in a free manner to be able to extend self toward another member seen as "different."

Some groups may gain cohesion by accepting members with diverse concerns but may demand a common degree of "ego strength," or ability to cope with anxiety, from members (Yalom, 1975). The drawback to the generally effective strategy of excluding members who lack ego strength is that participants will not have a chance to learn that no unbridgeable gap exists between the strong and the weak. A person who is evidently strong can learn about his or her own hidden weaknesses by learning to accept a member who seems weaker, more unbalanced, or more fragile. Similarly, a person who is convinced that he or she is inherently weak or unstable may find that he or she has been denying strengths. Sometimes individuals suppress their abilities to cope constructively or creatively with anxiety because they are used to feeling victimized or out of control. Creative abilities can be evoked within the context of relationships formed with other members who can encourage the recognition of strengths. This recognition can occur if individuals are willing to share their life problems with others and are able to get feedback from others concerning how they handle stress and difficulties.

Heterogeneity may not be useful if participants are included who are likely to experience discomfort or hostility in a group setting (Korda & Pancrazio, 1989). Nevertheless, the more heterogeneity that is acceptable within a group, the broader the base becomes for interpersonal learning and mutual work on personal problems or unfinished business (Wolf & Schwartz, 1962). Initially, the degree of heterogeneity is defined by differences in overt characteristics such as nature of presenting problem, age, income, education, religion, ethnicity, and skin color. As a group develops, heterogeneity is demonstrated by differences in less overt characteristics, such as life themes, emotional concerns, attitudes, perspectives, and values. This subtle evidence of heterogeneity is likely to emerge even if overt characteristics initially appear to be similar. Heterogeneity becomes increasingly tolerable in a group as norms are established that allow the norms themselves to be challenged and as these norms provide acceptance of diverse views, perspectives, and feelings.

Therapeutic groups may be conducted in institutions, such as prisons or hospitals, that may tend to force norms, values, and expectations on participants. The recognition that institutions sometimes impose structure and that people are sometimes more comfortable in that event does not necessarily negate the opportunity for a therapist to employ the principles of unstructured therapy within a given situation. If members of a group come to see themselves as responsible for the direction of therapy and become aware that relationships within the group are providing important learning, the two basic process goals are likely to emerge as central foci for the group.

Authenticity in the Group Therapy Setting

What group members do to move toward the two process goals is work that requires authentic communication. If members are not honest about their concerns, they will minimize the potential of their group to assist them to deal with these issues. Similarly, if members communicate in a manner that is not authentic, they will develop relationships that are distorted rather than healing. They also limit their ability to develop open communication in their relationships. Thus, working on problems has the potential to enhance relationships, and developing relationships allows members to feel free to discuss problems.

People generally avoid disclosing their concerns and difficulties as a result of past learning or to protect their self-image (Egan, 1970). The images that individuals project to others may involve conscious decisions about which attitudes and feelings a person will express. These decisions are the result of an intention to influence the perceptions of others. A projected self-image can also be the result of habituated patterns of behavior that involve very little conscious attention. In either case, the self-image that people project to others can play an important part in their overall sense of identity. Identity, one's sense of oneself, includes self-perceptions that have formed into a coherent image over time. Perceptions of self generally include both an image of how one believes one has been seen by others and one's hopes or expectations of how one will be viewed. The self-image is therefore not the portion of one's sense of self that arrives from immediate awareness or from present sensory experience; it results from the processing of past experiences and projections into the unknown future. People generally learn that the image of self that is shown to others will influence their success at work and can have a powerful effect on personal relationships, especially insofar as certain roles are involved in these relationships.

Sometimes people can develop a strong attachment to negative self-images that have influenced their survival. One of the authors once worked as a counseling psychologist in a drug treatment center, and one responsibility of this consulting job was to lead therapy groups. For about a year, a client named "Larry" attended an unstructured therapy group at the center. Larry had been a heroin addict for at least ten years prior to being imprisoned for armed robbery.

Larry described a life-style on the streets that was completely at variance with the way he acted in his group. On the streets, there were several people who wanted to kill Larry because he had stolen drugs or money from them. Larry described himself as being a bad actor when he was a member of the drug culture prior to entering the treatment center. He had developed a strong identity as a "bad

guy who people should not mess with." The author had the impres-
sion that Larry developed this type of self-image when he was a
drug addict because having a negative self-identity was better than
having no identity; also, of course, showing others in the drug
culture that he was dangerous was related to his own survival and
to his ability to get money to support a drug habit.

People often have a great emotional investment in their projected self-image. Because the two process goals require authentic
communication, movement toward them provides a challenge to
manipulative or habitual attempts to project a certain image.
Members are likely to confront their emotional investment in their
self-image as they move toward the process goals, regardless of
whether this image is positive or negative or is consciously chosen
or unconsciously habitual. It is not uncommon for group participants to find that their consciously chosen image is only projected
to a limited extent, whereas unconscious patterns of behavior affect
others' perceptions to a greater extent than was imagined. As
members learn about their investment in a self-image, they may
assume responsibility for meeting needs that contradict that image.
These unmet needs have an impact on relationships, although people may choose not to be aware of it. As members learn how they
affect others, they can use this learning to change previous patterns;
they can disinvest themselves in the past or future orientation and
can reinvest themselves in present-centered communication. Their
interpersonal process can become self-actualizing rather than
"image-actualizing" or "role-actualizing."

People tend to devalue spontaneity as they learn that society
(beginning with the family and extending through various other
social institutions) rewards consistent enactment of certain images.
As people learn that performing a role can be essential for their
social identity, they can come to believe that individuals *are completely defined* by their roles. They may believe that "who one is"
is identical to the role that one plays (Jourard, 1971). If people
identify with a role, they have inevitably disowned aspects of self
that do not conform to it. People can, for example, disown their
childish aspects to play the part of an adult or can disown their
adult aspects to play the role of a helpless child. People frequently

repudiate feelings and thoughts that they have learned to perceive as negative.

People can disown aspects of their experience by minimizing the intensity or importance of feelings, by attributing their own rejected thoughts and feelings to others rather than to themselves, or by diverting attention from uncomfortable feelings or perceptions within ongoing encounters. Other members in an unstructured group are often able to see the aspects of self that an individual is attempting to disown. These members can provide reactions concerning the nature of thoughts or feelings that a participant is denying and can show this participant how repudiating these affects who and how he or she is with others. This type of authentic feedback can greatly help members to move toward the two process goals. If they can be aware of feelings or behaviors that they have denied, members can become more honest about problematic historical events (for example, family relationships or sexual and romantic concerns) and can develop relationships with others that are not based on image projection.

It has already been said that the client named Larry was able to develop new roles in the unstructured therapy group that was conducted by one of the authors. These new forms of relationship were at variance with the types of roles and images he had projected while living as a heroin addict. When Larry was a member of the therapy group, he consistently displayed concern with the welfare of the other members who also had drug abuse problems. He was one of the members who could be counted on to support and empathize with other members who were experiencing distress in their lives.

Larry was able to gain new perspectives about the possibilities of human relationships from being in this unstructured therapy group. Of course, learning new roles and perspectives is not a guarantee of permanent change. When Larry left the drug treatment program, he became involved in familiar relationship patterns and eventually started using heroin again. He did reenter another drug treatment program voluntarily at a later time. Once he reentered this program, this author lost contact with him.

Denial and Self-Image Protection

Members may discover that they have denied certain problems to feel secure and comfortable about themselves. If they have learned that others will respond positively to their self-control and competence, participants probably learned to deny those feelings and experiences that led them to feel out of control or incompetent. If their group leads them to communicate authentically about their experience, members often discover the existence of "unacceptable" memories, attitudes, thoughts, or feelings. They also may discover that they have avoided awareness of the price that they had to pay for their denial of unacceptable feelings or realizations. This price is often found to include one or more of the following: emotional deadness, occasional experiences of panic or dread, recurrent anxiety, persistent feelings of frustration, uncomfortable internalized tension, and estranged relations with significant others.

Patterns created in past relationships are carried into present ones when these patterns affect present perceptions, modes of communication, and strategies for dealing with needs and feelings. Perls (1973) refers to these patterns that originate in the past as "unfinished business" because individuals' awareness and energy can be bound up in incompleted transactions from significant past relationships. The present and past become intertwined as people repeat past patterns of emotion and communication. Unfinished business can become finished only when members find a new form of relationship in the present that allows them to feel finished with a past form. However, individuals can generally grow from acknowledging the power of unfinished past relationships and dealing with whatever feelings and perceptions they have denied. Others in their group can facilitate a member's confrontation with unfinished business if they are able to be honest about how they react to that person.

The self-image that interferes with an authentic present encounter has been described as arising from an accumulation of experiences over time that affects how a person attempts to survive, to gain rewards, and to avoid punishment (Berne, 1964). Social conditioning and introjected values can be seen as central to the formation of the self-image (Perls, Hefferline & Goodman, 1951/ 1980; Rogers, 1961). One aspect of this conditioning process is that people may learn to keep thoughts and feelings to themselves. Over time, they may well have learned to discount their own feelings and perceptions and to misrepresent to *themselves* what they have felt, experienced, and thought in the past.

To maintain aspects of the sense of self that they have created by misrepresenting experience, people will habitually deny whichever feelings and thoughts are incompatible with their self-image. Maintenance of the self-image therefore is a central factor in many individuals' personal and interpersonal problems, as well as in the difficulties that they have in disclosing these problems to others. The self-image is a construct that will become reified insofar as an individual identifies this image with continued survival. The self-image will then be protected against feelings or thoughts that threaten its cohesion. Group members can help each other to learn that they can survive together and accept one another without relying on rigidly maintained self-images.

The Importance of Feedback

As members discuss problems and participate in interpersonal encounters in a free environment, they invite feedback from others in their group. Feedback is a key aspect of the process by which group members can take advantage of the therapeutic potential of their interactions. As members share problems, they demonstrate trust that there will be value to the feedback that other members may contribute. Without this trust, members would hesitate to disclose problems that might reveal some of their inadequacies, questions about themselves, and difficulties in relationships. If members believe in the value of others' feedback, they are far more likely to move toward the two process goals.

Although the term *feedback* is useful, it tends to minimize the multilevel nature of interpersonal communications. At the same time that a member is receiving information in the form of feedback, that person is sensing whether the other member genuinely cares and understands. The member who appears to be providing the feedback may simultaneously be sensing whether the other member is trustworthy. On one level of communication, there is a process of information exchange; on another level, there is nonverbal interaction of an intuitive and emotional nature whereby members learn whether they can have confidence in one another and be open with one another. Members are not always looking for information that will help them to correct ineffective patterns of relating to others; they are often hoping for experiential awareness that others are "with them" and can understand and care (Leszcz, 1992; Rogers, 1970; Yalom, 1975).

Some aspects of nonverbal communication are subtle, and the impact of these communications may be distorted or diminished if they are made the focus of verbal exchange. For example, subtle nonverbal signals may indicate the beginnings of friendship; however, to focus on these messages verbally would create unnecessary anxiety and inhibit the development of the friendship. If there is a contradiction between verbal content and nonverbal cues in communication, members can become uncomfortable with one another without clearly understanding how their unease has arisen. At the same time, members may feel accepting of one another in spite of apparently critical exchanges if there is an experience of mutual understanding based on congruence between verbal and nonverbal messages.

The full nature of an interaction cannot be comprehended if it is judged by the exchange of content alone. One member may appear to be providing feedback, but may actually be seeking to gain information from the other during the exchange. Additionally, the member who is offering feedback may simply be communicating in a nonverbal way, "I care about you" or "You're someone worth knowing." Often, the nonverbal interpersonal awareness that members explore during interactions is more important to them (and more difficult to address at the time it occurs) than is the surface content. Nonverbal messages may generate a cumulative impact that develops over several interactions, and these messages may need to be addressed verbally at that moment when their impact has become noticeable.

Feedback is essential to the process by which the two basic process goals are approached and developed. According to Corey (1990), "feedback that is specific and descriptive rather than global and judgmental is the most helpful" (p. 67). When information is accurate and specific, it allows members to focus on problems in a direct manner and to understand clearly how other members see them. Feedback can also help participants to question the labels or stereotypes that they may use to evaluate themselves and others.

Members who disclose problems often value the unexpected perspectives that other members may bring to their awareness through the process of feedback. Learning about others' points of view can help members look at options for forming values and behaviors that they had not previously considered. People outside the group who are closest to members may hesitate to be direct or may present their perspectives in a controlling manner, simply because they are being personally affected by the problem with which the member is dealing. Group members may have become habituated to a view of reality that is reinforced by others with whom they have formed close relationships. Participants in a therapy group engage themselves in a situation that allows them to receive new information from others outside their problem situations or relationships; an unstructured group thus becomes an important source of change in members' perceptual maps of reality.

Problem Solving and Awareness

Group experience is likely to confirm some aspects of a member's perceptual map of reality and challenge other aspects. This map tends to become a self-fulfilling prophecy. By acting as if a certain assumption is true ("people find me annoying"), a person finds that those expectations are indeed confirmed. A person develops certain core beliefs that form guideposts for the interpretation of experience. If a high level of trust has been reached in a group, members begin to give and receive feedback that may be far more direct and honest than they will receive elsewhere. The group has the potential to confirm or challenge core beliefs and interpretations of present and past experience. Feedback from other members has generally been identified in the literature as a factor that can promote healing and growth if it is used by a person constructively to change assumptions and expectations about self and interpersonal interactions (for example, see Leszcz, 1992; Morran, Stockton, & Harris, 1991; Rogers, 1970; Yalom, 1975).

The stress associated with living in a society that is competitive, and that can also be isolating and confusing, can be at least temporarily alleviated by an unstructured group. A successful unstructured therapeutic group can serve as an integrative emotional experience that helps members feel stronger and better about themselves when they leave their group to reenter their daily world. We cannot judge a group as truly successful if members have not found some new learning and if they have made no changes in their process of being that might be applied outside the therapy situation. If groups are ongoing, it is easier to judge whether this kind of learning is taking place.

A leader's recognition that group members use the therapeutic setting to disclose and discuss personal problems can lead to different conclusions about treatment. One possible conclusion is that groups should be oriented around one specific central and shared problem. The members of such groups might be expected to have a degree of prior consensus in their evaluation of life circumstances and their concepts of desirable and undesirable life goals. Another possible conclusion is that groups should focus on how members process information and perhaps assist these people in developing needed problem-solving skills. This conclusion would lead to organizing groups that are cognitively oriented, with the goal of improving members' effectiveness in dealing with their life problems. A third possible conclusion, which relates specifically to any theory of unstructured therapy groups, is that people can individually find ways and means to use their group constructively. A group setting that has not been specifically structured to address certain problems or problem-solving processes can still be useful for these purposes.

If predetermined structures are imposed on the manner in which problems or problem solving will be addressed, members may miss out on some of the resources potentially available in their group. On the one hand, if problem solving is defined as a cognitive activity, members might only focus on cognitions *about* relationships and miss opportunities for experiencing present emotional relatedness. On the other hand, a cognitive focus might be appropriate for a member who is able to be involved emotionally with others but who has problems understanding the patterns involved in these involvements. Because unstructured groups do not have a predetermined focus, members learn that they can help each other in ways that are individually appropriate.

Another difficulty that can arise from predetermined structures is that "problem areas" can be defined beforehand in a manner that restricts self-exploration and that may inhibit disclosures of problems that do not fit the agenda. Members may feel "steered" toward certain preconceived forms of interaction and thus will not assume responsibility for discovering their own unique mode of interacting authentically, helpfully, or caringly. An unstructured setting thus requires that members take relatively equal and mutual responsibility to determine how to address problems together.

Part of the benefit of unstructured groups is that they allow members to learn about ontological dynamics that are often addressed only covertly, and sometimes not at all. An unstructured group can move what is "background" in most groups into the "foreground." Many families, businesses, and social interactions are governed by unspoken rules that regulate what can be said, who can speak, and to whom it is appropriate to speak. Members can use the freedom of an unstructured setting to address personal problems in a manner that helps them to see how their own awareness (and lack of awareness) of these issues affects them.

Some problems derive from a situation and simply require new information and skills. Problems that are more psychological generally require a new perspective along with new information or skills. In reality, of course, there are many occasions when psychological and situational factors are joined in an ambiguous manner. Because there is no authority who has decided for group members whether their problems are situational or psychological, the participants learn to rely on their own judgment whether new information, skills, attitudes, or awareness of self would be most useful. Members often use their observations of how each participant forms relationships in their group to help determine whether psychological factors may be influencing that person's problems. Members can use feedback from others, but ultimately they have to decide whether they are creating unnecessary problems for themselves or whether they simply lack essential skills.

Members and the Group as Fields

Members can use exploration of problems to discover that self-esteem can be enhanced by abandoning a secure position that requires denial and distortion of many thoughts and feelings. Integration of the self with others occurs as members encourage each other to be revealing and as they let go of self-views that unnecessarily restrict or inhibit health and growth. The unstructured group becomes therapeutic by creating an atmosphere wherein members feel free to reveal themselves, their struggles, their achievements, their mistakes, their joys, and their problems to others.

Members often spontaneously choose to discuss their problems with others if an atmosphere of trust and acceptance is established (Polster & Polster; 1973; Rogers, 1970). An unstructured group allows individuals to change their perspectives as they become aware of changes in their process of being, especially those that occur through an experiential process of relationship. Problems and distress within an individual's life that are not simply the results of situational factors can be viewed as symptoms of disequilibrium, disintegration, and disharmony. If the individual is considered as a field of activity, then disharmony in one area of this field affects other areas. Psychological problems do not exist in isolation. Thus, a difficulty that a member has in a present romantic relationship can involve unfinished business with a family member. A problem related to dealing with feelings of intense anger can be associated with unrealistic expectations of self and others, and so on. A group setting can provide evidence to participants that they exist as fields since difficulties that they encounter with others in their group are often seen to be related to other concerns and problems that they bring to the experience.

Members also may observe that their group itself functions as a field. For example, problems between two particular members usually affect other participants. The influential theoretical perspective that persons and groups function as a dynamic field of interacting forces (rather than as a collection of separate elements)

can be traced back to the theory of individual and group functioning developed by Kurt Lewin in the 1940s (see Agazarian, 1992;
Yalom, 1975). If a group is viewed as a field, then as one person
works on a problem, other individuals and the group as a whole
will be affected. Conversely, others' reactions and the reaction of the
group will influence how an individual continues to work on and
perceive a particular problem.

A common means of coping with a perceived problem is to
compartmentalize the problem, to keep it outside awareness, and to
avoid relating the problem to other events and perceptions. Meta-
phorically speaking, humans treat problems the way that organisms
treat noxious internal substances; people separate problems from
the rest of themselves. This strategy can assist adaptation and survival to a degree. However, just as organisms can benefit by expell-
ing a noxious substance or by breaking it down and assimilating
it in a manner that allows the development of immunity, people can
expel introjects that distort perceptions and can assimilate problematic feelings and experiences that have interfered with an integrated process of being. By compartmentalizing or encapsulating
unhappy feelings and experiences, people construct rigid structures
of being that render them vulnerable to stress and unpredictable life
events.

Problems often exist as collections of elements in perceptual
fields that have not been successfully assimilated and integrated into
experience and ongoing encounter. For example, a person may
think, If I have experienced being sexually molested in the past,
then I cannot be a good person. This person may strive to feel like
a good person by denying the feelings associated with being molested. By keeping experience separate from self-concept, integration is prevented, and the person never truly feels good about self.
A variety of life problems can be created as a result. He or she may
undermine relationships at work or at home, take unnecessary risks,
hurt others to gain revenge, and so on.

If members change their behaviors, values, and assumptions
about who they are in relationship to others (which means changing who they are within their own perceptual field), these changes
tend to arise primarily from ongoing experiential learning. The
verbal content that is learned in discussions is far less important

than how one sees oneself, others, and oneself being with others as
these discussions take place. Members may learn to relate differently
than they have in the past, and this experience opens new possibilities and alternatives. In unstructured groups, epistemological
changes are not construed to occur separately from ontological
changes. People therefore alter their beliefs, attitudes, and perceptions as there are changes in their ongoing experience of being.

There are several key questions that are raised in an unstructured group context. What is the relationship of I and we? Who am
I with you? What do I learn in being with you? How does it feel to
be with you? Who are you being with me? To what extent do I
perceive myself with other members becoming we? Do I and you
assist each other's strengths, process of becoming, and well-being?
To what extent are we a part of something together? Awareness of
one's process of being can lead to changes in perception. Unstructured group process does not necessarily aim at changing a process
of being by altering specific thoughts and beliefs. These may be
consequential to changes in the integration of being oneself through
being with others. A person's attitudes toward problems can sometimes change due to the awareness of the context of the interpersonal
field. The person's self-understanding can shift from an isolated entity who "has" (in other words, carries) problems, to a more integrated being whose past problems do not interfere with current
participation with others.

Personal Problems and Group Process

The strength and courage to cope with stress and uncertainty are
associated with a unified awareness that can center itself within
moment-to-moment experience and being (Bugental, 1978; Fromm,
Suzuki, & DeMartino, 1960; Perls, Hefferline, & Goodman, 1951/
1980). If awareness is unified, specific strategies or beliefs can be
created to respond to particular situations. However, specific strategies may not be important if the activity of a unified awareness in
and of itself permits a person to move through difficult situations
with confidence. New confidence can be gained simply through the
healing of intrapersonal and interpersonal splits (Perls, 1973;
Polster & Polster, 1973).

Because members are unique individuals, it is difficult to generalize about which types of interaction are most empowering for those who are dealing with problems. Hill (1965) has performed research on unstructured group therapy with the intention of discovering which interactions are most therapeutic. He has devised a scale to measure group process and has concluded that therapy can be viewed as a continuum wherein members fluctuate in their commitment to therapeutic work and to developing relationships. The most significant therapeutic work of groups, according to Hill, is to establish and deepen present-oriented relationships with other group members. Personal problems were therefore assumed by Hill to be addressed most therapeutically if they are shared in the context of an ongoing relationship with one or more other group members. Problems can be shared less therapeutically when they are expressed in a manner that avoids or diminishes a member's awareness of a current relationship with other participants (Hill, 1969).

Hill also indicates that disclosure of problems can be used to create unequal relationships wherein one participant becomes an identified patient. He refers to these interactions as speculative because members tended to speculate about causes and solutions (Hill, 1965). Additionally, Hill observes that problems can be shared to avert attention to oneself, to draw focus away from the emotional impact of immediate events within group relationships, and to use intellectualization to distance oneself from immediate experience and feelings. Problems can be revealed in a manner that invites others to become helpers and problem solvers, thus providing roles that allow the person being helped to avoid responsibility and the helpers to be distracted from revealing themselves to others. Hill (1965) also notes that members can disclose problems in a manner that connects one participant to others and promotes constructive interpersonal interaction. To be therapeutic, the sharing of problems must occur in an atmosphere of equality, as well as in the context of a meaningful interpersonal relationship between members (Hill, 1965).

If problems are being discussed in a manner that promotes contact and mutual respect, then finding a solution to them tends to become secondary to the enhancement of mutual awareness within the context of present communication. Members may become aware that their deepest psychological problems are in some way being acted out within ongoing group relationships. In fact, one sign that trust is developing in a group is that members will be willing to expose the difficulties that they have in contacting others. Group participants may not be able to resolve long-term problems that affect being with other people, but openness about these concerns may itself be an important change. Members are likely to find that being honest helps them to feel accepted and to accept who they are able to be with others. Acceptance leads to changes in patterns of relationship, and members may then view their problems from a new perspective—one from which the existence of problems is less "problematic."

Interpersonal Learning in Unstructured Group Therapy

Much of the significant learning that takes place during therapeutic groups has been observed to have an interpersonal focus based on present relationships (Agazarian, 1992; Foulkes, 1957; Leszcz, 1992; Rogers, 1970; Yalom, 1975). The interpersonal aspect of learning becomes more prominent as members find that they experience growth and healing within the process of revealing who they are to others, revealing how they respond to others, and discovering how others react to them. Interpersonal learning that is likely to be constructive and meaningful can be differentiated from interpersonal learning that has less impact or is even potentially damaging.

Therapeutic communication is likely to be oriented toward personal experience within the present. The nature of the impact of communications and the meanings that participants draw from the act of communication (verbal and nonverbal) determine whether interactions contribute to growth. Rogers (1967b) notes that although a therapist might feel and communicate empathy, this may not be healing if a client feels threatened or intruded upon. No form of communication in and of itself can be considered as essentially therapeutic. To know if a communication is therapeutic, one must have an understanding of the relational and perceptual context in which it is offered and interpreted (Barret-Lennard, 1985).

Understanding the interpersonal context in which communication occurs is necessary to understand how effective therapeutic relationships develop (Bozarth, 1984; Friedman, 1992). Empathy seems to grow from a mutually interactive form of dialogue and cannot be considered a commodity that is provided by one person (the therapist) to another (the client) (O'Hara, 1984). The experience of empathy can be seen as an important aspect of interpersonal learning that occurs through a context that is mutually constructed by participants in unstructured therapy groups.

As members come to value the interpersonal learning that is possible in a therapy group, they begin to explore how they relate to others and may initiate personally untried or unusual ways of relating (Page, 1984). Explorations of new forms of communication and relationship arise naturally if trust and openness are established between members in a group. This motivation toward exploration of relationships is reminiscent of a child exploring an environment that he or she deems safe enough to investigate. There seems to be an innate curiosity that leads people to be interested in how others see them, to want to find out what others may have to contribute to their experience, and to discover what they may have to contribute to others.

Beyond the factor of curiosity, people also have an understanding that it is through others that they learn who and how they are. The self is formed in relation to others and to an environment. The exploration of relationships in a group is one aspect of individual members' lifelong endeavor to create themselves, an exploration that begins in infancy and ends only with death. Interpersonal learning is therefore a form of joint creation. If members investigate unfinished business from past relationships, this process is often an adjunct to the learning they gain about cocreation within present relationships. Members may come to realize through their experiences with others in a group that their sense of who they are is not really separate from their experience of who others are. Members who experientially realize how their sense of self involves others are likely to form new understandings and interpretations of past as well as present relationships.

The Theme of Estrangement Versus Integration

A broad range of therapists from various orientations have noted that clients in group therapy benefit from the interpersonal learning that is gained by developing relationships with other members. Generally, theorists tend to acknowledge that it is valuable to work toward authentic communication and confrontation with self-limiting patterns of interaction. Different theoretical schools use various terms and strategies to encourage and support members who are coming to grips with maladaptive or stereotypical relationship patterns. These have been conceptualized as maladaptive behaviors, transferences, games, roles, inauthentic communications, or evidence of inadequate self-concepts. We have observed a striking agreement among the theories about the idea that groups can assist members to effectively confront these patterns. We may infer a basic ontological grounding to this idea if we consider that its acceptance may indicate that it is part of a central process that occurs as people encounter other people. This fundamental ontological process can be interpreted as the mutual construction of themselves by participants in relationships.

A central ontological theme is one that affects the life of every human group. One way that people can affect others is by assisting each other to become aware that being together can be meaningful. People can help each other to discover meaning within a shared process of being by affirming and enhancing each other's awareness of how they are mutually affected and by being aware of patterns in relationship. As people grow in awareness, they change. From an ontological perspective, greater awareness is itself a valuable change in the form of relationship, a change that may or may not affect behaviors in a manner that is noticeable to an outside observer.

Anxiety about revealing oneself and learning how others view oneself can lead to estrangement—that is, distance from others and avoidance of authentic interaction. Tillich (1954) uses the term *estrangement* to refer to the process of separation that can lead in particular interactions to alienation of a person from others and ultimately to separation from the ground of being. The development of barriers within individual awareness and within the process of being can be viewed as a process of estrangement. Estrangement plays a vital role in the basic ontological theme of unstructured group therapy. The potential to move toward either an estranged position or one of relatedness is always present within interpersonal encounters, either overtly or covertly. The work done in this area affects the degree to which members make contact with one another and the degree of cohesion they experience as a group.

Members can either use or avoid using their ability to assist others to move beyond estrangement. An individual can be helped to learn about his or her own dynamic process of being and to understand what it means to be a person who exists with others. Group participants often feel estrangement as they encounter others. To experience estrangement is to feel blocked from contact and inhibited from full utilization of one's resources. If estrangement is experienced in its larger sense, members may be feel separated from the ground of being, however they individually understand this ground.

Individuals sometimes perceive themselves as separated from reality, God, humanity, nature, and all that is beautiful in life. One of the authors worked in a hospital where he conducted an unstructured therapy group. One of the members of this group was a person named "Joan." Joan was extremely bright, but she had a difficult time completing even the simplest of tasks. She could not make herself get up for work because she felt that others were laughing at her. Joan would not go out with boys because she felt extremely ugly in spite of assurances from others that she was quite pretty. Joan literally thought that God had created the universe solely to make a mockery of her. Although Joan may have thought that she was significant in God's scheme of things, she felt doomed to a life of failure no matter what she did because she thought that God was out to get her. Joan was trapped by her avoidance of the meaning of her feelings of loneliness and insignificance to others. The nature of this trap was endlessly repeated fantasies and feelings of persecution.

Members move from estrangement toward integration through a process of awareness within relationship. Awareness seems to develop by recognizing that blocks or barriers have been created (and disowned) toward aspects of experience that were uncomfortable or threatening. If these barriers can be recognized, a person can begin moving into the blocked area and start to integrate split-off aspects of experience. Estrangement is a reaction to the anxiety that is experienced if awareness itself is perceived as threatening to self. Awareness and self are essentially one, and it is through awareness that the self recognizes unity with "other." The self can attempt to disown awareness to escape relationship and responsibility. However, attempts to divorce self from awareness create an inescapable bind. Estrangement is evidence that the self is in a bind, that attempts to avoid relationship have depleted the self, and that awareness has become split in a manner that interferes with recognition of relatedness.

Psychological barriers to anxiety-provoking aspects of awareness are formed by retaining anxiety as chronic contractions against further explorations of contact. Reich (1960) recognizes that the anxiety that Freud had viewed as central to neurosis exists physically as chronic contractions of muscle tissue that he terms "character armor." Character armor inhibits those expressions of natural energy that might create contact in a manner that the person has learned to mistrust. Because the person's essential life energy is involved in these inhibited expressions, the feelings and needs involved never disappear. Thus, if a person restricts expressions of feeling continuously over time, chronic muscular contractions are created. These contractions keep the person in and keep others out. They protect the person from the world; more importantly, they keep the world from knowing the person. People are often more concerned with protecting the world from themselves than with protecting themselves from the world.

The estranged person suffers from disconnection from others and from nature, but typically repudiates the act of awareness that created the disconnection. Awareness must be disowned because in itself it embodies the potential to dissolve the protective barrier. If interactions in a group enhance awareness, members may experience a pull toward greater integration. The act of integration is motivated by the attraction of awareness. This attraction can be experienced as love or courage and helps people to move through barriers to reconnect with others and with disowned aspects of experience. Thus, integration can be considered as a movement into and through anxiety that opens a person to the experience of relatedness with others and with nature.

The Healing of Estrangement in Therapeutic Groups

Therapeutic process encourages members to experiment with boundaries—to allow in more of who others are and let out more of who one is. To create this process, members must risk accepting what previously was viewed as unacceptable and to question assumptions about the unacceptability of certain feelings and persons. Therapeutic process occurs, not when participants have no boundaries regulating the expression of feeling, but when the boundary is determined by mutual awareness of what is valuable in a situation. Openness allows people to construct flexible boundaries, whereas judgments based on acceptability versus unacceptability are often rigid and lack adaptability to various challenges in life.

All human beings feel estrangement from being at one time or another, especially at times that involve significant losses and heightened perceptions of vulnerability. These experiences lead people to create a basic polarity in the way they react, a polarity between what they can tolerate and what they cannot. Some examples of estrangement that often appear in problems that members share are the separation of self from experience, thought from feeling, intention from action, person from person, and self from the larger society. Unstructured group therapy is designed to allow members to encounter and express estrangement and to move toward reintegration of elements that have been separated. The essential learning that members gain through interpersonal encounters and relationships concerns both their own estrangement and their potential for integration.

Although past history, family relationships, and personal characteristics play a part in estrangement, it would be incorrect to blame its existence on these factors. To be estranged may be perceived as an evil or aberration, and this perception and its attending anxiety can lead people to attempt to find a cause for their feelings. Anxiety that can be explained is instantly under more control than inexplicable anxiety, which has no possibility of being understood or controlled (Frank, 1963). Estrangement, in a sense, is a fall from grace. One might want to blame this fall on a "serpent in the garden"—for example, a family member, a group of people viewed as destructive, or certain historical conditions. However, although family members and historical events often contribute to it, estrangement can also be considered an inescapable aspect of human lives. We may want to create environments that help ameliorate and heal estrangement, but we recognize as absurd any attempts to eliminate it from life experiences.

The image of the T'ai Chi figure, in which yin and yang intertwine, helps explain why estrangement is an inevitable aspect of human life. The Taoist philosophers invented the image of T'ai Chi to represent the psychological awareness of a dynamic interplay and balance of opposing forces, a perception that polar opposites gain their existence in relation to one another (Suler, 1991). Because persons can be aware of closeness, they can also be aware of losing it. Because trust can be established, it can be broken. Estrangement and reintegration are aspects of a spiral of human growth generated through the development and transformation of relationships. In a group setting, rhythms of contact and withdrawal, closeness and distancing, form the context for communications and relationships.

Gestalt theory demonstrates that group dynamics are involved in the process by which attention is focused on individual issues that become "figural" for the group's attention at certain phases of a group's life (Polster & Polster, 1973). When a group's attention can be constructively focused on individual members' experiencing of estrangement, the inclusiveness and healing power of the group are expanded (Gemmill, 1989). If an estranged individual is scapegoated by other members, they may be blaming this person for their own potential for estrangement, and the group's healing dynamics will be diminished (Gemmill, 1989). By excluding a scapegoat, other members ensure their own belonging; however, by accepting and working with the person's experience of estrangement, a group enhances its ability to encourage authentic intimacy based on recognition of differences (Agazarian, 1992).

Attempts to deny and escape estrangement create a great deal of psychological stress, so the simple willingness to encounter these feelings honestly can reduce the sense of being overwhelmed. Much of the persistence of estrangement comes from a split in awareness that is based on avoidance of feelings and relationship patterns. Thus, individuals and groups of people grow in awareness and personal power as they come to terms with patterns of estrangement, express and assimilate related feelings, and move toward reintegration. Growth of awareness can lead to new learning and growth, to new life within relationships, ethnic groups, and cultural and political systems. Estrangement can be a challenge rather than an evil.

A client named Joan was described earlier in this chapter. After an initial period of individual counseling, Joan expressed some interest in becoming a member of an unstructured therapy group led by one of the authors. Joan came to the group regularly and gradually began to think of herself as making a contribution there. Joan also began to like some of the group members and even began to think that they were showing some acceptance of her as a person. Joan never completely abandoned the idea that God had created her as a joke on life itself, but she did begin to develop some constructive relationships with the other group participants. While Joan did continue to experience personal and interpersonal difficulties during and after the group, she considered this unstructured therapy group to be a personally meaningful experience. Her awareness of self had enlarged to include others to a greater extent than before. She had somewhat relaxed her restricting perception of self as contemptible and worthless.

People generally enter therapy groups as initially estranged. These individuals usually have had no previous experience with each other. In the beginning, they tend to view others as unknown quantities who may prove to be helpful or hurtful. How they confront their estrangement and use their group to create forms for relationship will depend on their individual resourcefulness, the cooperation of other group members, and perceptions of responsibility. As members move toward mutual responsibility and authenticity, they move from estrangement to integration. Members can extend their sense of being and of self to include others and the experiences of others as their group progresses. This extension is expressed by changes in the nature of relationships with others in the group. These changes move in the direction of greater self-disclosure and openness in giving and receiving feedback. Members may find that they are capable of mutual confirmation, of moving from I-it relationships toward I-thou relationships (Friedman, 1963, 1992).

Interpersonal Learning and I-Thou Relationship

In conducting a psychoanalytically oriented version of unstructured group therapy, Wolf and Schwartz (1962) were focused on helping members to move from seeing each other as objects to experiencing each other as persons. These concerns are similar to Martin Buber's (1970) philosophical observations about the nature of worthwhile human relationships. Buber was an existential philosopher and theologian whose views on human relationship affected Rogers (Freidman, 1986); Perls, Hefferline, and Goodman (1951/1980); and Yalom (1980). Buber believed that a central life issue for each person was whether to relate to the other as a thou or as an it. To experience one other person as a thou makes it possible to experience anyone in that way.

The characteristics of an I-thou relationship have to do with perceptions of mutual involvement. This form of relationship is therefore the basis for a dialogue in which there is listening and understanding, mutual respect, and perception of the other as a being who is unique and yet shares the same qualities of humanity and awareness that one feels are basic to oneself. I-thou dialogue is a mutually creative act.

The I-it relationship is based on inequality (Buber, 1970). The world is not sensed as a living environment, but rather as a world of objects that may have their uses. Other people are not perceived as fully alive or real. Since others are viewed in a manner that objectifies them, I-it dialogue lacks the qualities of listening, caring, and empathizing.

Buber believed that I-thou dialogue, by contrast, leads to mutual confirmation of individuals' existence. His discussion of human relatedness and dialogue points to the recognition that there is a common basis for relationships that can arise from therapy, friendship, and love. These may take place in different situations, but each serves as a way through which people can learn about the fundamental qualities of I-thou relatedness. Though unique limits pertain to each form of relationship, the dynamics of each can assist participants to move toward I-thou relatedness.

One way to understand how roles affect therapy is to view interactions in terms of overt and covert dynamics. The *overt* dynamics of interaction revolve around the differences in participants' perceptions of the responsibilities they have within the relationship. Essentially, roles reflect the assumption that the therapist is there to offer help and the client is there to seek and receive it. In a group setting, participants may take certain parts that revolve around a "script." Such roles have been analyzed in terms of facilitation (in other words, initiator, elaborator, or evaluator), maintenance (encourager, harmonizer, or compromiser), and antigroup (aggressor, recognition seeker, or monopolist) (Vander Kolk, 1985). Antigroup roles can apparently be very useful for the development of therapeutic dialogue if new learning can be gained through interaction, confrontation, and acceptance (Gans, 1989; Unger, 1990). These roles may reflect past learning and present interpersonal dynamics.

The *covert* dynamics of interactions do not concern projected images and roles but rather participants' awareness or lack of awareness of others as persons. Although the overt dynamics of a therapeutic group are likely always to show some evidence of differentials in power or status, the covert dynamics can increasingly move toward mutual acceptance and confirmation. Thus, within the situational limits that affect unstructured therapy, participants in effective groups can move toward a more full awareness, acceptance, and inclusion of one another (Cohen & Smith, 1976; Rogers, 1970).

Because much of the interaction in a group is between participants other than the leader, the overt dynamics that accompany the therapeutic role are less likely to have a constant influence on ongoing interactions. Group therapy settings can provide rich learning about the covert dynamics that affect members' perceptions of each other as objects or as persons. Since the status barrier between a therapist and client is not present in many interactions, group members can encounter their own dynamics in establishing relations with others with whom they are on an equal initial footing. In individual therapy, covert relationship dynamics may not be as clearly observable or may take longer to become apparent.

The I-thou relationship is most congruent and powerful when the overt relationship dynamics are not inconsistent with the covert ones—that is, when participants' roles do not interfere with their perception of each other's humanity. Although many psychological theorists have valued the potential for therapy to lead to I-thou communication, there is much variation among their descriptions of the nature of this communication. For example, Van De Riet, Korb, and Gorrell (1980) have written, "The essence of Gestalt therapy is *I* and *Thou, Here* and *Now*" (p. 95). Gestalt therapists follow Buber, according to these authors, by differentiating between "using" (I-it relations) and "experiencing" (I-thou relations). Experiencing is a form of relationship in which an "I" encounters another "I" (p. 32). In Gestalt therapy, it is also traditional for the therapist to provide direction and focus for clients in a manner designed to assist clients to come to greater awareness.

Van De Riet, Korb, and Gorrell (1980) believe that it is possible to have an I-thou form of relationship in spite of roles that develop from the therapist's use of methods and techniques that are designed to lead clients in a certain direction. The therapist facilitates I-thou relatedness by making direct contact with the client and working on a shared task that has the goal of increasing his or her awareness. Korb, Gorrell, and Van De Riet (1989) have described I-thou contact as a process in which participants "become unmediated presences *to each other* through an act of faith" (italics in original), participants' conscious processes of cognitive control may be temporarily suspended, and a loving experience is created that is a "healthful, healing, and contactful state of confluence" (pp. 113–114). This description indicates that participants in an I-thou relationship experience sufficient distinctness for contact as well as a merging of boundaries (confluence).

James Simkin, another Gestalt therapist, has depicted the "I-thou" relationship as a "horizontal" relationship (1976, p. 79). A "vertical" relationship in which the therapist maintains a "superior" role as director or expert can discourage the confluence that can occur in a horizontal relationship. A horizontal relationship is described by Simkin as one in which the therapist can also share of self and can allow the client access to the world of the therapist. The therapist encourages the client to ask to "invade the privacy" of the therapist if the client wishes to learn something, just as participants often assume that therapy will invade their privacy. Although participants, including the therapist, always have the right to refuse to answer questions, a therapist who insists on retaining a vertical position remains emotionally hidden and may encourage dependency by projecting the image of an authority figure.

In unstructured group therapy, members can move toward awareness of themselves within a group that supports the personal expression of meaning and feelings. To begin this movement, they make authentic contact with one another and gradually relax self-protective modes of interaction. They may then begin to perceive that they are not separate from others. Of course, interpersonal learning does not necessarily or automatically move people toward this perception.

Aloneness and I-Thou Relationship

Members may continue to perceive themselves as isolated beings throughout a group, especially if they do not feel sufficient trust and openness to relax habitual modes of defense. They may need to learn to trust their defenses before they can allow themselves to extend themselves to others. They may need to learn that they can say no to others who want closeness so that their yes can have meaning and can affirm a spirit of freedom. The ability to say no is necessary for people to learn that they can differentiate their own perspective from that of others. Introjects from early childhood are powerful because parents project values and experiences at a time when children are not yet able fully to say no. Therefore, human development depends as much on learning how to say no and to exclude as it does on learning to say yes and to include. A person whose relationships are based on introjects is not able to say yes in a way that fully expresses personal choice and power.

The realization of individual uniqueness does not necessarily lead to a sense of separation from others. If participants accept and integrate feelings of aloneness, they may recognize that these can be a basis for contacting others. The experience of loneliness that often accompanies recognition of what cannot be shared also often leads to an understanding that distinctiveness leads to relationships. If a person communicates vaguely, never meaningfully declares feelings or thoughts, and avoids a distinct presence with others, the person will also avoid relationships. The recognition that "I am I and you are you" is therefore vital. Of course, some sameness of feelings and perceptions is necessary for communication and is indicative of the universality of being human, but distinctiveness is equally essential.

Members often initially experience their individuality in a group as aloneness. They are especially likely to feel that way if their distinctiveness arises through expression of feelings or thoughts that others do not support. Members may feel lonely because they have reached out to others and have been rebuffed or misunderstood. They may also experience existential aloneness if they realize that being with people means being distinct from as well as sharing with others.

The experience of existential aloneness can arise through emotional and cognitive awareness of limits inherent in the process of being (May & Yalom, 1984; Yalom, 1980). Anything that comes into being can, and eventually will, cease to exist. Therefore, individuals must contend with the physical and emotional consequences of limitations such as illness, loss, and death. Perls (1969) has found that clients in therapy need to move into and through aloneness as they encounter an impasse. The impasse typically involves the realization that environmental support is not available and self-support is not currently sufficient (Perls, 1969). An individual moves through an impasse into new growth by creatively forming a new gestalt, a new awareness of meaning, within an experience of meaninglessness and emptiness (Perls, 1969; Tillich, 1952).

Thus, awareness of aloneness can attend the recognition that no one else can completely accompany one through the dilemmas that are encountered in the process of personal growth. Individuals may also encounter loneliness if they are aware of needing to define personal ethical values to guide and limit their behavior in certain situations or if they feel that the limits of language and communicative abilities have restricted the degree to which experiences can be shared. Any of the previously discussed limits may initially be experienced as isolating or constricting. If, however, they are viewed as necessary aspects of human existence, they may paradoxically become liberating (May, 1981).

This realization is part of the basic learning that can be gained from participation in a therapeutic group. For example, when members struggle to manage time so that different people get to share the attention, they may recognize that they are helping to create a unified field for interaction. Similarly, as members struggle to define norms for interpersonal behavior and communication, they may also learn that these form the basis for expressing self and forming relationships. Limits are definitions, definitions are distinctions, and distinctiveness is a basis for relationship. Persons as individuals and as members of a group grow through recognition of the differences that form distinctions and awareness of similarities that form connections within distinctions (Agazarian, 1992).

If members retreat from the experience of existential aloneness, they are simultaneously (and usually unconsciously) retreating from being. Members can retreat from aloneness by setting up the leader or another member as an authority figure, by forming group norms that stress cohesiveness through conformity, or by pursuing contact with others in a manner that avoids disclosure of self. In the last case, I-it dialogue is likely to result. A person who is using contact with others to escape aloneness is likely to feel uncomfortable simply to be with others. Such a person is likely to use these others as a way to escape unwanted feelings of aloneness and therefore will have difficulty responding to others receptively.

Members who examine those patterns of relationship in which they may have sought to dominate others, have sought to be dominated by others, or have experienced being addicted to others often find that they were using their interactions with these others to avoid confronting themselves. People avoid confronting self when they fear the sense of aloneness and emptiness they may find within themselves. If I-thou dialogue is established, this dialogue will inevitably bring the person into awareness of the very aloneness he or she is attempting to avoid. By contrast, if I-it dialogue is used by individuals to avoid awareness, their communications may seem anxious or even desperate to others. I-it interactions will, at least temporarily, distract these individuals from experiences of aloneness, but the lack of interpersonal communion in these relations will eventually make itself apparent.

The essential difference between I-it dialogue and I-thou dialogue cannot be understood simply by attention to verbal content. The content of communication is an element to be considered because overt verbal content can reflect to an extent whether a participant is aware of the other as a person or as an object. However, verbal content that seems caring and appropriate can be contradicted by nonverbal messages that convey lack of contact or respect. Verbal content and nonverbal messages may also not be interpreted as the communicator had intended. If members perceive themselves to be involved in I-thou contact, they are likely to interpret communications differently than if they feel estrangement. Communication with innocuous content can thus be perceived as caring and contactful; communication with "deep" content can be perceived as distancing or inappropriate.

Nonverbal communication can be used when participants recognize that there are aspects of an experience that cannot be verbalized and when they want to signal that there is more to their feelings and perceptions than they can convey with words. Nonverbal expressions of meaning can be conveyed by tears, laughter, sighs, tone of voice, silence, facial expressions, gestures, and positioning of oneself in space. Participants may use nonverbal communication when they have experiences that they sense would be diminished by attempts to articulate them. To attempt to verbalize fully an experience requires a degree of analysis and judgment that can detract from the presentness and wholeness of that experience (Perls, 1973). From certain kinds of events, participants may learn to appreciate aloneness and can gain understanding about the limits of what can be verbally and nonverbally shared.

A person can understand and accept the aloneness of others if he or she understands and accepts his or her own. At the same time, this acceptance creates a basis for understanding the most shared aspects of human existence and awareness. For example, if one has struggled through the feelings of loneliness involved in the ending of a close relationship or in the loss of a loved one, one can respect and understand the grieving process of another person. As group members learn to sense when and how others need space and contact, a sense of connection develops that includes an appreciation of aloneness as well as an understanding of the process of sharing.

The dynamics of unstructured therapy groups form a kind of rhythm. Members tend to seek contact at times when they perceive value in contributing, gaining support, learning by interacting. If they make and complete the kind of contact that they intend or if they feel unable to establish connection, participants will withdraw from interaction. Members may move toward I-thou connectedness and then move toward a more distant posture. If members disconnect from interactions that form the center of a group's attention, they may want to learn from observation or they may want time to process what they have experienced previously. It is necessary that members move from expression of self to silence. This movement creates spaces within the process of a group that allow freedom for other members to communicate and for the group as a whole to form new foci.

The rhythms of a group's process can contain many levels of intensity and many themes and subthemes. One theme may be explored, then dropped, and then picked up again later. A group may move from a theme that involves all members to a concern of one particular member and then back to a more universal issue. Members may focus on here-and-now encounters, may move toward exploring relationships outside the group or past family relationships, and then may go back to a discussion that reflects present relationships. The intensity of I-thou relatedness varies throughout the life of a group. The complexity of the rhythms and patterns of relationship that occur in an unstructured group allows members to seek the degree of contact with others that they need and to create the degree of emotional space that they also require.

The interpersonal learning that takes place in a therapy group allows participants to recognize the value of I-thou communication, but it also permits them to see that timing is an aspect of intimate communication. Members come to terms with perceptions of existential aloneness as they realize that it is impossible to hold onto moments of I-thou relatedness and to force intimacy to occur on demand. There are times during the life of a group, and the life of a relationship, when I-thou communication emerges spontaneously and naturally. There are other times when such communication is absent, and any attempt to force such a level of intimacy into being would undermine whatever genuine contact is available. I-thou relatedness can occur between members during a given interaction or within a given period of their relationship and may then recede.

The Creation of Shared Psychological Space

The ebb and flow of I-thou contact is part of the overall ebb and flow of closeness in interactions. Closeness and distance are both essential aspects of relationship and the process of living. Members can grow from confronting and accepting feelings of distance as well as feelings of communion with others. Acceptance of individual uniqueness and difference allows a person to establish a "space" in which to form connections.

Psychological space, unlike physical space, is not possessed or owned (as physical territory is). Psychological space is established as individuals explore experience and use this exploration to enhance their awareness. This kind of personal space is the ground in which various aspects of experience can be integrated. This ground can be extended to include others and can become shared. The perception of shared psychological space enhances the richness and meaning of communications. This space enables people to use awareness mutually to develop gestalts of meaning within experience. Because a sense of shared space is constructed by extending personal space, the former depends on the latter. If people lack a sense of personal space, they may be greedy for new experiences and sensations but may not be able to appreciate what they already have or what others are offering. They may unconsciously discount aspects of experience that another brings to communication because they have not established a basis for learning from what is presented.

The establishment of psychological space does not require any particular kind of activity. In fact, certain mental activities can distract from the openness that establishes psychological space. People can use mental or physical activities, chemicals, or excessive verbiage to fill up their psychological space. People who have truly established a sense of psychological space, however, do not need to fill it up because they appreciate the openness that exists when one is simply receptive and "there." Developing comfort within psychological space is an antidote for addictions and compulsive mental activities. There are many ways that people can develop this sense of existing as a receptive space as well as a physical body. For example, people can increase their sense of psychological space as they go fishing or hiking, listen attentively to music, learn to listen to their "inner voice" and their feelings in therapy, participate in various forms of meditation and contemplation, or silently view works of art at a museum. All of these activities offer opportunities to empty oneself of preoccupations and internal chatter, to listen and observe, and to improve appreciation of events within present awareness.

The key factor in the development of this personal sense of space is that individuals learn to value the simple act of being silently aware. No activity per se is necessary; the person may release any sense of striving to get "somewhere else" and is likely to be open *to* experience without demanding things *from* it. Maslow (1962) refers to this kind of openness as a part of "peak experience"; but in less dramatic fashion, silent awareness can become a part of everyday activity and being. Group members who can relax and be open to experience can also relax and be open with others.

Members who have a sense of personal psychological space can demonstrate for others how people can interact in ways that communicate respect for one another's space. This respect is an aspect of the development of loving contact that underlies I-thou relatedness (Korb, Gorrell & Van De Riet, 1989; Simkin, 1976). Group participants who are dealing with patterns of relationships developed in families that were enmeshed or rejecting can benefit when other members communicate respect for and caring about one another's space. Members will feel and be affected by a sense of inclusivity and acceptance. A group then begins to function as a whole that is more than the sum of individual parts. Members experience cohesion and belonging with others, as well as support for their uniqueness and individuality.

Receptivity and acceptance are attitudes that are essential for the generation of psychological space. Within a shared physical space, two people can be considered as separate "objects." Within a shared psychological space, people can be within each other. The presence of one person enables another to disclose who he or she is, and vice versa. Shared psychological space is created as people begin to accept each other's presence without judgment and to disclose thoughts and feelings. People then become comfortable with themselves being with others and with experience as it unfolds.

Shared psychological space also allows all members to feel that they are actively involved with one another, even when certain members are temporarily "center stage." This kind of space allows the focus of attention in a group to shift as needed. Members are seeking to assist one another and view each other as equals within a shared process. Participants are not using their group to provide drama, except insofar as genuinely helping one another to enhance awareness can sometimes be dramatic. Members can become comfortable with silence as well as speech. They can enjoy simply being together as well as sharing thoughts and feelings. As they create psychological space, group members are not pressured to reveal thoughts or feelings but offer these naturally. Natural sharing occurs as members use communication to increase understanding of self and others. Members are not trying to *make* something happen when they communicate in this manner but are communicating something that *is* happening. Communication within shared psychological space can creatively heighten awareness of what is happening and of the fact that their joint experience is rich with possibilities for exploration.

Chapter Three

Self-Actualization
as a Central Theme

Theorists have ideas about the nature of human beings that affect their assumptions about human behavior in groups. Assumptions lead theorists to focus on various aspects of group process, to diverge in their interpretations of observations, and to vary in their descriptions of typical occurrences and themes in unstructured therapy groups. Theorists' descriptions of events in therapy vary in part because they are oriented toward different central themes. It is worthwhile to review some of the concepts that influential theorists have used to focus their observations. An underlying or basic idea involved in unstructured therapy groups may be found within the divergent themes that theorists have observed and described.

One concept that certain theorists have viewed as an underlying or basic theme is self-actualization (for example, Maslow, 1962; Patterson, 1980, 1985; Rogers, 1951). Although some have hoped that self-actualization could serve as a unifying construct for understanding healing and growth (see Patterson, 1985), others have observed that self-actualization has not lived up to its promise to become a truly integrative concept (see Daniels, 1988; Geller,

1984). One persistent criticism of self-actualization theory has been
its reliance on a biological metaphor for human growth that does
not fully address the impact of dialogue and the mutual construction of experiential realities between partners in dialogue (Arnett,
1989; Friedman, 1986; Geller, 1984). Recent attempts to revitalize the
concept of self-actualization have attempted to move toward a
process-oriented view that can integrate awareness of biological aspects of personhood with dialogical, experiential, and social aspects
of personhood (Daniels, 1988; Frick, 1990). Using a process-oriented
and integrative conceptualization, *self-actualization* can be a useful
term for describing self-directed human movement toward growth.
From this perspective, growth harmonizes personal and interpersonal realities (Daniels, 1988). Thus, to achieve a viable conceptualization of self-actualization, we must move beyond either-or
thinking in which individual is pitted against group, self against
other, inside against outside. Instead, opposites can be viewed as
arising in mutual definition (Suler, 1991).

Individuals arise with and within groups, and groups are
defined by their members. Self arises with and is enhanced by others
(Watts, 1961). Self-actualization can therefore be understood as a
process, a resonating movement that harmonizes polar forces,
which allows these to work together well and with mutual benefit.
The perceptually conflicting forces of "I" and "them" can become
the mutually enhancing forces of "I" and "we" as movement toward self-actualization occurs between persons in a group.

The frequently criticized idea that an "a priori," "essential,"
or "core" entity is being achieved (see Geller, 1984; Smith, 1973) is
not necessary for a useful conceptualization of self-actualization.
Following the lead of Wilson (1988), we view the "real self" or "core
self" experientially, as an integrative unity of mind-body and social
and physical awareness of being. We propose that individual movement toward wholeness occurs within awareness, a joining of intrapersonal and interpersonal forces that may sometimes clash but
which yet can be experientially integrated. The self can become a
stronger self by giving itself to others, by including more of others,
and by experiencing itself with others. This self that becomes
stronger is not an entity that exists separately from experience, from
others, and from nature. Rather, the self can be conceptualized as

an integrative potential that arises as relationship and that potentially includes all of experience, all others, and all of nature (Tillich, 1954). This kind of conceptualization of the self can be enhanced by the integration of Eastern and Western psychology (Daniels, 1988; Page & Berkow, 1991; Watts, 1961). One purpose for such an integration is to provide a workable framework (an effective "myth") that can coherently reconcile human experiences of self-expansion and self-transcendence (see Daniels, 1988).

The movement of the self between polar conditions (for example, aloneness and contact, estrangement and communion) is a process by which relationship is developed and enhanced (Perls, Hefferline & Goodman, 1951/1980; Schneider, 1990). Thus, the self uses experience to integrate and differentiate (Frick, 1990). The self does not exist as an entity apart from experience and relationship. Thus, an individual's self-actualization inevitably includes others. Mythically, self-actualization can be viewed as "quest" that is a "shared adventure" (Daniels, 1988, p. 35). Variations of this mythic theme can be found in various theories that attempt to explain how individual human growth can be enhanced through group therapy.

Integration of Theories of Self-Actualization

Eastern perspectives about psychological well-being have portrayed awareness of one's original nature as consistent with a harmonious integration of self with the world of nature (Page and Chang, 1989). Individuation, if it includes integration of self and nature, will also include the possibility of communion with others. The uniqueness of personhood does not separate the individual from others because awareness of harmony with nature and others is part of realizing one's self. A theory of self-actualization can evolve that is compatible with Eastern as well as psychodynamic perspectives. Such a theory would view potentials that are realized as uniquely individual and universally human. *Self-actualization* can be defined as a process that resolves self-other tensions and polarities; therefore, self-actualization can occur within activities that people use to communicate with one another. Group therapy then becomes understandable as one of the human activities through which a process of self-actualization can be enhanced.

Participants in therapeutic groups often ask questions that refer to themes of identity, direction, and experience. Directly or indirectly, people ask, "Who am I, where have I been, where am I going, who am I going with, and what is my experience of being here and moving there?" These ontological themes continually surface and resurface, revealing self-actualization to be a process, a movement, a creation of self within the act of relating oneself to others. As the individual relates self to others, the individual also relates ongoing experiences and aspects of experience within the act of being. Addressing questions of an ontological nature leads a person to create psychological space. Within this space, people can discover resources of which they were not previously aware. Such resources include awareness to determine directions for growth and abilities to act effectively in one's world.

Self-actualization is expressed in different ways in various cultures. Because self-actualization is creative, it is never completely defined by any person's or any culture's myths and symbols. Individuals can become excessively invested in cultural symbols that provide positive self-representations if these people have become creatively blocked in their self-actualizing use of encounters. Cultures themselves can be viewed in terms of collective self-actualization. Cultures define themselves in relation to other cultures. If a culture is insecure, it may affirm itself aggressively against other cultures or may become isolationistic. A self-actualizing culture, according to the definition used in this text, is willing to form constructive and confirmatory relations with other cultures. A therapy group's culture can also form constructive relations with the other cultures in which members may participate. In a group therapy setting, members' self-definitions include those that these participants have achieved in other groups in which they have been involved. By defining oneself in relation to others in a group, one tends to use past definitions of self that are present within one's continuing acts of relationship.

Theories of Group Psychotherapy and Self-Actualization

To be understood as an underlying theme in human activity, self-actualization must be conceptualized in a manner that can account for the negative as well as the positive aspects of human self-direction. Some psychological theorists have focused on ideas such as unfinished business (Perls, Hefferline & Goodman, 1951/1980), compulsive repetition (Freud, 1920/1955), games that people play in relationships (Berne, 1964), and communication (Bateson, Jackson, Haley & Weakland, 1956). Persons' acceptance of unsatisfying or self-limiting patterns in relationships, even when other options are available, is a factor in therapy (and life) that is difficult to deny.

The movement toward self-actualization can be severely distorted, although never totally negated (it is too basic to the process of being). Some relationships can be seen to lead to the diminishment of participants' self-esteem and self-efficacy (sense of self) and to tragedy and hurt. Others strengthen and enliven the participants. A valid theory of self-actualization should account for people's willingness to engage in destructive game playing as well as mutual affirmation. Psychoanalytic thinkers have been among those theorists who have attempted to understand how people create and maintain self-defeating patterns in relationship. It is useful to examine how these thinkers have viewed group therapy.

Psychoanalytic Influence on Theories of Group Therapy

The concepts conceived by psychoanalytic theorists have played an important role in many therapists' views of unstructured therapy. The influence of psychoanalytic thought is due in large part to the impact of certain key theorists, trained in psychoanalysis, who were pioneers in the use of unstructured groups to promote improved social and personal functioning. Though they have thought critically about many of the central issues involved in conducting therapy groups, psychoanalysts have placed certain limitations on the themes on which they have generally focused. Human nature is assumed to be governed by unconscious motivations that are essentially oriented toward obtaining pleasure without concern for the needs of others or toward causing destruction for its own sake. These assumptions lead to reductionistic and negativistic descriptions of human motives for interacting with others. Negativistic descriptions of people maintain a core focus on the potential of people to hurt themselves or each other through pleasure-seeking behaviors or through unchanneled aggression.

The psychoanalytic view of human beings invites us to look at ourselves and others without illusions and to be suspicious of our innate ability to organize our thinking around palatable self-deceptions. At the same time, it tends to minimize persons' potential to help each other to grow and succeed. Of course, a viable explanation of self-actualization needs to account for destructive interpersonal patterns of relationship without being naive and without placing all responsibility for destructiveness outside the person. Yet we would like to be able to recognize and to account for destructive behavior without necessarily *expecting* negative behavior and without seeing interpersonal destructiveness as inevitable and inherent in human nature.

For Freud (1926/1953a, 1934/1953b), the id was the basis and origin of human personality. The *id,* as described by Freud, is an essential driving force in human nature that is fundamentally instinctual and that strives for immediate satisfaction and relief of tension. The structure of identity, which Freud termed the *ego,* and the structure of moral conscience or guilt, termed the *superego,* arise because external reality frustrates the desires of the id for immediate satisfaction of its drives for pleasure and destruction. The ego and superego can be viewed as portions of the id whose functions have become differentiated to cope with aspects of reality external to the person (Alexander, 1961).

One implication of Freud's view of the person is that the psychoanalytic therapist needs to represent a somewhat authoritarian image. This image is necessary insofar as the therapist represents the impingement of "external reality" on clients. The therapist needs to exert control to strengthen the egos of clients (Freud 1940/1964). Within the context of Freudian theory, we do not find explanations of how clients can move toward greater integration without direction from a leader or authority figure. The therapist is required to encourage the appropriate channeling and expression of needs, so that the ego of the client does not become overwhelmed by denied and repressed impulses from the id.

Because repressed life energies are thought to be related to past experiences that have not been integrated, the psychoanalytic therapist helps clients recover memories that have been buried or denied (Greenson, 1967). At the right time, the therapist can interpret for the client how her or his present relationship with the therapist is a reenactment of themes connected with the forgotten past (Greenson, 1967). If therapy is successful, the client will release previously bound-up energy and will become more free to choose modes for self-expression and directions in relationships that are not compulsive repetitions of past patterns.

Psychoanalytic therapy emphasizes a causal relationship between the past and the present; it therefore becomes necessary to discover "the truth" about the past. However, in reality, the only truth that is available in the therapy session is the client's reconstruction and memory of past events and the therapist's guesses and opinions about these memories. The importance of past events in the process of counseling is therefore a matter of subjectively experienced meanings rather than objectively verifiable ones. The client's present mode of being affects how he or she focuses on certain past events and how these are remembered and reconstructed. The effect of past patterns on present encounters is a matter of the personal meaning attached to previous events. Whether a person is reacting inappropriately to current relationships because of unfinished business is ultimately determined by the person's own present awareness, although feedback from others can be helpful.

Group Work and the Legacy of Freud's Theory

Psychoanalytic theory can perhaps be differentiated from psychoanalytic therapy. The latter offers clients opportunities to explore experiences freely and openly. It is believed that people can use this self-exploration to become more effective and more fulfilled in work and in love. Clients are encouraged to relate aspects of experience (especially the present to the past) in ways that they have previously not been able to do. They are asked to reflect on themselves, their feelings, and their patterns of being with others. This form of therapy implies that people can become more aware, more self-reliant, and more effective (in other words, more self-actualizing) by exploring who they are in an atmosphere of freedom. The theory of psychoanalysis seems to be far more pessimistic about the basic nature of human beings than is the actual therapy employed. Psychoanalytic theory presents human beings formed by the past and motivated by greedy and hostile feelings that make other people into objects for individuals' desires and aggressions. Although the therapy pursues the idea of awareness in an atmosphere of freedom, the theory negates it by conceiving of it only as a device to allow people to delay gratification and to redirect drives.

In application to groups, psychoanalytic theory indicates that members are not likely to assist each other's growth unless the leader maintains a strong presence. Freud's pessimism about human nature was based in part on his observations concerning human behavior in groups. If people are in an unstructured group that lacks direction from a leader, they would likely act out unresolved feelings of aggression or sexuality that are prevented expression in other social situations (Bion, 1959). Even if there is the presence of a strong leader, the group members are expected to have deeply conflicting feelings about that person. Freud was in fact pessimistic about the long-term ability of humans to survive collectively. He feared human beings' tendencies to unleash aggression as a group activity (Freud, 1930/1961). Increased technological abilities for destruction, combined with the regressive instincts of people that Freud observed emerging in group situations, led him to take a dim view of the future.

Freud (1921/1948) has written that people in groups may regress to a disinhibited mob psychology. A human mob tends to find a leader with whom they can obtain power through identification. They may compete for the leader's affection or may wish to view the leader as loving everyone equally. The expressed desire for the leader's love is largely an illusion to reverse the phylogenetically inherited murderousness of the primal horde (Freud, 1921/1948). This theory is an attempt to explain how mobs of people can be fused into a unified group through identification with a leader who is able to rouse their hatred and channel their aggression toward an outside enemy, an occurrence that has not been historically uncommon.

Human psychology in unstructured groups tends toward regression, according to psychoanalytic theory, and is therefore a problematic environment in which to assist individuals to establish ego strength. The phenomenon of regression in group situations leads to such human inventions as carnivals and orgies, which can temporarily ease the tension between ego and ego ideal and may thus have an anxiety-reducing effect (Scheidlinger, 1980a, 1980b). Freud did not advocate the practice of psychoanalysis in group settings, a view that is consistent with his theoretical beliefs. However, later psychoanalytic therapists made various attempts to modify Freudian theory in a manner conducive to treatment in a group situation (Scheidlinger, 1980a).

As previously noted, some of the earliest and most significant authors who wrote about therapy in an unstructured situation were trained in psychoanalysis. S. R. Slavson, S. H. Foulkes, W. Bion, A. Wolf, and E. K. Schwartz were some of the pioneers. These theorists had to reinterpret facets of Freudian theory and had to explain the nature of group identity in a manner that was consistent with their observation that groups have a potential to assist members to become strong and healthy individuals. These theorists also had to contend with the diminished control of the therapist over the therapeutic process that is inherent in a group situation. These theorists varied in their allegiance to Freud's view that the central themes of human groups revolve around the control of aggression, individuals' desires to regress, and the need for the leader to provide direction and channeling for the instincts of group members. In coming to terms with Freud's hypotheses about human nature in groups, these authors addressed basic concerns about conducting group therapy that are relevant for group leaders of any theoretical persuasion. These psychoanalytic group leaders saw opportunities for individuals to grow through interacting with others in a group, although they had considerable differences concerning how growth might take place. Though none of these theorists used the term *self-actualization*, their work implied that an individual needs interactions with other people to become more individual and more whole.

Conceptualization of the themes around which helpful interactions occur in a group evolves from assumptions about the basic nature of a human group. A group may be characterized as a collection of separate individuals or as a whole that has unique qualities that cannot be described solely as the sum of separate parts. Foulkes (1953, 1957) and Bion (1959) have taken the latter position and have gone so far as to characterize the group as having an identity or personality. They both speak of the group personality in a manner that is identical to references made to individual personalities. Therefore, the group personality is viewed either as being expressed consciously or as manifesting itself on unconscious levels. This personality is said to arise whenever individuals join together.

Though agreeing that the group could be considered a personality, Foulkes and Bion disagree about the nature of this hypothesized group personality. Bion's (1959) view is closer to Freud's pessimism concerning the potentially destructive nature of the human unconscious. He expects the group's unconscious motives to become evident in expressions of dependence, in acts of overt rebellion against the leader, or through covert noncooperation with the leader. Bion believes the leader will have to confront and interpret the resistance of the group as an entity. The group as a whole will resist working together to solve problems. In addition, there is also the resistance of individuals who interfere with growth toward their functioning as conscious and aware persons. Bion foresees the likelihood that individuals will use the group as a means to flee from the demand to work on problems or to fight the leader or each other rather than work together. Members could imagine external or internal enemies that were nonexistent or feel themselves as dependent on the leader or on the group for survival. Individuals could also attempt to form pairs with each other or with the leader and thus resist cooperation and unity.

Bion (1959) also believes that the leader functions as the ego of the group, regulating the destructive capacities of its unconscious. The leader could forge the group into a work group by preventing any one of the basic tendencies (fight-flight, dependency, and pairing) from becoming dominant. The leader, as described by Bion, does not involve himself or herself in the mutuality of group relationships. This approach allows the leader to function as an objective observer who can interpret the activities of the group and who can maintain control of the group process against the unconscious forces that threatened to promote regression. Bion's theory suggests that any kind of self-actualization that is possible must use a perspective dissociated from emotional trends in the group.

Foulkes (1951), also influenced by Freud, takes a much more positive stance toward the personality of human groups. Foulkes believes that the group unconscious could move in constructive directions without the imposition of controls by an external source.

The leader is viewed as more of a guide than an authority. The leader can function as a participant who guides the group toward constructive work and does not need to function as an emotionally removed commentator on group process. The conductor, as Foulkes refers to the leader, can accept a leadership position but actually desires to surrender this role as members assume more responsibility. The leader does not concern himself or herself with setting goals that would make the group efficient and is instead interested in generating a free-floating discussion (Foulkes, 1948).

Within this discussion, the therapist might notice conscious and unconscious levels of meaning, called *resonances* (Foulkes, 1975). Although it is important for the conductor to interpret these, such interpretations should not have the effect of moving the group away from its present interaction or from an atmosphere of free-floating discussion. The therapeutic group that functions as a healing group becomes a matrix for the development of the identities of its members. The members begin to sense themselves as part of a whole and are not threatened by group dynamics in the manner suggested by Bion. In fact, the group that is functioning most therapeutically is one where the leader exerts little overt control on the direction of group process (Foulkes, 1951). Foulkes is far more confident than Bion that human self-actualization could arise from the emotional and cognitive matrix of the group process itself.

Wolf and Schwartz (1962) agree with Foulkes and Lewis (1944) that group treatment has therapeutic potentials that are not available in individual treatment. Wolf and Schwartz also agree that the leader's proper role is to exert little control on group process; they advocate the use of alternate sessions where the members meet without the leader. However, Wolf and Schwartz emphatically deny the existence of a group personality or group mind. Although they acknowledge the importance of understanding group dynamics and process, they tend to view concepts of a group personality as mystical and countertherapeutic. The group personality is seen as an illusion that could be perpetuated to promote conformity and mediocrity at the expense of autonomy and genuine I-thou relationships.

Foulkes (1951) finds a healing power in the group itself that transcends its individual members. It is therefore conceivable that individuals who function pathologically elsewhere could create a healthy group norm that reinforces their ability to relate and that corrects their neurotic reactions. This idea of Foulkes's is regarded by Wolf and Schwartz (1962) as a "deification of the group" (p. 20). They criticize this idea as encouraging an "I-group relatedness." This is described as an I-it relationship; the group itself functions as a substitute for the development of I-thou relationships between responsible individuals. Thus, Wolf and Schwartz indicate that groups could further individual self-actualization if self is clearly differentiated from group and if the group was not viewed as a kind of self.

Slavson (1957) is also mistrustful of the attempts of individuals to respond to the group as if it were an entity. Although Wolf and Schwartz are relatively trusting of individuals' abilities to generate I-thou relationships without the intervention of a group leader, Slavson (1953) views interpretation by the therapist as being essential to prevent group members' inevitable attempts to give up their egos, or portions of these, to the leader and the group. Slavson believes that bonds between group members, even if they appear cooperative or collaborative, have the effect of promoting regression and neurosis. Although there are many means for members to escape or resist the therapeutic process, group members can experience healing through relationship, catharsis, insight, ego strengthening, reality testing, and sublimation (Slavson, 1951). The group is a setting that allows for the therapist's analysis of individuals in a situation where their modes of relationship are apparent. For Slavson, self-actualization can only occur if members develop sufficient ego strength to avoid merging self with group.

Object Relations and the Human Group

More recent developments in psychoanalytic thought have come about through investigating dynamics (relations to human objects) that occur earlier in individual human development than the dynamics that were most important for Freud (see, for example, Mahler, 1968; Winnicott, 1958). These object-relations theories tend to show that healthy independence cannot occur without a developmental process that includes healthy dependence on healthy human objects (represented internally as "good" objects, sources of security). Development toward self-esteem and autonomy is often impaired by experiences of anxiety associated with persecutory fears (represented internally as "bad" objects). These theoretical constructs are used by group leaders to help members experience being cared about by others (reinforcing and developing good internal representations); at the same time, feelings of anxiety and anger can be contained within the group, and members who experience these feelings can be gradually assisted to understand how defensive strategies related to internalized bad objects are the basis for much fear and anger (Ganzarain, 1992).

Developments in object-relations theory support the concept that therapeutic benefit can arise from members receiving a kind of protective motherly warmth and acceptance from their therapist or group (Ganzarain, 1992). Object-relations theory indicates that early developmental difficulties with internalizing a strong and nurturant maternal presence underlie much psychopathology. Individuals may need to view the group as a strong and nurturant presence to internalize this image and thereby to develop a more positive sense of self. Individuals who see the group as a "bad mother" who cannot meet participants' needs for recognition and sustenance may resist the group.

According to object-relations theory, much of what is useful for participants is the extent to which the group can satisfactorily meet previously unmet needs (for example, to feel cared about, to feel significant to others). These needs are transferred into relationships in the group through unconscious fantasies (Bach, 1957). If needs are distorted by game playing, group members are generally relied upon to sense when and how to confront games played by other members. These games typically involve attempts to meet unmet needs without consciously acknowledging their existence and nature. A healthy group will tend to develop intermember relationships that have increasingly less distortion, less defensive exploration of issues, and more accurate self-correction by group members (Bach, 1957).

Individual maturation can occur in a group if its power as a whole is used to support individuation. The individual's relationship with the group as an entity can be positive if this relationship allows the individual to internalize feelings of self-esteem. A person

can be seen as having a need to experience belonging and acceptance within a cohesive group as a way to establish and maintain
a sense of internal unity (Bach, 1957). Members may attempt to use
the group as a whole to gratify unconscious fantasies that reflect
unmet needs, but the desire to maintain group cohesion and acceptance from others will result in self-exploration, less defensiveness,
and growth toward positive relationships. Bach (1957) views the
individual as capable of using the group in ways that either negate
or enhance the development of self-esteem. Object-relations theory
has moved in a different direction than many of the earlier psychoanalytic group theories by associating the power of a group to exist
as a cohesive entity with the development of members' perceptions
of individuality. Interpretation by the therapist is less important for
moving toward individuation than is the establishment of interactions that meet authentic needs.

In object-relations theory, group atmosphere becomes an important factor, perhaps an excessively emphasized one. It is possible
to treat the group atmosphere as if it were a personality, a being in
its own right, to which members may look for nurturance. This kind
of perception can lead to a kind of dependency that inhibits individuation unless members feel that it is safe to disagree with others in
their group and to gain support from sources other than their group.
From the perspective of self-actualization, this theory emphasizes
that human potentials can be actualized most effectively in an environment that provides supportive and caring communication.

Self Psychology

Self psychology, based on the psychoanalytic theorizing of Heinz
Kohut (1971, 1977), places the development of a cohesive sense of
self at the center of the therapeutic enterprise. Kohut (1971) indicates that the self develops through internalization of early experiences of merging with the mother (or other care giver) and being
mirrored by the mother. Merging provides experiences of security
and well-being that gradually become internalized as a sense of self-
esteem. Communications that mirror a child reflect the care giver's
awareness of the child as a valued being and thus contribute importantly to his or her sense of self and self-value. Additionally, the

child's sense of self is built upon the process of idealizing someone who is perceived as omnipotent and whose strength and ideals are gradually internalized by the child. Furthermore, a person who has deficits in self-esteem may move toward greater strength of self by developing a "twinship" relationship with another—that is, a relationship in which the other is experienced as being very much like oneself (Kohut & Wolf, 1978). Thus, Kohut is more optimistic than Freud about people's ability to repair damage that they have suffered and to generate new "self-structures" through relationships at various times in the life cycle.

Kohut's theory, among other ideas derived from Freudian thought, probably comes closest to an overt conceptualization of a self-actualizing process that occurs through relationship. However, Kohut implies that the self can only be formed by passively transmuting and internalizing aspects of others. The ability of a person creatively to invent self through initiating new forms of relationship is minimized in this theory.

Object-relations theories and self psychology support the view that the group can provide a corrective emotional experience that can respond to previously unmet needs for love and significance. Self psychology places less emphasis on fantasies about internalized representations of objects compared with object-relations theories. The felt experience of relationship, especially its empathic aspects, is stressed by Kohut (1977).

Applied to groups, the feeling-level reactions of participants become important (Bacal, 1985). Relationships are experienced and felt by individuals, and these feelings and experiences determine who they become. Self psychology applied to group theory also attempts to explain how interpersonal dynamics can enhance or detract from the development of a positive sense of self (Berry, 1991). The human being is not so much a separate unit with biological drives as a being that exists through relationship, an entity who needs others to construct its perception of self. Applying Kohut's theory to group practice, it becomes plausible that a person could become stronger and healthier from experiencing him- or herself as a member of a cohesive and accepting group (Berry, 1991).

The use that members make of the therapeutic group has been understood, in object-relations theories and self psychology, as largely being activated by narcissistic motives (Bacal, 1985). The analysis of persons in a group focuses on how these individuals attempt to form relationships that will restore, maintain, and increase the sense of self. Self psychology indicates that members want to establish a feeling of belonging in a group as well as a feeling of being special. They may seek mirroring responses, may attempt to merge with others or with the group as a whole, or may establish a twinship relationship with another. Since members have typically been hurt in the past, their resistance to forming intimate relationships is properly understood as their attempts to protect themselves from expected hurt or from the possibility of reopening old wounds.

Self psychology pictures psychological health as derived from the establishment of a cohesive self, which is necessary for the recognition of a cohesive self in others and an understanding of how to respect the self of others. Narcissism, or self-love, is viewed as playing an essential role in developmental maturation. The development of a cohesive self is achieved through transmutations of narcissism and is necessary for participation in mutually empathic relationships (Kohut, 1977).

Humanistic and Existential Themes in Group Therapy

Humanistic theories, such as those of Maslow and Rogers, value the realization of human potentials and use the theme of self-actualization to affirm human beings and their possibilities (Daniels, 1988). Humanism thus emphasizes trust in the human organism, based on a belief that innate potentials for physical, emotional, and spiritual well-being, as well as innate motivation toward prosocial interpersonal interactions, exist. Humanistic theories can be seen as a reaction against Freud's pessimism. At the opposite extreme from Freud, this philosophy declares that human beings are essentially motivated to achieve caring and prosocial relationships. However, like Freud, the humanistic school tends to validate its assertions about human nature by appealing to biologically rooted, pseudoscientific metaphors (Daniels, 1988). Human beings are considered to have an innate nature that unfolds in a predictable manner, that moves unerringly toward inherent goals.

The existential movement in philosophy and psychology

does not react so much against Freud's pessimism as against his determinism. The existential position generally places great importance on persons' abilities to make choices that influence who they become. The existential philosopher Sartre (1956) describes persons as creating themselves through their acts. Most existentially oriented thinkers would not view the person as essentially either destructive or prosocial (although people can make destructive or prosocial choices). One key difference between Buber, the existentialist, and Rogers, the humanist, is that Buber (in spite of his respect for Rogers's therapeutic work) philosophically rejects Rogers's belief in a universal core predisposition toward constructive directions (Friedman, 1986). Buber feels that this belief in a positive core could inhibit therapists or other participants in relationships from engaging in certain kinds of growth-enhancing interpersonal dialogues. These dialogues would allow one participant, as an individual who has chosen values, to enter into another's struggle between constructive and destructive possibilities within that person's self. Buber uses the term *confirmation* to describe an effective interaction in which this kind of dialogue has occurred. Confirmation may result from a struggle between and within participants (Friedman, 1986).

One means to integrate existential and humanist views is to recognize that both are compatible with the assumption that the person is capable of constructing self and world creatively. Along with existentialism and humanism, the epistemologically oriented thinking of radical constructivists also emphasizes the human being as an active creator of reality (Watzlawick, 1990). Existential thinking tends to place more emphasis on individuals' confrontations with those factors that inevitably place limits on individuals than does constructivism, and existential theorists often see creativity as growing out of these confrontations (May, 1981; Perls, 1969). Relative to constructivism, the concerns of existentialism and humanism are generally more ontological (being oriented) than epistemological (knowing oriented). However, the view of the person as a creator of meanings, an organizer of perceptions, and a determiner of values seems to bridge the worlds of being and knowing. Within the process of being, knowing is integrated with action, and creation of meaning is inseparable from openness within perception (Perls, Hefferline & Goodman, 1951/1980). In the continuous activity of moment-to-moment existence, being is not separated from knowing, and emotion is not distinct from cognition.

A *central* assumption can be made in unstructured group therapy that integration occurs as being and knowing come together. This assumption will give a present-centered focus to therapy. Integration of being and knowing is evidenced by spontaneous actions and feelings as well as by intuitive awareness of self and others. In self-actualization that is promoted by unstructured therapy, knowing and being are one immediate process. Members can be encouraged to think, to feel, and to know—and they can be encouraged to know their experience as they experience it. Knowledge that is separated from being is less stimulating than knowledge that embraces being. From this perspective, experiential knowledge is preferable to attempts to formulate abstract "truths" that are separate from ongoing experience and existence (Bugental, 1978).

An example of being and knowing coming together occurred in the case of "Celia," a thirty-year-old woman who had suffered from mood swings and manic episodes that disrupted her life severely. Celia was a member of both structured and unstructured groups offered at a community mental health clinic. She attended these groups at a low point in her life—a time when she had lost her job, her relationship with her mother, and her fiancée. These losses were largely due to compulsive and grandiose ideation that revolved around themes of her power and importance, erratic behavior such as spending sprees, and outbursts of aggressive emotionality. Early in her therapy, Celia was able to recognize intellectually that one aspect of her problems involved her attempts to compensate for very negative feelings about herself and denial of her difficulties relating honestly with others. However, Celia did not realize fully that she could accept and value herself until she had gone through a process that allowed her to give to and receive from others. She stated at a later point in her therapy, "I thought I was better than everyone. But I met people, some of whom were worse off than me. And I found that I could value them and that sometimes I could help them feel better about who they are."

Through a process of giving and receiving, Celia's knowledge about the importance of self-acceptance came together with a new way of being with others. In both structured and unstructured situations, she made choices that involved her in a healing process. Her structured groups, generally forms of activity-oriented therapy offered by the center, provided opportunities to cooperate and involve self with others. In her unstructured group work, she was able to give and receive feedback in a way that confronted her limitations, and also to acknowledge her genuine caring about others. Celia eventually left therapy at a time when she was able to recommit herself to the academic work she had previously left, was working part-time, and was in the process of forming new friendships and a more adult relationship with her mother.

The more that a group has a structure imposed by the therapist, the more possible it becomes to treat knowledge as a goal that is separate from awareness of being—that is, imposed structuring often implies that there is some kind of predefined knowledge that members are expected to get from their group experience. This knowledge exists independently of what a group becomes through the process of interaction, and interactions are therefore aimed toward this knowledge. Misuse of structured group formats is far more likely to occur if the group leader is using the structure to assert his or her own importance to others. A group setting can be used by a leader to demonstrate that he or she has something special to give, that he or she is therefore a powerful and worthwhile being. Of course, one danger of this approach is unnecessary dependency; another is that members will be deprived of opportunities to find out how they are unique and what they have to contribute. Even in unstructured formats, it is possible for therapists to manipulate their groups so they (the therapists) appear to have knowledge or status that makes them more valuable or worthy than other members.

Unstructured groups can be based on a view that knowledge exists within a context that is continuously created by participants. Participants grasp their creativity by learning that their knowledge is relevant because it arises out of and is never separate from present experience. Present experience changes, brings about beginnings and endings, confronts people with their limitations, and discloses possibilities.

Since beginnings are not possible without endings, awareness of loss and limitation is as central to human self-actualization as is a sense of possibility and potential (May, 1981; Yalom, 1975). Members can learn to recognize choices that they make, to experience how they create themselves by choices that affect relationships in their group. These choices do not take place in a nonhistorical void. Members' past and present context for awareness affects their choices; thus, what is determined and what is nondetermined come together in a present act of being (May, 1981). Members of therapy groups often wrestle with the limitations of their personal and social contexts as they struggle to make choices that affect relationships and lives. Limitations such as poverty, loss, or physical handicaps or shortcomings can affect recognition and opportunities for actualization of potentials. Freedom to create within present experience is freedom within these limits.

Contributions of Rogers and Person-Centered Therapy

One major commonality of humanistic and existential theorists has been their recognition that the themes that evolve during groups are most effectively and therapeutically treated if these issues are confronted in the context of authentic present relationships (Rogers, 1970; Yalom, 1975). Carl Rogers's (1970) theory of individual and group therapy has had a significant impact on many leaders of therapy groups (Corey, 1990, 1991). One aspect of Rogers's influence is his emphasis on the importance of present-centered communication that is genuine and empathic. His emphasis on the importance of congruent perception and communication leads him to question whether psychiatrists and psychoanalysts have access to any special knowledge about human beings that make these professionals the sole proper authorities to conduct individual and group therapy.

Rogers's (1967a) theory proposes that the quality of communication is far more important to therapy than any special knowledge contained in the communication. Rogers was the first theorist to advocate that his own and others' sessions be taped and reviewed to discover what *is* therapeutic, rather than relying on what experts *say* is therapeutic (Garfield & Bergin, 1986). His analysis of the events that he observed to lead to experiences of healing and growth resulted in his departure from some of the premises of Freudian psychotherapy.

Rogers (1980) came to emphasize what is genuine and exists in the present, whereas psychodynamic therapy attempts to analyze and expose resistances to a free flow of energy and experience, especially focusing on the transference of early relationship patterns and needs. Rogers's method of working with clients focuses attention on the present dynamics between participants in therapeutic situations and builds on whatever authentic communication is occurring. The recognition of avoidance behaviors and strategies of communication is not considered necessary for therapeutic personality change (Rogers, 1967a). Avoidance can be assumed to diminish automatically as trust and openness become operating principles for communication. Analysis of past behaviors and situations is not required. Individuals move toward health and self-actualization as they learn that they can trust themselves, their perceptions of experience, and others (Rogers, 1977).

The experience of trust and openness is also important in psychoanalytic psychotherapy. In a healing psychoanalytic therapy session or group, the client also develops trust, often through sharing his or her "dark side" or perhaps by disclosing significant past events whose importance has been denied or avoided. Yet Rogers's theory diverges from psychoanalysis in that Rogers suggests that it is possible fully to trust oneself, one's whole organism, and one's actual experience.

The trustworthiness of human nature emerges as a central theme in therapy groups. Clients struggle to learn whether they can have confidence in themselves and others. They may find that other members and the leader support their ability to be open to their experience, or they may find that others discourage openness and self-revelation. If the group expects participants to be fully open to their own experiences and evaluates members negatively if they appear to be self-protective, members who have difficulty being open may be discouraged. If there is excessive interpretation or evaluation of a client's experience by the leader or other members, clients who wish to become more open to experience without feeling evaluated may become discouraged.

Interpretation is not an important therapeutic element in

Rogers's theory. Rogers (1970) stresses that interpretation generally leads to a devaluation of the client's own judgment. The client is considered by Rogers to be the expert on her or his own experience. The empathy of the therapist is considered far more helpful than the therapist's interpretive ability. Empathy is viewed as the means by which the therapist can understand the world of the client from that individual's perspective (Rogers, 1967a). This kind of understanding supports the client in his or her own self-exploration. Kohut (1971) also stresses the importance of empathy; however, he primarily sees it as a means to gain information that could assist effective interpretation.

Rogers may have underestimated the extent to which communication with another person tends to involve simultaneous interpretations of one's own and the other person's experience. Clients often use the interpretations of others as the basis for their own interpretations of themselves. They may seek out others' understanding and reactions and then will filter these through their own interpretations.

Self-actualization is often equated with experiencing one's "real self" (Wilson, 1988). However, this linguistic terminology does not mean that some type of static entity is involved (Wilson, 1988). The "real self" is not static; it can be viewed from many perspectives and can change, depending on such variables as time, point of view, and focus of awareness. If members see themselves as disclosing who they are from their "core," they generally mean that they are not hiding feelings or disguising their needs or reactions. Finding one's center within experience gives more freedom to change, not less. When clients self-actualize in a group, one aspect of this process can be the realization that they are perceived differently by various participants and that all of these perceptions or interpretations have some degree of validity. One's own disclosures to others are also one's interpretations of oneself. Although self-actualization thrives on simple and honest disclosures of self, these should not be taken as concrete and irrevocable evidence of who a person is or who that person will become in a group. Self-actualization also thrives when members do not try to stereotype each other and do not rely on preconceptions about who each other is or how each participant is expected to respond to interpersonal events.

A core belief in Rogers's (1987) understanding of human beings is that people are essentially constructive beings; they are prosocial and motivated toward health and growth. As individuals come in contact with who they genuinely are, each person can be expected to find vast inner resources to direct his or her behavior, relationships, and movement toward growth (Rogers, 1980). The group as a whole thus also has the potential to become an expression of a universal movement toward self-actualization. Rogers indicates that if a group is functioning therapeutically, something universal begins to emerge. This process involves a loss of the experience of oneself as separate; the sense of "me" and "you" becomes less distinct (Rogers, 1980). Rogers (1980) reports that people in such groups have expressed highly positive feelings arising from the sensation that their consciousness is not separate from others in the group.

Wood (1982), a theorist of the Rogerian, or person-centered, school of thought, has also found that a therapy group tends to evolve as a distinct entity that influences its individual members. Bozarth (1981) has concluded that person-centered groups can work well with an unusually large number of people. As many as one hundred people have found they could function successfully and grow as a group. Person-centered groups are conducted with the premise that individuals are the best authority for choosing situations that will assist their own growth. Therefore, group leaders would have little investment in trying to guide or direct members in any particular direction (Bozarth, 1986).

Contributions of Perls and Gestalt Therapy

One possible problem with the belief that people will always move in a constructive direction is that it may make it difficult to recognize when individuals or groups are struggling with avoidance or hurtful patterns (assuming that such struggles can occur). Perhaps people can benefit from an atmosphere in which constructions are questioned and challenged up to the point where a person decides to destroy the construction. This possibility would be consistent with the theory of Gestalt therapy.

One core concept in this view of healthy human functioning is that people need to accept their ability to destroy in order to become creative (Perls, Hefferline & Goodman, 1951/1980). This insight can serve as a reference point for many aspects of therapeutic encounter in groups. For example, people may need assistance from others to sort out and integrate their potential for destruction and creation. It may not be helpful simply to assure these people that we will support their choices, whatever these are, because we know that no one else could possibly know what would be best for them. They may benefit from some awareness of how we would go about making decisions. Of course, the possibility of imposing values on clients becomes more acute as a therapist offers more of his or her own perspective and ideas (Polster & Polster, 1973). Therefore, a therapist who uses this approach also needs to be able to convey respect for a client's strength and ability to make choices in a free environment (Polster & Polster, 1973).

Gestalt therapy has tended to view self-actualization as an activity that integrates polarities within the person. Integration is often seen in this theory as an individual rather than universal activity of awareness (Page & Chang, 1989). Perhaps for this reason, Gestalt therapists generally conceive of the group as a setting wherein members explore their experiences individually while others observe, rather than as a setting wherein members cooperatively share explorations and develop a relationship with their group as a whole (Polster & Polster, 1973). Perls (1969) always used the "hot-seat approach" when conducting therapy in groups (see also Polster & Polster, 1973). The hot-seat approach places one individual in the center of attention, and this individual works on his or her unfinished business—that is, unresolved personal issues. Other group members are placed in the position of learning vicariously from the experience between the therapist and the client. One can conclude that Perls (1969) relates to a group as a collection of individuals, and his focus is on the resolution of individual issues rather than on the development of cohesive group process.

Polster and Polster (1973) have found that therapists can apply Gestalt theory to group work so that the leader surrenders more control to the group than Fritz Perls did. Polster and Polster (1973) advocate a "floating hot-seat" approach, a natural movement of members in and out of the center of their group's attention as they learn to attend to salient issues without the intervention of the therapist. Currently, Gestalt therapists vary greatly in the degree of control exercised by the group leader (Korb, Gorrell & Van De Riet, 1989). This variation in leader styles arises from the Gestalt emphasis on individual creativity, an emphasis that allows much freedom for the group leader to define his or her own role in the therapy situation.

Though it supports the concept of self-actualization, Gestalt theory stresses the individualistic and creative aspects of self-actualization more than the social and universal aspects (see Korb, Gorrell & Van De Riet, 1989; Perls, Hefferline & Goodman, 1951/ 1980). A consistent emphasis of Gestalt therapists who work in groups is that clients have individual needs and issues to resolve. The concept of a shared group spirit tends to be emphasized less in Gestalt theory than in person-centered theory. Person-centered therapy focuses on individuals but includes social and universal aspects of self-actualization (see Rogers, 1980). Gestalt theory and person-centered theory can be integrated by noticing areas of contact between the theories (for example, both intend to assist movement toward wholeness), valuing differences in emphasis (autonomy versus empathy), and reconciling these differences within a broader framework that creates a relationship between the theories (O'Hara, 1984).

Divergent Views of Self-Actualization

As participants use their group to affirm their individuality and universality, certain recurrent themes emerge. The theorists that we have investigated thus far in this chapter have noted the importance of several ideas but have arrived at different conclusions concerning how to treat them. We have identified certain differences concerning theorists' views on these key themes: (1) the need of group members for authoritative leadership, (2) perceptions of the group's existence as a coherent totality or as an entity, (3) the possibility of members being fully open to experience, (4) the possibility of attaining an authentic, present-centered focus in communications, and (5) the trustworthiness of human nature. We have noted that the varying assumptions and biases of leaders can affect group process and thus can influence what is observed in the process of therapy. Yet it is still hard to believe that trained observers of human interaction could come to such divergent conclusions.

Differing interpretations of human behavior in groups may have occurred because observers have focused on different facets of human growth, aspects of the process of estrangement and reintegration. Therapy groups take place to help members heal their interpersonal and intrapersonal estrangement and become more integrated through the process of relationship. If theorists focus on the activities that are evidence of estrangement, they may stress the apparent untrustworthiness of human beings, their perversity, their interpersonal games, and their self-destructiveness. If theorists focus on events that demonstrate reintegration, they may emphasize the trustworthiness of persons, the emergence of the group as a coherent unity, and the potential for authenticity, self-direction, and growth. It is therefore as incorrect to say that people are essentially untrustworthy as it is to say the reverse. People who feel estranged may behave in untrustworthy ways, but they can begin to move toward reintegration and trustworthiness when they can fully experience the dilemma of their estrangement.

Self-actualization has generally been associated with the assumption that there is a universal tendency to move toward growth and enhanced integration. Theorists such as Rogers (1977) and Patterson (1985) have viewed self-actualization as evidence that there is a constructive core to all human beings. Patterson has postulated that self-actualization is an underlying motivation shared by all persons, evidenced by a continuous striving to maintain and enhance ourselves. This idea of self-actualization as a *core motivation* can be traced back to Kurt Goldstein's use of the term in the 1930s, when he observed how brain-damaged individuals strove to maintain their organismic viability (Korb, Gorrell & Van De Riet, 1989).

Maslow, Rogers, and Patterson share the view that self-actualization is an innate, biologically inherited potential. Unlike Patterson, Maslow (1962) perceived only a small portion of the human population as being authentically involved in a self-actualizing process. Maslow's theory depended on a differentiation of deficiency needs from "beingness" needs (Goble, 1971). While he viewed self-actualization (a beingness need) as a potential that is latent within all persons, he thought that this potential could only emerge as a central concern after lower-order needs for safety and self-esteem had been met. Rogers and Patterson did not differentiate higher- and lower-order needs and were thus able to view self-actualization as a central and omnipresent organizing principle for human development.

On the one hand, Maslow's model of self-actualization is problematic because it is based on a predetermined hierarchy of needs contradicted by observations of unique patterns of individual growth and development. This theory also artificially dichotomizes the human race into "actualizers" and "nonactualizers" along lines that many view as arbitrary and reflective of personally and culturally bound value judgments (Geller, 1984; Lethbridge, 1986). The model proposed by Rogers and Patterson, on the other hand, is also problematic because it attributes human activities that foster growth to sources within organisms and harmful activities to sources in the environment. Explaining hurtful behavior according to environmental influences alleviates guilt but avoids issues of responsibility (Yalom, 1980). For example, a person can blame his or her parents for creating a hurtful environment, and these parents can blame their parents, ad infinitum. Basic questions remain unanswered concerning how individuals who are assumed to be essentially good can consistently and repeatedly make decisions to wound others or themselves.

Toward a Viable Construct of Self-Actualization

Self-actualization needs to be understood, not as a rigid prescription or formula for growth, but as a concept that helps us to understand how people and communities establish patterns of relationship that lead to or away from growth. This concept should not be confused with self-conscious attempts to better life according to a predetermined plan for growth; similarly, self-actualization has nothing to do with egocentric gains for oneself at the expense of other people or at the expense of one's relations with them. Self-actualization should be understood as (1) a process of relationship; (2) the ability to affirm one's distinctiveness as a basis for caring about others, giving to others, and receiving from others; and (3) the affirmation and confirmation of one's own being, the being of others, and the source of being, which connects oneself with nature and with others.

Ultimately, self-actualization is the recognition that one's distinctiveness and one's universality are not opposed to each other. Distortions of self-actualization are therefore based on avoidance of either distinctiveness or universality. Individuals stifle their own growth if they are afraid to stand out and be noticed (Yalom, 1980) or if they are afraid to let go of themselves and experience a larger totality than their usual sense of self (Maslow, 1964; Wilson, 1988). Individual growth is moderated by a kind of contraction into distinctiveness as an individual and a kind of expansion into a more universal and infinite awareness (Schneider, 1990).

Distorted Forms of Self-Actualization

Self-actualization can be viewed as a primary psychological process that establishes the integrity of human personhood. Self-actualization can never be totally blocked or denied because any one who is alive will have some degree of integrity. However, as we have seen, self-actualizing processes can become severely distorted and perverted.

Individuals may tend to perpetuate distorted dynamics as they form new relationships. If the relationships that have contributed to who a person is have been hurtful or constrictive, people may have only a very vague sense of how to formulate constructive relationships. People may also have chosen modes of relationship that they believe helps to protect them or ensure their power. These choices can blind people to opportunities for constructive relationships of which they are indeed capable. Persons may need to acknowledge that they have committed their energy and awareness in a misguided or self-destructive direction before they are able to form new and better patterns.

Commitment to a distorted form of self-actualization can be disguised by self-deceiving perceptions. People may perceive that negative interpersonal and intrapersonal dynamics "have a life of their own" or just "always seem to happen that way." Individuals may feel that they are possessed by negative forces beyond personal control. For example, patterns of drug abuse, fearfulness, or hurtfulness to self or others can become powerful compulsions against which individuals feel powerless and by which they feel controlled. A person can "know what is right" and yet can continue to perpetuate a pattern that is leading to unhappiness, anxiety, and lack of fulfillment and success.

Nonetheless, the environment should certainly be considered as a factor in the perpetuation of negative patterns of relationship and behavior. Environments can support or hinder self-actualization. If individuals are taught to fear or ignore experiential possibilities, they are likely to mistrust their own awareness and creativity. Environmental support is helpful for the self-actualization of individuals, and some degree of support is essential. However, the individual as well as the environment can create distortions of self-actualization. Individuals can choose a distorted form of self-actualization due to anxiety about emerging as a distinct individual or to avoid the responsibilities that emerge from awareness of universality. Self-actualization is therefore possible in adverse environmental conditions and can be avoided even given a supportive environment. Apparently adverse conditions can bring a person to a greater appreciation of the importance of relatedness, and supportive conditions can be misused to avoid self-confrontation that would enhance self-actualization.

Such factors as past conditioning, social prejudices, financial stress, and lack of emotional support in a community can make it difficult for individuals to thrive. Therapy generally focuses, however, on what an individual can do to create change—things such as attitudes, relationship patterns, and experiences. This focus should not blind us to the very real effects of environments and should allow us to enhance the ability of persons to recognize whatever personal power and responsibility are possible within given circumstances and situations. Without negating the role of the environment, therapy can assist people to own the negative dynamics by which they often feel "possessed" and through a process of integration can help members to reframe and redirect energies that have been misapplied. Reframing involves the recognition that "this is I" rather than "this is outside me," and redirection involves making connections where there were previously disconnections, interpersonally and intrapersonally (for example, see Yalom, 1975, 1980; Perls, 1969, 1973).

The persistence of negative interpersonal patterns when there are options in the environment for change and growth is often due to an investment in and a commitment to a distorted form of self-actualization. Self-aggrandizement or self-hatred can become habituated forms of experiencing and relating. This habituation derives from identification with a negative pattern that has been established in the person's perception of "reality." The person may emotionally need to perpetuate a pattern of being with others that he or she intellectually recognizes is causing self-destructive or self-limiting behaviors.

As we have seen, groups can either move toward healing or away from healing and can either create an environment that enhances or avoids self-actualization. This movement within groups is largely associated with members' perceptions of the possibility and desirability of realizing their ability to communicate relatedness within the psychological environment provided by the group. The actualization of these potentials may involve risk taking; there are likely to be risks involved in becoming distinct—for example, criticism or rejection. Members tend to heal and grow if they perceive their environment as one that is encouraging and trustworthy. Yet their self-actualization reflects personal decisions and choices that are influenced but not controlled by the environment. Members' collective choices and decisions within relationships help create what their environment is and what it becomes. A group that becomes an optimal environment for self-actualization thus provides sufficient support for trust to develop and sufficient challenge to assist members in questioning their complacency and static systems of belief.

Self-Actualization and Guilt

The choice to realize the potential to experience and communicate relatedness can disturb the psychological status quo of the person who communicates, the person who receives the communication, or the group in which it takes place. Actualization of increased awareness and involvement is often difficult because homeostatic stability is affected. Secure roles that have been established to regulate transactions may be called into question.

However, the decision to maintain an avoidance-based status quo at the expense of self-actualization is also a risk. The hazard is that estrangement from the process of being will become an entrenched way of life and that it compulsively will govern responses within ongoing encounters. Because the universal process of being is essentially unified, this process exerts a "pull" on aspects of individual processes that are disunited or split.

The pull toward reunification can be denied, but the price that is paid is ontological guilt. Similarly, cultures can resist the pull toward integration of estranged members and groups, and this resistance creates ontological guilt on a cultural scale. Ontological guilt is not tied to feelings of shame due to introjected values. Ontological guilt is the anxiety that attends disconnection from being. This disconnection arises from refusal to be distinct and refusal to be aware of universal values that connect people to each other and to nature. Disconnection from being leads individuals to experience estrangement and attendant guilt. Yalom (1980) refers to this kind of guilt as "existential," a guilt that "is a positive constructive force, a guide calling oneself back to oneself" (p. 280).

Differentiation of ontological guilt from guilt that is created by the imposition (and subsequent introjection) of others' values and others' expectations for conformity assists effective therapy. Perls, Hefferline, and Goodman say that "an introject consists of material—a way of acting, feeling, evaluating—which you have taken into your system of behavior, but which you have not assimilated. . . . you take it on a forced acceptance . . . as if it were something precious. It is actually a foreign body" (1980, p. 23). The experience of ontological guilt can lead to potentially corrective experiences that can be worked through until changes in patterns of being allow guilt feelings to be dropped. Ontological guilt can permit an enhanced process of self-actualization to be realized.

On a cultural level, ontological guilt alters patterns of relationship within the culture. These changes do not occur to meet expectations or legal sanctions imposed from outside sources (which leads to introjected guilt) but take place because the culture has learned to question its own assumptions and biases. Since culture is an abstraction that expresses a collective dynamic formed by individuals, it cannot question its assumptions unless individuals within the culture are questioning theirs. Constructive change will occur if individuals feel guilty because biases against others are recognized as having disconnected individuals from a potentially inclusive process of being. Therapeutic groups are minicultures that can be models for how a group atmosphere can encourage self-questioning by members of assumptions and biases. Therapeutic self-questioning is encouraged, not when members attempt to instill guilt, but when they help each other to recognize potentially constructive aspects of guilt that have arisen within the life experience.

Dynamics Involved in Distortion

Lack of such basic elements as empathy, caring, and respect within primary relations in childhood can play a major part in the establishment of the patterns that lead to deep estrangement from the process of being. However, persons can also develop problems that lead to distorted forms of self-actualization if they become estranged later in life and in spite of a rewarding childhood. On a deep, often unconscious level, the estranged person senses that he or she cannot be truly alive until he or she reunites with the process of being and regains a sense of power within self and fulfillment in relationship. However, the estranged person has learned to mistrust being in relationship, often due to hurts or disillusionments, and so resists the attraction of the process of being. This resistance is typically expressed as a rigidly maintained desire to be in control and can also be expressed as a desire to avoid responsibility (an effort to feel a sense of control by avoiding blame). The ability to be in control is substituted for authentic creativity as the form of power that is perceived to be self-actualizing.

One of the authors had a client who illustrates how people can resist the pull of being, or the messages provided by ontological guilt, in their efforts to maintain a semblance of being in control of their own lives. "Robert" was a member of a therapy group led by one of the authors that was conducted in a hospital setting. When Robert was young, he was a member of a gang in a large metropolitan area. As he described himself later, he felt completely crazy in the ways that he acted. He was continually fighting with the members of other gangs and was regularly breaking the law to obtain money to support a life in the fast lane. Gradually, Robert became extremely unhappy with himself as he lived an increasingly antisocial life-style. Robert eventually decided that life was not worth living, and he ended up trying to commit suicide by shooting himself in the head while looking in a mirror and laughing at himself.

Though Robert did not kill himself, he did sever his optic nerve and became totally blind. He spent some time in the psychiatric ward of a hospital. Yet, as Robert himself later said, becoming blind completely changed his life for the better. When Robert made this statement, he did not appear to the author to be in denial of being blind; instead, he seemed to mean what he was saying. One way of explaining why Robert was glad to be blind is to show how ontological guilt contributed to the general lack of meaning he felt when he was living the life of a hustler.

Robert gradually became more and more unhappy with himself because of his basic estrangement from the process of being until he reached the point where he attempted suicide. Once he was blind, his life slowed down, and he was forced to develop new and more satisfying interests and relationships. One of Robert's activities once he became blind was to become involved with associations for the blind. His therapy group assisted Robert to reconnect with others in ways that allowed him to contribute and receive. Reconnecting with others occurred simultaneously with Robert's reassessment of the meaning of being with people in the world.

Robert was able to develop a new sense of being worthwhile. A person capable of authentic creativity and aware of power within self responds positively to evidence of creativity and power within others. A person whose awareness of power is distorted strives to control others' power and to dominate others' creativity. A twisted awareness of power never truly senses power within self; power is only experienced when something outside oneself is controlled.

Thus, a person one does not control becomes a threat. The threatened individual may try to control the other through intimidation or punishment or through manipulations and rewards for compliance. Distorted power can lead a person to invalidate spontaneous expressions of feelings or creative approaches to situations.

People may fear that if they stop controlling others, they will lose authority over self and life; they may even fear that they will totally lose their identity or their sense of psychological balance. Such individuals are likely to repress feelings of ontological guilt and to perceive such feelings as possibly overwhelming to their sense of reality and their ability to survive. Yet if group members are willing to explore strong needs or desires to control others, they often receive helpful feedback. Members can also learn vicariously from observing others that it is possible to express feelings of ontological guilt, as well as related feelings of grief or vulnerability, without going crazy or losing their identity.

Estrangement often leads people to seek means of protecting themselves from the experiences of insecurity and anxiety associated with the perceived threat that their reality could be diminished, engulfed, or annihilated by the process of being. These perceptions can play a part in intimate relationships and can arise either subtly or overtly within relationships between members of therapy groups. In this situation, members (including the therapist) are likely to bolster their sense of security by communicating in ways that hide self from others and by establishing role-oriented interpersonal games. These strategies are based on a hidden desperation, a desperation that has not been experienced and integrated, but that drives one to maintain a hold on a controllable and predictable reality. These distorted forms of self-actualization hurt others and oneself because they are governed by rules that prohibit openness to experience and are aimed at the goal of avoiding reintegration with the process of being.

Distorted forms of self-actualization also run the risk of becoming self-perpetuating vicious circles. Defensive maneuvers and resistance to ontological guilt may lead a person to avoid communicating relatedness, a failure that engenders more ontological guilt, which then must be defended against, and so on. Awareness must be fragmented and aspects of experience split off in order to maintain this vicious cycle. In extreme forms of distortion, often termed "psychotic," awareness can become tortuously twisted. For example, persons can deeply hate themselves for attempting to exist, can annihilate their own attempts to organize experience, or can attempt to refuse any communication of relatedness. Although research shows evidence of an organic component in severe forms of psychotic experience, distorted family relationships as well as feelings of self-devaluation and often intense self-hatred are also typically involved (Arieti, 1974). Seriously distorted forms of self-actualization are evidenced by repetitive and compulsive patterns of behavior that often seem beyond individual control. The individual's attempts to suppress the experience of ontological guilt play a part in these self-created vicious cycles. Attempts to be in control lead to experiences of being out of control.

Before they can end a vicious cycle, persons may need to reach a point where they perceive that control has been lost to the extent that self-control is impossible. The person can then let go. This letting-go experience has been reported in Zen Buddhist descriptions of satori, or enlightenment (Watts, 1961; Wilber, 1980), in Gestalt-oriented (Perls, Hefferline & Goodman, 1951/1980) and person-centered descriptions of movement toward health (Rogers, 1980), and in descriptions of the path by which members of Alcoholics Anonymous generally have to "hit bottom" before they can change destructive patterns of behavior and relationship (Lewis, Dana & Blevins, 1988). Descriptions of letting-go processes that lead toward health and wholeness are so pervasive that an ontological basis for these experiences seems likely. Therefore, therapy groups assist members' movements toward self-actualization if these groups become settings wherein members feel safe to release some of their self-control and wherein members can reveal their impasses or the ways in which they have experienced hitting bottom.

Historical Manifestations of Distorted Self-Actualization

Distorted forms of self-actualization have been evident throughout human history. Politically, these have often revolved around political parties and group leaders who espouse slogans that verbalize the importance of unity, power, and growth at the same time that forms of relationship are instituted that eliminate individual freedoms and responsibilities. Language that encourages identification with the party or group is used simultaneously with dynamics that undermine abilities to resist the party or group. The followers of such leaders often wish to identify with a powerful figure; they may want someone to control them, and they are willing to surrender their own distinctiveness to become part of a collective mass movement that promises actualization for the group (Fromm, 1964). These dynamics are a distortion of the dynamics of authentic self-actualization. Letting go to control by a leader is substituted for letting go to experience within awareness. Power achieved through identification and subjugation is substituted for personal power that arises from responsibility. The necessity of maintaining law, order, and control of deviants is generally a central theme in these movements. Such movements tend to arise when chaotic situations bring out people's anxieties about their own capacity for destructiveness.

The same dynamics that work in social and political situations can be evident in therapy group situations (Yalom, 1975; Leszcz, 1992). A group leader can operate in ways that are similar to political leaders who encourage dependence by undermining opportunities for responsibility. Group members may also look for authoritative leadership if they experience too much anxiety or perceive the beginnings of chaos as conflict emerges. A leader can present him- or herself as a powerful figure, assist members in avoiding becoming distinct individuals, and encourage participants' willingness to believe that they need someone to be in authority to keep them in control of themselves.

In extreme forms, this negative dynamic produces cultlike interpersonal patterns of relationship. Leaders and organizations may attack members' self-integrity by creating double binds that are resolved through conversion and by inducing altered states of consciousness that are used as "proof" that a new person has emerged through a miraculous process (Cushman, 1989). Thus, the ability of the self to form directions and make sense of the world is undermined in a manner that fosters allegiance to the organization's program and a willingness to adopt a new more "positive" ideology.

An example of the process of distorted self-actualization occurred with the Synanon movement in drug rehabilitation. Charles

Dederick, Synanon's leader, gradually assumed a hierarchical position of near-total control in this therapeutic community. Therapeutic process became subordinated to a structure that encouraged certain members to control other members who were viewed as morally inferior (Yablonsky, 1965).

Because the pattern through which distorted self-actualization occurs has aspects that are repeated across situations, cultures, and history, an ontological basis for this dynamic can be postulated. The basis of this pattern is the use of charismatic or authoritarian leadership, offers of miracle technologies or cures, and exploitation of the anxieties and emptiness of selves to assist individuals in undermining themselves (see Cushman, 1989).

In less extreme forms, distorted self-actualization encourages conforming and role-oriented relationships as well as judgmental attitudes about members' contributions. These milder forms of distorted actualization occur in those groups that McClure (1990) calls regressive (or immature), as opposed to generative (or mature). According to McClure, the members of a regressive group abdicate responsibility, become numb to feelings, use hatred of enemies and out groups to generate cohesion, rely on allegiance to a myth of intragroup harmony and lack of conflict, and react negatively during stressful situations. Generative groups are characterized by curiosity, openness, respect, love, and trust. Participants feel safe and are free to express themselves. They sometimes feel a sense of surrender to a greater whole that differs from the loss of autonomy that occurs in regressive groups. Individuals do not lose their identities, but "integrate the 'I' with the 'We.' Group members become spontaneous, rather than autonomous, and are engaged and carried along, not in spite of themselves, but beyond themselves" (p. 167).

Enhancement of Self-Actualization in a Group Setting

When people make the decision to join an unstructured therapy group, they are usually willing to confront their own distortions or their anxieties about being open with self and others. However, in spite of their positive motivation, they are likely to introduce these distortions and anxieties into their relationships with others in their group. People tend to repeat what they know rather than move into

an unknown form of relationship. A therapeutic group is therefore
an opportunity for members to work through their relationship
patterns rather than simply to gain cognitive information about the
possibility of trying new forms.

Members may make changes in their relationship pattern if
they can acknowledge its limitations. If a member experiences these
limitations and risks new forms of relationship, he or she can become aware of different possibilities for expressing caring about
others or for allowing others to care about self. Robert, the client
who was discussed earlier in this chapter, illustrates how group
members can take interpersonal risks to develop new forms of relationships. During the unstructured therapy group that Robert
joined, he consistently showed the ability to develop helpful relationships. He also served as a model by trying to change his life
outside of the group. Robert was ultimately successful in turning
his life around by becoming creatively involved with others and by
obtaining a personally rewarding job.

A group becomes a setting that encourages the self-actualization of its members if they feel free to experience estrangement
without being judged negatively and if they sense they will be accepted even if they move away from predictable patterns of being
with others. Someone who knows a person only casually may have
difficulty recognizing whether that person is choosing or avoiding
the actualization of potentials for creativity and integration. However, these choices are often apparent to others in a group because
self-actualization involves relationships and can be seen in changes
in the quality of these. Changes are likely to include movement
toward authenticity, enhanced awareness of self and others, trust in
self and others, and acceptance of mutual responsibility to form
directions. Of course, if members become too intent on making
"meaningful" changes in their patterns of relationship, they can
lose a sense of simple acceptance of self within the moment. A
balance is therefore desirable between acceptance of who members
are and who they are becoming.

Whether members wish to risk changes in their usual pattern
of being with others or whether they are relatively content with
themselves as they are, their interactions help create a group atmosphere. This atmosphere is formed by the individual members' per-

ceptions of the other participants and themselves and by the quality of freedom in group communications. If a group atmosphere is promoting the self-actualization of members, the themes that arise in interactions will likely be affected. Rogers (1970), a careful observer of group atmosphere, notes that certain themes emerge in groups that tend to help promote self-actualization of members. The following themes are in general agreement with Rogers's (1970) observations about constructive groups and are likely to characterize interactions as the group encourages growth: (1) the members do not seek authoritarian leadership from any one participant but become flexible in taking leadership roles themselves; (2) the members often make comments that reflect their perception of other members as individuals; (3) participants express willingness to be open to experiences in their group; (4) members value an authentic, present-centered focus in communication; and (5) they move toward the view that they and others in their group are trustworthy.

The development of such basic themes as authenticity, the nature of the group as an environment that can support individuality, and members' awareness of each other's strengths and trustworthiness reflects the degree of support for self-actualization. It is impossible to predict how or if self-actualization will occur for members; they themselves often do not know beforehand. Self-actualization is an integrative movement that brings individuals into contact with others in ways uniquely meaningful for those involved and that must develop from mutual perceptions rather than from preconceived labels, roles, predictions, or explanations. This movement of people in a group context toward mutual contact can reintegrate love, power, and justice as a gestalt in being. This gestalt has a unique configuration for each individual and relationship.

Members may not realize in what direction they need to move before they have experienced the potential of the group to establish openness, trust, and honesty. Yet we assume that people are capable of providing their own direction for self-actualization because no other source can force this unified movement. *Imposed* concepts of self-actualization, "healthy" behavior, fulfillment, and the like may well lead to introjected guilt and detract from spontaneous present-centered interactions. By definition, self-actualization cannot be imposed on an individual from outside and cannot be imposed on a group by either a leader or external institutional forces.

Self-Actualization and Temporal Orientation

We have indicated that an individual's process of self-actualization is encouraged by a focus on the present in communication and relationship. This focus may be a different temporal orientation than that promoted in many settings outside the therapy situation. Many cultural institutions in the West emphasize a future-oriented perspective that aims toward growth based on what one can expect to become if one works hard or sacrifices for a cause. Because members of therapeutic groups also belong to society, it is important that their group generates a present-centered atmosphere that includes exploration of future concerns. These concerns are worthwhile topics for discussion if they are personally relevant and reflect a member's relationship with society. Nevertheless, a focus on the present is conducive to change and growth because change occurs through action, and action only occurs in the present. (Action can occur in terms of perception, which is difficult to observe, or in terms of behavior, which is easier to see.)

There is a rationale—one with implications for self-actualization—for focusing on present experience in group therapy. Although past patterns influence the present, people can spend endless hours gaining understanding of the past while remaining stuck in the present. Change in the present tends to come when a person breaks, at least to a degree, with the past. Dwelling on the past extensively can make it more difficult to risk change; people can become habituated to ruminating over past events in a manner that detracts from recognition of present opportunities.

Individuals can also use a focus on what will happen in the future to avoid awareness, action, and change that can occur in the present. A person can avoid changing by focusing on all the possible disasters that could occur. People can also discuss wishes or hopes for the future while their present behavior remains inconsistent with these ideals. Additionally, goals can become impositions associated with introjects if these objectives are not congruent with present experience and awareness.

People often underestimate the options that are available within the present. If they can learn to be more open to current possibilities, they will be open to future ones. Individuals also learn about their capacities for spontaneity and creativity in relationships and problem solving when they allow themselves to be present with one another.

Resistance to present-oriented awareness can be evidenced by excessive storytelling that lacks emotional involvement and experiential reality, by theatrical dramatics that are used in ways that prevent the establishment of relatedness, by abstract intellectualization that masks noninvolvement, or by an insistence on focusing on general events outside the group. Resistant members may find ways to distract others from current interactions. They are likely to characterize an emphasis on here-and-now encounters as an undesirable use of time in the group and as inappropriate or falsely intimate.

This kind of resistance is understandable; if norms that would regulate most social situations involving strangers are applied to the therapeutic group, present-centered interactions might be deemed risky or inappropriate. Resistance to focus on present interaction needs to occur. If group members begin to recognize their own avoidance as an obstacle to what they would like to gain, they can confront resistance constructively. Typically, group members become bored with avoidant forms of relationship and begin to confront tired interactions. A group leader can support members who risk a here-and-now focus (while not necessarily discouraging other forms of communication) and can encourage discussions in which members are willing to reveal their perceptions of the quality of interactions in their group.

Participants can interact in the present without excluding their awareness of the past and future—excluding the past and future is itself a form of avoidance. Past events and possible future events can be discussed either in the context of the present or in ways that avoid the current relationship. For example, one member may share his or her memories of past events with another in a manner that says, "I want you to know who I am, what I am struggling with, where I feel really stuck." This sharing can be vital to therapy. Another member can reveal memories in a manner that says, "I want to focus on these past events so that I can avoid forming or acknowledging connection with you now." This kind of sharing can be an obstacle to therapy if it becomes a pattern and may need to be acknowledged as a barrier.

A here-and-now emphasis in therapy can present problems, of course. Present centeredness becomes stale if it leads to stereotypical responses or simplistic answers to serious problems. Focus on the present can become artificial, a "should" that is an imposition on members and that can limit relatedness. A leader may equate a here-and-now focus with therapeutic work and make demands on members to "bring experience into the present," to "stop avoiding what you are feeling right now," and so on. Self-conscious efforts to stress the present are likely to interfere with whatever flow of energy is spontaneously emanating from current encounters. Members may learn from the leader that emphasis on the present is a formula for therapy and may respond to direction from the leader by complying with this formula. Member responsibility is then diminished and the potential for authentic I-Thou relatedness limited.

Part-Whole Relations

As members feel increased permeability of interpersonal barriers, they may sense that their own existence is a process of mutual definition that includes others and nature. In this event, they are increasingly likely to accept experiences that others present as demonstrating aspects of themselves as well as others (Agazarian, 1992). An unusually intense perception of part-whole relatedness joins the individual and collective aspects of group functioning so that individuals experience a sense of surrender to the flow of interaction in their group (McClure, 1990). We have noted that this unusual kind of openness occurs if the group's atmosphere is experienced as safe, trustworthy, and free.

Group members are affected by the atmosphere in their group, which they create through the process of their interactions. This environment does not necessarily lead to a perception of the group as an entity, but it does support a perception of universality, of a collectively shared reality. As we have already seen, awareness of differences between members' individual worlds does not interfere with their sense of a shared world if the group atmosphere supports indivi♭uality and universality. Adler (1969), Buber (1970), Jung (1958), Maslow (1962), Tillich (1954), and Yalom (1975) are among those who have found purpose, meaning, and well-being to be associated with perceptions of universality within human experience. Group members rarely seem to experience universality in their relations with other participants if they are trying to make their group into an entity that can negate aloneness (Wolf & Schwartz, 1962; McClure, 1990). The theme that existential aloneness is an essential aspect of the experiential encounter of individuals with the ground of being can be found in the writings of Bugental (1978), Jung (1916), and Rank (1945) and in the psychologically oriented philosophies of Buber (1970) and Tillich (1952). All of these authors share a recognition that congruence within the process of being is simultaneously an awareness of relatedness and an acceptance of aloneness.

Although members of therapeutic groups may experience aloneness as they come to terms with their own questions about themselves and the process of being with others, this aloneness should not be taken as evidence that people exist as separated beings. Members often wrestle with feelings of aloneness as they come to terms with their awareness that they are not as separate as they had believed. In recognizing that one's existence is not separate from others, an individual becomes more vulnerable. This vulnerability can bring feelings of aloneness. Members can experience themselves as part of a shared process with others; yet within this unitary process, I am nonetheless I and you remain you. Although I do not exist as an enclosed entity that is separate from you, my "I-ness" is distinct from your "you-ness." This distinctiveness is the basis of our uniqueness, of our ability to learn to share empathically (Friedman, 1986). At the same time, awareness of our uniqueness can be experienced as aloneness or even isolation (Yalom, 1980). This sense of aloneness can become particularly poignant for members who are dealing with a serious loss, who are experiencing terminal illness, or who are dealing with a particular personal limitation that is not shared by other members.

Members struggle with the relationship of their limitations with their ability to grow, of their distinctiveness with their universality, and of their self with their group. This struggle may bring sorrow or frustration or joy. Sometimes, individuals work through the feelings related to perceptions of themselves as a part within a whole and come to experience a kind of self-transcendence (Maslow, 1964; McClure, 1990). Self-transcendence is appropriately considered as an aspect of the development of self-actualization (Daniels, 1988; Vaughan, 1991). Experiences of self-transcendence can occur if a person reaches a new awareness of relationship between self and a larger totality. *Transcendence* of the self is a paradoxical and somewhat confusing term. Who other than the self could even talk about such an experience? How can the self have been transcended if it remains to talk about its experience of transcending?

Transcendence has been discussed by Frankl (1966) and Yalom (1980) as a movement of attentional focus and involvement toward others and away from oneself. Maslow's (1964) research into peak experiences and Jung's (1933) work on the collective unconscious led them to believe that integration was possible in which the usual feeling of self was transformed. Both of these theorists viewed such experiences as being essential to growth toward full humanness. Transpersonal psychologists have generally followed Maslow's lead and have discussed self-transcendence in terms that indicate the desirability and importance of this kind of encounter with the ground of being (Vaughan, 1991; Wilber, 1980).

In both interpersonal and transpersonal terms, transcendence is a construct that portrays individuals as capable of gaining new perspectives, more comprehensive forms of awareness—a new center for experiencing life and others. Transcendence, going beyond one's limits, implies that an individual has reoriented and formed a new perspective, a new gestalt within awareness. Transcendence in this sense is neither self-negation nor a means of making a person more "special" than others (Vaughan, 1991). Rather, the centering of ongoing experience around an enclosed and separated self is transformed so that more attention can be given to experiencing others and the world. It is thus possible to assert that members of therapeutic groups can experience degrees of self-transcendence as part of their self-actualization within group process.

Participation in a group can provide learning about part-whole relations. In an effective therapeutic group, the whole (group) exists because of its parts (members), and the parts communicate within the context of the whole. Because the whole provides a context that would not be possible without others, the whole is more than the sum of parts. The individual's sense of self can be enriched and recreated through participatory acts that involve others. Group members may gain a sense of "belonging in the universe" that can enrich their contact with people and their confidence in living.

Chapter Four

Awareness, Freedom, Responsibility

Awareness, freedom, and responsibility act as a gestalt within human experience that affect human perception and action in the world. Awareness, freedom, and responsibility are all interrelated because they cannot operate effectively in isolation from one another. For example, unless people are aware and act responsibly in human relationships, they will not enjoy the full benefits of human freedom. Unless people recognize their abilities to make responsible choices in life, they may not take the necessary steps to expand their levels of awareness in a manner that promotes their self-actualization. And unless people realize that they can make choices in a self-aware manner, they will not have the wisdom to act responsibly. Therefore awareness, freedom, and responsibility all are directly related to the goal of unstructured therapy groups of individual growth.

Awareness

In part, *awareness* can be viewed as the activity of registering, maintaining, and connecting aspects of experience. This activity leads to the formation of perceptions, cognitions, affects, and actions. The idea that awareness registers experience is incomplete because a separation of awareness and experience is implied. The point where awareness meets experience without separation is extremely difficult to convey linguistically; yet this meeting point is essential to the function of awareness. Here awareness simultaneously receives and creates experience, and awareness and experience are aspects of one process. Recognition of a human ability to experience certainly implies awareness as the basis for this ability (Egan, 1970).

To a considerable extent, experience is "given" by biological and physiological processes that predetermine forms for sensation and perception. Awareness constructs experiences, relates and links them to one another, defines them, creates boundaries or splits within these, and can open areas of experience that were previously compartmentalized.

Manifestations of Awareness

Self-actualization includes the realization that one can change one's perceptions, way of experiencing self and life, and quality of one's awareness (Rogers, 1980). Influencing one's experience does not mean that one can create whatever experience one desires. Avoiding or denying unpleasant aspects of experience is in many ways an attempt to fulfill wishes that one could make whatever reality one wants. Therefore, self-actualization is not likely to be enhanced by the belief that one can create any desired experience. This kind of belief could easily lead to holding people responsible for their hardships.

Construction of experience connects the person with the world by permitting the expression of various forms of activity. This construction allows for interactions with others who are also creating experience. Because each person's experience can affect another's, self-actualization leads to a mutually interactive mode of experiencing. This interactive and transactive form of experiencing is a creative sharing between self and world. As a process of being and becoming, awareness from individuals implies the potential interactive awareness of communities, cultures, and humanity as a whole. In an unstructured therapeutic group, the challenge for individuals to make a commitment to awareness is one that affects each person and the group as a whole.

As a uniquely individual activity, awareness involves the creation of personal meaning within experience by forming gestalts of perception-cognition-affect-action. The more an individual can relate the uniquely personal world of awareness to interpersonal and universal awareness, the more that person's construction of meaning becomes related rather than isolated (May & Yalom, 1984). Therapeutic groups provide opportunities for participants to learn about the relationship between the personal and interpersonal worlds of experience and potentially to connect individual with universal aspects of experience.

Awareness is far more likely to be actualized if individuals perceive psychological freedom to be real (Polster & Polster, 1973). Unstructured groups whose members are able mutually to construct an atmosphere of freedom are far more likely to experience their group as capable of enhancing the self-actualization of members than groups that are not able to create this atmosphere. Freedom, however, is essentially meaningless for individuals unless awareness of responsibility is also accepted (May, 1969, 1977, 1981; Yalom, 1980). Without responsibility, freedom can only become an exercise of actions that are random, behavior that cannot be focused toward integrated relationships.

Relationship of Self-Actualization to Awareness

Actualization is an inherently ontological concern of human beings, or as Rogers (1980) puts it, "a way of being" that thrives on congruent awareness of experience and empathic communication with others. A way of being is a way of being aware. Awareness is necessary for being as a person because awareness allows us to recognize our potentials and enables us to find ways to actualize them.

Experientially, self-actualization involves healing through reunification of the self with all aspects of present experience. Persons integrate themselves within present experience as they become open to their own potential to be fully aware. The activity of awareness becomes evident as people perceive meaningful wholes, or gestalts, within experience. This activity is also evident in human perceptions of groundedness within the process of being. Awareness can be seen in persons' abilities to be empathic with others and to recognize the world of experience communicated by another person. Awareness can potentially integrate the self with the other while preserving and enhancing the distinctiveness of persons.

From both person-centered (Rogers, 1961) and gestalt (Perls, 1971) perspectives, growth is related to openness to present experience. Both of these theories imply that abilities to be interpersonally open and related are associated with abilities to experience life fully. When persons become open to their experience, they use fewer strategies and techniques designed to avoid, split, or compartmentalize experience. Theorists have noted the deleterious effects of such strategies as repressive defenses organized against naturally occurring wishes and feelings (Freud, 1926/1953a), intellectualization (Perls, Hefferline & Goodman, 1951/1980), projection (Jung, 1916, 1956), habitual physical tensing (Reich, 1960), and interpersonal games (Berne, 1966). Any of these strategies may become evident during different events within group process as members attempt to avoid awareness. If participants accept the challenge to embrace awareness in their group, they will decrease their reliance on defensive strategies that restrict aspects of the experience of being with others.

To grow in awareness, people need to have a kind of faith that there is more to be gained by acknowledging experience than by denying it. People can be externally forced into a new experience, but they will reassert defensive strategies unless they are truly ready for increased openness (Perls, Hefferline & Goodman, 1951/1980). The person who is not ready for integration will find ways to reinstate the same patterns of distortion and blocking of perception that worked in the past. Attempts to coerce a group member into greater awareness are generally counterproductive, if not literally impossible. Although one can invite a person to explore experience, acceptance of this challenge is ultimately a matter of personal responsibility and subjective choice.

The Gestalt of Awareness, Freedom, and Responsibility

Awareness, freedom, and responsibility can be imagined as three points that form a triangle. The triangle can only emerge as a stable form when all three elements are present. Thus, stability and groundedness require the integrated functioning of all three elements.

A group therapy setting is simultaneously a social organization and a gathering of distinct individuals who have different concerns. The gestalt of awareness, freedom, and responsibility has implications for the functioning of the group, as well as for the individual functioning of members who compose it. Structures and directions that define interactions are not imposed by the leader or the institution that is sponsoring such a group. Therefore, an assumption is being made that the unstructured group setting can potentially allow awareness to function without the imposition of restrictions.

Frankl (1965), the creator of logotherapy, gives the creation and discovery of meaning a central position in his therapeutic framework. Frankl found that survivors of concentration camps in World War II, of whom he was one, were able to maintain their sense of personal integration if they were able to focus on events that were meaningful. By contrast, those victims of concentration camps who saw their experience as completely without meaning became hopeless, lost their former sense of identity, and sometimes gave up struggling or turned on others. The ultimate human choice is not the determination of what one will encounter but the meaning that will be given to or discovered within that experience (Frankl, 1963).

If regarded as equivalent to the formation of perceptual wholes and associations within experience, meaning can be viewed as simultaneously discovered and created by awareness. The idea of awareness, freedom, and responsibility as a gestalt assists us in connecting individualized forms of making meaning with collective processes that form meanings. The individual gestalt interacts and resonates with the collective one.

Human awareness is never truly separate from nature, although people may feel a split between themselves and nature. Nature can be considered as a gestalt within which individuals and communities form subsystems of meaning. Group members generally have a sense of sharing a collective gestalt, a sense that is allied with awareness of sharing a common nature. Those who are unable or unwilling to acknowledge this gestalt will sometimes create difficulties or conflicts within group process. If members are to deal constructively with these difficulties, they need to draw on their awareness of their group as a whole and its place within a larger whole that includes humanity. Conflicts can lead a group either toward disorganization or toward awareness of universality within distinctness, depending on members' abilities to clarify issues, accept and value differences, and integrate differences within a shared dialogue.

The authors had an experience that illustrated to them how members can have a sense of a collective gestalt. We were both members of a person-centered group or workshop that included more than fifty members. Much of this particular group seemed fractious and interested in playing games to avoid discussing personal issues or their reactions to one another. The group was not particularly meaningful to either of us until a turning point occurred after at least four hours of talking.

At this moment, everyone in the group suddenly decided to be quiet. The group came together during this silence and developed a bond that is difficult to explain. One aspect of the "coming together" was that by mutually deciding to become silent, members tacitly acknowledged that trivial chatter and melodramatic expressions of opinions had outlived their usefulness. The two coauthors felt as if they were a part of a collective whole that somehow felt personally meaningful. One of the members who had previously been dominating the group finally broke the silence because, as he later indicated, he was feeling uneasy. According to subsequent disclosures, most of the participants had similar experiences to ours when this silence occurred. We felt more connected with the group as a whole after this experience.

As we have seen, awareness can be considered an activity that is simultaneously individual and universal in its functioning. Because awareness is the basis for choices, particularly choices in the formation of gestalts of meaning, awareness has an individual aspect. At the same time, awareness arises from within nature and is based on an intrinsic organization given by nature, reflecting a universal aspect. Yalom (1975), a group theorist who has recognized universality, interpersonal learning, and interpersonal cohesiveness as important therapeutic factors, has also noted the importance of more individually centered activities (for example, catharsis, self-understanding and personal responsibility and control). Although Jung acknowledges transindividual aspects of being (archetypal images that represent potentials of the collective unconscious), he (1936/1968) generally mistrusts the conformity engendered by groups and strongly associated growth in awareness with individual self-reflection (Iling, 1963).

Awareness as an Integrative Activity

The creation of meaning is often conceptualized as occurring at different levels of awareness. For example, Freud (1940/1964) and Jung (1936/1968) refer to conscious and unconscious aspects of human psychology. Different levels of meaning form conscious and unconscious aspects of human functioning. The *conscious* mind can be viewed as a system of meanings that can be held, reviewed, and changed intentionally. *Unconscious* meanings are outside the conscious system or have been blocked from interacting with conscious meanings. Unconscious meanings affect experience but cannot be intentionally reviewed and changed. Awareness of intentionality defines the boundary between conscious and unconscious processes. Changes in perceptions of intentionality (shifts in awareness of responsibility) can alter the boundary between conscious and unconscious levels of meaning.

The unconscious represents those aspects of functioning that a person has been unable to "own." Unconscious thoughts or feelings are things for which a person does not feel responsible. The work of therapy groups is to assist members to allow more of their experience into the sphere of self-disclosure and self-reflection and to recognize themselves as more fully responsible for their perceptions and actions. Thus, we could conceptualize therapeutic work as changing the boundary between conscious and unconscious aspects of self. This idea seems limited because we can never be precisely clear about what exactly is being defined by the terms conscious and unconscious. More adequately, we can conceptualize therapeutic group work as activity that helps members to move toward integrated awareness. Members can learn to be alert to aspects of their process of being that they had ignored or of which they were unaware.

Unstructured group therapy lends itself to a treatment of the person as a whole being. Because structures are not imposed, members may have an opportunity to move toward a unified experience of self. Rather than helping members to use one level of awareness to control another, unstructured group therapy assists them to accept themselves as whole beings within an ongoing process of relationship. As people move toward integration, the quality of their awareness becomes more extensive and intensive. Awareness becomes more extensive when individuals are able to form distinctions without creating splits.

Awareness is always working to form distinction, gestalts, and relationships within experience. If this work occurs within self-imposed barriers, awareness is blunted and tends to create tensions related to self-contradictions. Awareness constructs wholes from the level of sensation to the level of abstract thought. Self-created barriers exclude aspects of awareness, interfering with self-organization, and also affect the formation of relationships between people. Thus, awareness can be said to exist simultaneously at a social level and a personal level. Members extend their personal awareness of one another to include one another and thus create a social aspect of awareness through their interactions. Conversely, members' personal level of awareness has been formed through their previous interactive experiences.

Polarities and Splits

A primary polarity that many members deal with in therapeutic groups is the split caused by the categorization of thoughts into "good" or "bad." If experiences are evaluated as bad, they are often rejected, and awareness will not be able to complete its work of integration. Bad experiences may be maintained within gestalts of unfinished business that have an impact on ongoing patterns of relationship and perception (Perls, Hefferline & Goodman, 1951/1980).

For example, one of the authors worked with an unstructured group conducted in a woman's prison for two years. The story of one member of that group illustrates how hurtful experiences of rejection can contribute to having unfinished business. "Nancy" was a heroin addict who was ignored by her alcoholic parents as a child. She started dating a man who was a heroin addict when she was thirteen years of age and quickly became addicted to heroin after she married this person. Nancy engaged in a lot of personal exploration during her group experience. When the group was finished, evaluations of the group experience were filled out by the participants. She wrote out a statement that was quite simple: "The group helped me to accept reality." What this statement meant to Nancy (based on what she had discussed in the group) was that she was finally able to accept the fact that her parents had treated her horribly. Nancy finally had developed the courage to give up her illusions about them; she then became free to quit trying to hurt her father and mother by hurting herself because they did not live up to her expectations. She was able to accept some of her life experiences that she had previously denied.

Individuals can attempt to escape negative experiences that haunt them by denying their existence or by projecting the badness outside themselves and onto others. These tactics require people to minimize the costs of failing to integrate these experiences. The work of therapy groups may lead members to feel uncomfortable if feedback from others brings awareness of the costs of denial and projection. Such feedback is most likely to be useful in an atmosphere where members can expect that they will not be seen as bad if they acknowledge negative feelings and attitudes or experiences of having hurt or been hurt. The group moves toward an atmosphere of freedom by accepting members and their experiences and by developing a nonevaluative ambiance for self-disclosure. Members' acknowledgment of their evaluative feelings can be a vital step on the road to the development of a free atmosphere.

Many theorists have recognized that therapy encourages participants to recognize and integrate polarities. One of the central polarities that has been addressed in existential therapy is clients' split motivation between authenticity versus conformism (Maddi, 1985). Perls (1971) focuses on those aspects of a person's internalized dialogue that involved the "top dog" (representing internalized "shoulds") versus the "underdog" (representing resistance to "shoulds"). Freud (1923/1962) emphasizes the polarity created between the instincts of the id versus the rationality of the ego. Jungian therapy works with polarities such as the persona (or social self) and the shadow (rejected aspects of self), as well as the ego (personal center) and the self (transpersonal center) (Jung, 1964).

The reason that so many influential therapists have focused on this area is that the tension created by a polarity exists as potential energy that can be tapped and released through therapy. As tension is released, it can be used to formulate a new gestalt, a new organization of experience. The means to tap this energy is to increase awareness of the polarity and to work toward acceptance of both sides of it. The work of therapy is not to make the polarity disappear but to explore it in a manner that enhances self-acceptance and the growth of awareness and that allows access to emotional and physical energy.

During a therapy group for college students conducted by one of the authors, a female member indicated that she had been abused by her parents who had continually exposed themselves to her when she was young. These experiences were traumatic for her, and she developed many phobias that revolved around her attitudes toward sex and seeing the human body. "Mary" began to think of her own body and sex as being something alien to her and as being essentially bad. Much of Mary's energy was spent in trying to avoid thinking about anything sexual or that involved the human body. By participating in an unstructured therapy group, Mary was able to make progress toward openly discussing issues related to dating and sex and her past erotic experiences with her parents without feeling uncomfortable. Mary began to accept her own sexual feelings as not ugly and bad by discussing these in the group.

Awareness becomes rigidly self-limiting when it accepts internal splits as being necessary for self-maintenance. Exploring polarities that appear in relationship patterns or experiences of self can reveal these self-limitations. Group members can then explore these splits and help one another to "heal" them through increased integration. Integration is facilitated by the acknowledgment and acceptance of a split. Acceptance becomes integration as the person gains experiential understanding that both sides of a split have been affecting the person's interactions and sense of self.

Because experiential understanding plays a major role in the process of integration, members can benefit by directly acknowledging feelings, perceptions, and memories that play a part in the split. A member can be encouraged directly to verbalize thoughts and feelings. Perls (1969, 1973) advocates techniques that encourage individuals to make hidden splits overt and that use individually oriented psychodrama to create a present-centered focus for the energy involved within a split. Other therapists have employed psychodrama techniques as advocated by J. L. Moreno (1964) and Z. T. Moreno (1965) to involve more than one member in an "acting out" process to explore internalized conflicts or splits. Although psychodrama role playing that involves two or more members (as well as individual acting out of internalized dialogue) can be helpful techniques to facilitate exploration, these techniques may not always be comfortable or perceived as appropriate by members of a group.

Members may be able to generate present-centered dialogue that assists explorations of splits in awareness without recourse to specific techniques. At times, a great deal of emotional energy can be released simply because a person talks about an event to others who are relating to her or him in a concerned manner. When a person feels that others really care and are attempting to understand, a situation evolves that can be highly conducive to releasing emotional energy and physical blocks of tension. It is the experience of oneself being accepted by others that seems to be the essential dynamic involved in the process of healing. An individual can then move toward experiential understanding and integration of a polarity within awareness.

For example, in a group of college students dealing with eating disorders, a woman named "Rhonda" was divided between the image she tried to maintain with others and her inward feelings of loneliness and unworthiness. This split between inward and outward selves was rectified through a group process conducted by one of the authors. Rhonda had always feared she would "go crazy" if she began to express her negative feelings about herself. When she took the risk to acknowledge and express feelings of sadness and anxiety about loneliness, she found that strong feelings do not equate with being crazy. She found that she could be accepted by others and could accept herself as a whole person. This improvement of a split in awareness formed the groundwork for Rhonda's subsequent work to change compulsive patterns in relating to people and food.

The Interpersonal Field of Awareness

The dynamics of unstructured groups lend themselves particularly well to a continuing assessment of the question "What is happening between us?" Individuals' connections and splits affect a group's atmosphere. Members develop connections and splits in their relationships with other members because of their experience of being with others and because of unfinished business. The unfinished business that members carry "within" is inevitably experienced "without" in the interpersonal realm of awareness. If members are able openly to confront their experience of being with others, they will be able to work on themselves by dealing with what is occurring *between* themselves and others. As members address the question "What is happening between us?", they increase their awareness of relational context—essential to the process of the therapeutic work in a group setting.

Awareness of a relational context is often manifested by explorations of the questions "How are you affecting us," and "How are we affecting you?" Underlying these questions is the awareness that "you" are an aspect of "us." The dynamic relationship between the "self" and the "we" is necessary to create group process. Questions about how an individual is affected by being in a group can be addressed in a general context, in terms of the effect of the group as a whole. Exploration of specific incidents in which members have affected one another can also provide important learning about the process of the self being with others.

Participants are likely to manifest their internal splits and polarities within the dialogues that emerge as relationships develop between members. Internal splits tend to make it difficult for individuals to move out of themselves and into the "between." Thus, individual splits in awareness mirror those that occur in the relations between members. Addressing differences of opinions or attitudes and learning about discrepant perspectives can become means to help individuals to move toward personal integration. Members can provide feedback to help each other learn about dynamics that either assist or interfere with the relationships that individuals are attempting to form. Such feedback is generally most helpful if it reflects observations and reactions on a personal rather than an abstract or philosophical level. Personal reactions enhance awareness of relatedness. There are times when abstract or philosophical feedback can be useful, but only when it does not foster intellectualization and distancing from awareness of present experience.

Members may validate certain kinds of disclosures while ignoring or responding inappropriately to other kinds. For example, disclosures that seem caring or empathic may be validated, whereas revelations about frustration or irritation may be ignored or quickly dropped. Members may learn to hide feelings of dissatisfaction with others in their group and may disguise their anger toward the leader or others. Anger may be about incidents in which a participant was hurt or treated unfairly; it may also be about unfinished business and targeted toward a scapegoat. If the group is not to be perceived as a safe place to explore feelings of anger or frustration, members will have diminished opportunities to learn about themselves and what is occurring.

The Goal of Awareness

Perls states that "in Gestalt therapy, *the goal is always awareness and only awareness*" (1969, p. 55, italics in original). This statement sets up the intriguingly paradoxical possibility that awareness is its own goal. However, this paradox disappears if we assume that barriers to awareness have been formed by activities of awareness.

Other theorists (for example, Adler, 1969; Berne, 1961; Moreno, 1947; Yalom, 1980), believe that awareness must be joined with a particular kind of insight that is based on cognitive understanding. To these theorists, simply being aware is not enough; one must know something about the contents of awareness. These theorists imply that participants in therapy must increase their awareness in order to grow, but they must also learn certain principles at the same time. Members can then apply these principles to events and relationships outside their group and their present field of awareness. Naturally, various theorists and schools of therapy recommend focusing on different types of insights or cognitive formulations.

A basic issue underlying differences between schools of therapy, as well as between individual therapists, concerns definition of the goals of awareness. There are also differences in how to define directions that assist clients to greater awareness and how to describe what should be done with this awareness (if anything) once it is achieved. An integrated therapeutic approach can be developed by learning from various perspectives about the importance of enhancement of awareness as a central movement of effective therapy. Recognition that there is no one "correct" approach is likely to lead practitioners to develop a flexible attitude toward these objectives. Perhaps there is no predetermined correct direction for awareness. In this case, situational, cultural, and historical contexts, personal issues and concerns of participants, and continuing modes of relationship must all be taken into account as directions are formed. Because these variables shift and change as group processes evolve, predetermined goals for awareness are of limited value.

Observation of therapeutic group work is likely to lead an observer to conclude that, in spite of the leader's opinions, each member seems to have a different perspective about what is important in a given situation. Of course, some leaders may help create an atmosphere wherein members are reluctant to express these differences. Nonetheless, an observer of almost any unstructured group is likely to find that individuals vary in how (and if) they want to use their group to improve their awareness, how and where they wish to focus awareness during a particular event, and in what direction they seem to want to develop that awareness.

Members constantly influence one another in creating foci for discussions, in pursuing events or aspects of events, and in making certain meanings out of events. Additionally, the theoretical orientation of the group leader and, what is more important, his or her perspective on awareness are likely to influence how and when the leader communicates and affects group process. This personal perspective is the ability to grasp the direction of the awareness of individual members, their effect on each other's awareness, and the effect of one's own direction and focus of awareness on others. This type of understanding of phenomenological events within group process involves an ability to sense many factors interacting simultaneously.

As we know, members often struggle with their ability to increase their own awareness. They may have trouble believing that their own feelings are important or may not feel that their own perceptions of events are valid. If one participant becomes a director for the others, they may not learn that they can trust their own ability to form meanings and directions. Rather than supporting the group's need for a director, norms can be developed that recognize the person as a creative, potentially self-directing being. The person can be assisted to find his or her own ability to form directions that make sense and that feel right. When members assist each other in forming directions, they tend to exchange leadership roles in different situations. Members begin to use their interactions to generate an atmosphere of freedom. They can use this freedom to learn about their mutual influence in the process of exploring awareness.

If members sense their shared field of awareness, group interactions begin to form gestalts of meaning that may develop into ongoing themes. One person alone does not determine the flow of energy and awareness in a group. As freedom develops, all members perceive themselves as able to influence directions at any given time. Areas of focus form according to participants' mutual perceptions of their own needs and wishes and those of others. The question of whether awareness within the present is itself a sufficient goal or whether some type of additional cognitive insight is important becomes relatively unimportant. Members learn that they are capable of attending to their own sense of events, can use this to assess each other's emergent needs, and can contribute to one another accordingly. Through finding out about each other, members learn if an individual needs to explore a new cognitive perspective, to express feelings, or to experiment with new behaviors.

Freedom

The perception of freedom within the field of experience facilitates opportunities for developing new learning (Cain, 1989; Rogers, 1983). Freedom can be experienced inwardly as an unconstricted investigation of thoughts and feelings and as the formulation of perceptions according to one's own integrity. Freedom can also be experienced outwardly as an openness in communication of thoughts and feelings (without interference from imposed values) and as interpersonal encouragement for investigation of experience. Ideally, a group atmosphere can support a merging of both fields. The personal and interpersonal fields of perception can then interact to create and develop gestalts of meaning. Freedom then becomes a shared and inclusive experience, one that members support and encourage.

The perception of freedom is a useful foundation for the recognition that the individual is responsible for forming her or his own meanings and directions (Polster & Polster, 1973). In the absence of freedom, a person would not be able to view self as responsible. If freedom is not within the group, the member might have to fight to assert the reality of freedom and to self-actualize.

History has not yet provided us with an example of a large society that has been able to surmount the limitations created when one group uses force to gain and manipulate resources at the expense of others. Therapeutic groups struggle to achieve on a microcosmic scale what has not yet been achieved in the social macrocosm of the world. Because members may have adapted to social systems based on exploitative norms, they may carry these patterns into relationships with others in their group (Yalom, 1975). When individuals have adapted to exploitation as a reality, they may have difficulty experiencing real freedom. Individual participants may struggle to understand whether freedom can be real in their group, and if so, what they would want to do with that freedom.

There are certain resources available in a group for which members may compete. These resources include attention, respect, sympathy, admiration, and control of themes and norms. Members' distorted patterns of self-actualization may present themselves as attempts to manipulate or dominate discussions in a group or to influence group norms to fit personal values. Group members may face conflicts or crises that evolve as they vie to gain attention or respect or as they try to sway the values that will predominate. Much of the therapeutic work done in an unstructured group has to do with recognizing freedom and learning to use it constructively. As members learn to use freedom for each other's benefit, they generally move toward more cooperative and less competitive modes of interaction.

No group will achieve complete freedom based on total awareness of mutual responsibility. In fact, if members insist that everyone in the group must be perfect and have total respect for each other's freedom, authentic thoughts and feelings are likely to be inhibited (Burnand, 1990). People, being imperfect, will create misunderstandings, will share power unequally, and will have disproportionate effects on the development of group themes and the use of group time. Growth does not often come by a sudden leap into a totally new way of being with others. Growth more often comes by learning how to compromise, cooperate, affirm oneself and others, and create win-win rather than win-lose situations. Competition becomes balanced by cooperation, and self-assertion is offset by respect for others.

A member's expression of self sometimes represents an imposition on or a misunderstanding of another, or it may be intended to establish control through imposition (Gans, 1989). Group members can move toward freedom by dealing with how an imposition or misunderstanding is experienced by others in the group (Yalom, 1975). If members are unnecessarily polite and avoid disagreement, they will not experience real freedom. If they are too concerned about infringing on one another in dealing with issues of freedom in their group, they will necessarily keep part of who they are hidden. The more of themselves that members feel must remain hidden, the less free is the atmosphere in a group, regardless of the norms that are consciously espoused. Group participants may not consciously perceive that they must hide aspects of themselves but may simply experience a reluctance to disclose feelings or a lack of any thoughts or observations to share.

Three related assumptions that underlie the formation of an unstructured therapy group are (1) that individuals are capable of choosing to be aware, (2) that an atmosphere of freedom maximizes opportunities to choose to be aware, and (3) that individuals will value that freedom and the relationships and new learning that result. An atmosphere of freedom reflects acceptance of diversity, openness to novelty, and a willingness to live without the certainty of prearranged outcomes. This atmosphere of freedom will not come into existence simply because a group leader has determined that an unstructured format will be used. Members must see themselves as free and must be willing to use their freedom to make choices to move toward awareness. As relationships in a group begin to develop, a group leader may help members to look at choices they are making to reveal themselves or protect themselves. Members can learn that they are making choices in the perceptions that they form about their group and in the ways that they choose to present themselves to others there.

Limits of Freedom

Although predetermined roles are not provided, members generally take on roles within their unstructured therapy group (Yalom, 1975). Members will also typically institute an often subtle system of rewards and punishments (using attention and feedback) and create ritual forms of interaction with predetermined outcomes (using politeness or a system of norms). Members tend to institute roles and norms that have prevailed in other social groups in which they have participated. Roles and norms form limits that regulate free expression. These limits are necessary insofar as interpersonal relationships require a degree of predictability concerning how others will respond and how one will respond to others.

Group process provides opportunities for members to observe how they create roles, rules, and rituals. They may learn that they have created these roles and rules through their own choices. If members can acknowledge choices that they are making, they become aware of their abilities to influence events in the group. An unstructured format, because it does not provide predetermined norms, allows members to learn about themselves as they observe themselves structuring their own interactions. If they learn about the patterns that they create by adopting certain roles and rules, members may then assume more responsibility within their interactions. They can learn that they do not have to repeat roles and rules that they used previously but can select new ways of interacting that are more authentic, that meet needs, and that allow for creative expression of self.

People tend to institute those roles with which they are most

comfortable when they are in an unpredictable situation with unfamiliar people (Leszcz, 1992). Group participants, being human,
will go through this process of attempting to create a social role in
their group. Some participants will be polite and agreeable to attempt to win the goodwill of others, to reassure themselves that they
can belong in their group and that others will support them. Some
may use wit or charm to gain attention. Other participants may
demonstrate a no-nonsense practicality, attempt to define group
tasks, and generally assert leadership. These participants may find
that others contest their attempts to guide their group, and some
members may compete by trying to show evidence of their own
intelligence or knowledge. There may be members who ask others
for something or who identify themselves as people who need help.
Still other members may find a place in their group by showing that
they can be empathic, supportive, or caring. Sometimes, participants withdraw from their group or evidence anxiety and uncertainty. Any or all of these means for creating a presence in a group
may be part of the interplay of dynamics by which members establish a role. As roles are defined, they help set the foundation for the
establishment of norms that will guide interactions.

In creating roles for themselves, members learn about one
another. Their roles are not created in a vacuum but in relation to
one another's presentation of self. Most, if not all, individuals are
capable of presenting themselves in different ways or according to
the perceptions they have of various situations. These perceptions of
the group environment will guide their decisions in creating a part
for themselves. The more that members establish roles with each
other, the more easily they can predict one another's responses. A
degree of security and certainty is created and can be the basis for
establishing trust. However, if trust depends on maintenance of
roles, participants will hide aspects of themselves from each other.
They can hide those aspects of self that would conflict with a role
or those aspects that might create conflict with others in their group.

To deepen the atmosphere of interpersonal trust, members
must be willing to reveal aspects of self that do not fit into group
norms or into roles and expectations that have been established. If
members value their group's potential to create an atmosphere that

joins trust with freedom, they will experiment with interactions that are "out of role."

Freedom, the basis for choices and decisions, is a fundamental quality of awareness. Individuals can choose to limit their awareness, to expand it, to focus it on certain events and situations, or to avoid attending to these events. Although there are many factors that determine our lives, we are also free to form perceptions and to explore awareness in ways that diverge from past patterns. At the same time, we are not free to do whatever we wish. For example, we will not be able to walk through a wall simply because we decide we can, and we can never control our environments totally, although some people might wish to do so. A common misconception about freedom is that it represents the ability to do whatever one wishes or to become whatever one wants to become. This myth represents an immature view of freedom, one that perhaps is appropriate in adolescence, when people may feel full of possibilities and have not yet faced the reality of mortality.

Mature awareness of freedom does not disregard limits and does not ignore factors that determine peoples' lives (May, 1981). The experience of freedom is that of one's own creativity within interactions. While acknowledging the impact of environments, physiology, and their own history, members find that they can create new perceptions of who they are and who they can be with others.

Limits on freedom are not only produced by physical factors or uncontrollable environmental ones. People limit their own freedom and thus create illusions of certainty and predictability (Perls, Hefferline & Goodman, 1951/1980). Of course, a degree of certainty and predictability is necessary for human interaction; yet, if the pursuit of security is compulsive and occurs outside awareness, actualization of potentials for growth and fulfillment will be curtailed. An overemphasis on security tends to undermine the potential atmosphere of freedom in a group.

Environments condition the perceptions of members. The members of groups may question the kind of conditioning that is being promoted. Women and blacks have attempted to form their own perceptions of valid roles and have had to struggle against the ways that society has framed their behavior and attitudes. As women and blacks have struggled in American society, they have helped focus the attention of others on the power of messages that are conveyed in families, through the mass media, and through the dynamics of power in social systems. We have come to recognize that other groups also may feel oppressed by social expectations that define the roles that they are offered. Homosexuals, men, and the elderly are some other groups that have found that social expectations limit their freedom to create themselves.

Unstructured therapy groups can become environments wherein it is acceptable to question whatever stereotypes have limited individuals' perceptions of freedom. Rather than using stereotypes, group members may feel free to step out of these roles or to experiment with new ones. However, in the process, members are likely to find that their own stereotypes and unfinished business affect the roles that they create. If trust has been established in a group, members can grow by sharing their own prejudices and preconceptions. Members can then learn to recognize each other's individuality and can validate each other's unique ways of using freedom in their group to explore awareness and experience. They can acknowledge the psychological, as well as the physical and environmental, limitations that have affected their life experiences. Members can help each other to see if they are responding to one another habitually—in ways that have been conditioned by environments in which they had to survive.

One key aspect of the experience of freedom is the sense of paradox. The experience has the potential to heal at the same time that it can overwhelm, and it can be threatening or exhilarating depending on a person's readiness for the experience. People can only be healed by experiencing freedom when they are intellectually, emotionally, and spiritually ready to accept the implications of freedom.

The anxiety of freedom may lead to attempts to gain security by imposing limits and restrictions on experience. The exhilaration of freedom may encourage tendencies to deny the existence of limits, even when these are real and unavoidable. Group members often work on learning how to be open to freedom without minimizing the risks and limits that are part of the experience of freedom.

For example, Rhonda (who was mentioned earlier in this

chapter) struggled with feelings of being overwhelmed when she expressed sadness and anger about how lonely and self-despising she had been. She gained in freedom, and this provided motivation to continue her therapeutic path. However, as she opened to the freedom of revealing feelings openly, she was concerned about the uncertainty of where she was going. New ways of expressing herself led to unknown areas of awareness and relationship that were genuinely scary for her. She ran the risk of being rejected as the person she really believed herself to be, a possibility far more frightening than that of being rejected for playing a role poorly.

Sartre (1956) writes of freedom as something to which people are condemned, and Fromm (1964) describes it as something from which people long to escape. People can be viewed as condemned to freedom because they cannot escape the responsibility of choice and as longing to escape freedom because it demands awareness of anxiety-provoking aspects of reality. May and Yalom (1984) indicate that intense anxiety can arise from perceptions of freedom. This anxiety is due to feelings of groundlessness related to lack of certainty and external authority and to a fear of dying (May & Yalom, 1984).

Group members may try to escape from freedom by making the leader an authority or guru. This escape may be instigated by the leader or by group members but cannot be accomplished unless there is collusion from all involved. Group members can also institute rigid norms to regulate behavior and thus escape the anxiety that comes with awareness of choices. Freedom seems to create anxiety because it reveals life to be a process that does not have absolute or final rules and regulations.

Personal and Interpersonal Freedom

People are free to the extent that they can change their lives by altering their perceptions of self and others, by creating new forms for communicating with others, and by generating new goals. This kind of change represents personal freedom. Participants in relationships explore interpersonal freedom as they learn how they can use interactions to explore ideas and feelings. If members accept the challenge of freedom, they often find that along with anxiety, they can experience excitement and fulfillment. Rogers has emphasized the positive aspects of freedom. He points out that as people learn to trust their own perceptions and their own ability to function autonomously, they can use freedom in ways that enhance growth and create fulfillment (Rogers, 1980, 1983). Though freedom may be associated with the anxiety of insecurity, it can also be used to release the anxiety that develops from adhering to unnecessary limitations. Freedom is a basis for the affirmation of creativity and for movement toward personal fulfillment in relationships.

As members explore possibilities for freedom in their group, they also learn about limits to this freedom. A person may be free to explore authentic communication, but this situation does not guarantee that everyone in the group will accept and admire this person's use of honesty. Peoples' freedom does not allow them to control the responses of others. Individuals may also find that if they strive to obtain the affection of others, they have sacrificed the freedom to express those aspects of self that others do not like. Freedom involves choices, and these mean that certain alternatives are sacrificed as others are actualized.

If members decide that they do not have the right to control others, they begin to move toward an ethic that can support the freedom of others as well as the freedom of self. This movement is associated with a shift from I-it relations to I-thou relations. As we have seen, freedom in I-it relations is that which comes when the responses of the other can be controlled and predicted. Freedom in I-thou relations is that which comes when participants can validate and affirm each other's creativity, self-direction, and spontaneity.

It is possible for a person to act spontaneously in ways that others perceive as hurtful. Examples include choices to leave a lover or spouse, decisions to reveal negative perceptions of others, and various communications and behaviors that do not meet the wishes of others. I-thou relations involve mutual affirmation of spontaneity, something that is usually diminished if one person perceives that another is acting in ways that seem unnecessarily hurtful. As members move toward I-thou relatedness, their spontaneity becomes tempered by their empathy. Self-created limitations on the use of open communication can assist the development of effectively therapeutic transactions (Kaplan, 1985). These kinds of boundaries to self-disclosure are most useful if they are motivated by a consideration for others that grows out of empathic resonance, rather than from attempts to conform to imposed norms. Group norms of consideration may not be an imposition if members genuinely respect and care about each other's feelings.

Empathy is itself an expression of freedom because people choose to enter the perceptual worlds of others. If spontaneity can be integrated with empathy, members can experience freedom as a mutually supported condition in their group. Empathy is not a magical device to protect people from being hurt. There are times when hurting another person can be unavoidable—for example, when people have conflicting needs or wishes. Empathy helps members to use freedom responsibly, so that unnecessary pain is not inflicted on participants.

Experiencing Freedom in the Group Setting

Members' experience of freedom in a group setting involves the perceptions of several individuals as they affect one another. If someone takes risks that enhance perceptions of freedom in the group, others may feel relieved and may themselves begin to take more risks. A participant may experience the reality of freedom, but others may dislike the way this person uses it to relate to others. Conflict will most likely arise at this point. Such a conflict represents an opportunity to enhance perceptions of freedom in a group. Group members will need to discuss their perceptions of events and will need to learn about each other's views of these events. If they can learn enough about each other to discover how they are affecting one another, the development of a therapeutic group atmosphere can continue.

The experience of freedom in a group can be threatening to some individuals. Freedom makes demands on people by involving them in interpersonal contact that is open to change and that does not have clearly defined rules that predetermine outcomes. When members perceive the reality of their freedom, they sometimes recognize the illusory nature of those conventions and proscriptions that are supposed to make interactions predictable. They may have learned from listening to others that everyone has had experiences that did not follow the rules. They may have learned by observing their group that interactions have often diverged from whatever norms had been established. Members who have invested themselves in a fixed set of beliefs often find these challenged by the diversity of life experiences and personal attitudes revealed in their group. Perceptions of freedom may challenge individuals' needs for security but may also help them to become more flexible within evolving relationships, more accepting of diversity, and less dogmatic in their conceptualizations of themselves and others.

As a group develops a therapeutic atmosphere and as members begin to value each other's freedom, a person who negates or invalidates others may be seen as detrimental. A group can be challenged to extend acceptance to those who are deviant according to group norms or to help these members understand how these experiences of rejection developed (Gans, 1989). Extending acceptance to a deviant member allows him or her the opportunity to choose a new approach. Without acceptance, such a member simply receives reinforcement for those stereotypes that allow him or her to picture others as members of a different species. Although group members may honestly disagree with, and even disrespect, the values of a certain participant, they need to validate that person's value as a human being capable of growth. If they are unable to validate the potential for growth, they have in effect given up on that person. Giving up on someone is an expression of a group's sense of their own inability to heal and to care. This awareness of an inability to accept will be a limitation that negatively affects the group atmosphere.

All groups have a limit to their ability to heal, of course. No therapist and no group can be all things to all people. In very unusual cases, the members or the leader may suggest that a member should leave a group because this person has repeatedly and frequently interfered with the work that others wish to do. Other group members are more likely than the leader to question whether a disruptive member should continue to participate in a group. If such a suggestion is made, it should be discussed with the member, preferably in the group. It is hoped that this individual can learn how the group perceives his or her behavior. Then, that individual can make a choice about whether to accept the responsibilities involved in group membership.

A member who is encouraged to leave should be given a coherent explanation for this course of action and should be supplied referrals so that he or she can continue to receive therapy. Asking a member to leave should only be a last resort in extreme situations. Even if a consensus exists in a group to expel a member, the group leader will sometimes intervene to assist members to explore the issue further. A participant should not be asked to leave as a "punishment" for misbehavior or to allow other participants to feel powerful or self-righteous. Some members may become demoralized after a participant leaves their group, either for voluntary or involuntary reasons. These members may perceive themselves as having been unable to include and care about all who were present. The future ability of a group to generate an atmosphere of freedom will be affected if someone has been asked to leave. Members will know that if one person can be told to leave, anyone may have the same experience.

Given an atmosphere of freedom, members will usually work out for themselves the question of whether and how to participate. Members are usually capable of understanding the needs of others in their group. They may decide to leave for a while and to return later when they are ready for group interaction. As we know, meeting others in a group setting can be a stressful experience. If people realize that their freedom includes the liberty not to attend, they may feel less stress. Attending an unstructured therapy group should be a voluntary commitment, should not represent an obligation or duty, and should not represent an imposition of values. The value of freedom underlies attendance and participation in these groups.

Freedom and Responsibility

Because awareness not only registers but also makes experience, freedom is not merely passively perceived; it too is actively created. Freedom, an aspect of nature, also is a potential of the self that it brings into being within its interactions and through its choices. To say that freedom is created by the self is to say that freedom is not bestowed by an outside force or entity. Freedom is not so dependent on environmental conditions that it is impossible for a person to realize freedom unless he or she exists in a free atmosphere. At the same time, freedom is not so independent of environmental conditions that these are unimportant. People need to discover freedom within their own experience of life and self to create freedom in their environment. Freedom originates from awareness and becomes real within awareness.

As individuals recognize their potential for freedom, they also realize their creativity. At the same time, they also can destroy (Perls, Hefferline & Goodman, 1951/1980). They can affirm their own possibilities and those of others, or they can also choose to negate their own and others' potentials. Freedom implies that we are responsible for nurturing our own capabilities and for producing a nurturing atmosphere for others. Individuals *cannot* be responsible for the choices others make regarding the development of potentials within their lives, relationships, and environmental interactions. Individuals *are* responsible for respecting others' capacities to choose and for contributing to a supportive environment.

People are thus responsible for bringing freedom into being, for encouraging it in relationships, and for respecting it in others. These responsibilities are inherent in living fully as a human being; to deny them is to deny the potential to be fully human. Unstructured therapy groups are essentially settings that confront members with their potential for freedom and with the choices they make to affirm or negate freedom.

If people avoid the responsibility associated with freedom, they inevitably distort their own processes of self-actualization. This distortion leads to estrangement from others and from nature. The movement through estrangement into reintegration always involves an acceptance and affirmation of one's own capacity for freedom. Freedom is the necessary foundation for the ability to make creative choices that can change one's perceptions, one's relationships, and one's life. Thus awareness of freedom implies responsibility, because this awareness implies that one can make choices that make a difference.

Responsibility

The individual's ability to be responsible is reflected by the willingness to choose, to own feelings, and to become distinct within relationships. Realizing the individual aspects of responsibility leads a person to become more aware of the possibilities of others. A person then recognizes and acts on an awareness of responsibility to others.

Responsibility and the Ground of Being

Responsibility allows a person to recognize a common ground that connects self, others, and nature. Thus, responsibility can be conceptualized as the activity by which a person establishes groundedness within the process of being and within the process of relationship. The experience of gaining a sense of groundedness is often described as a sense of "centering" within the flux of experience. To center is to balance and harmonize diverse sensations, thoughts, feelings, and perceptions. Through centering, the person creates an integrated wholeness within the multiplicity of feelings and perceptions. Awareness increases its intensity and extensity, and a totality can then be recognized by the centered person.

Centering is not the creation of a static structure or position for organization of experience. Centering can best be understood as integrative movement, as the forming of meaningful connections between and within experiences and persons. The development of empathetic resonance between members is therefore possible. They no longer need to rely on conformity to imposed norms to form a sense of connection and coherence. Members become centered within their participation in their group as they are increasingly able to trust their own experience and perceptions of themselves and others and to express what they feel. Centering becomes a basis for interpersonal grounding of the self as members are able to use interpersonal interactions to move into a shared field of awareness and freedom.

The person establishes and expresses responsibility within the context of a matrix of ongoing relations with others and in the context of relatedness to the ground of being. Ultimately, it is groundedness within being that is the basis for responsibility. Responsibility within the ground of being takes precedence over responsibility to a given relationship or to a system of relationships. A responsible person may decide to break connectedness because of his or her perception of groundedness in being (Fromm, 1964; Tillich, 1954). For example, a grounded person may resist the pattern of community relations in a society that is becoming totalitarian, may break ties to a group of others who have become destructively oriented toward nature, may leave a family whose norms require hurtful interpersonal interactions, or may leave a personal relationship that is thwarting centering. Groundedness in being provides the basis for awareness that one's own being participates in the being of humanity and in nature and that one is responsible for one's own and others' freedom.

A member of a human group expresses responsibility by recognizing the humanity of others in the group (Buber, 1970). The individual cannot exist without the relations with others that help form who the person is and who the person becomes. Each individual is formed within a complex web of human relations that begin at the moment of birth and that are developed throughout a lifetime.

The ground of being is not separate from the process of being. Group members may move toward groundedness within being by exploring the nature of present relationships or by looking at unfinished business involving relations with those who are not present. Participants can also move toward contact with the ground of being by gaining a sense of how their personal development has involved many significant relations with others. Members may gain important knowledge vicariously, by observing that other members also grow and develop through a process of relationship. Learning from observing can help members to become aware of the universality of the process of being and especially to be aware that it involves relationship.

As members discuss their past and their hopes for the future, they may gain an understanding of themselves as beings within relationship. Through exploring their involvement in beginning, moving into, and ending various forms of relationship, members become aware that their distinctiveness has evolved through an ongoing process of reciprocal connectedness. Throughout this process, they have related themselves to others, and others have related to them. As members learn from the process of being with others, they become encouraged to experience contact with the ground of being. This ground is no different from the universality that is accessible within any group experience in which members are willing to be open with one another. Awareness of the ground of being gives members a basis for the integration of various aspects of their experiences and relationships.

Learning About Responsibility

By experiencing various aspects of relatedness with others who are present, members develop an awareness of the connectedness and mutuality through which interactions gain meaning. As members make meaningful connections with others, they also tend to learn experientially about the importance of responsibility within relationship. This learning occurs because connections form opportunities for sharing and closeness and present occasions for responding actively to what is learned about others. Norms, rules, and prescriptions that define responsible behavior have limited value in helping members to learn experientially. If norms and rules are used to substitute for experiential learning, they are likely to form barriers to the development of authentic responsibility.

There can be no prescription that dictates how a person should establish himself or herself as a responsible being. To enhance responsibility, each person must begin where he or she is, become aware of life experiences and important relationships, and make connections between feelings and perceptions. Responsibility grows as a person becomes clearly aware of present situations and relationships, of unfinished business, of the being of others, and of the larger context within which individual lives unfold. Responsibility involves awareness of one's own needs and feelings and of the context in which these are expressed.

Members of therapeutic groups often do not discover how to interact responsibly until they are ready to face very simple truths about themselves and their relationships. These are often perceived when members allow themselves to be open to emotional aspects of being with others, to feelings that are powerful without being complex. These feelings must be integrated into awareness to contribute to the development of responsibility, and this integration involves forming direct connections within experience more than it involves abstract cognitive processing of information. An excessive degree of cognitive processing usually interferes with work on integrating simple experiential truths.

Responsibility and "Letting Go"

Awareness of a ground of being prevents responsibility from being mistaken for control over events or other people. Responsibility is equated by some theorists with control over one's actions, one's emotions, one's relationships, and external events that impinge on the self (see Yalom, 1980). This perspective obscures the role that letting go of control often plays in a person's movement toward responsibility. As we saw in Chapter Three, someone too intent on controlling others or him- or herself will maintain a split that prevents experiential awareness of freedom. A responsible person is aware of when controlling a situation or a feeling is appropriate and when letting go is the right course of action.

Awareness establishes the basis for understanding when and how a person can function most appropriately within a situation by releasing control of people, events, or the individual's own feelings. For example, it is sometimes necessary to let go of control over children so that they can recognize themselves as responsible. At other times, a parent needs to exert control over situations in which a child is unable to foresee consequences or is looking for guidance. The release of the tension caused by a false sense of responsibility based on control of self and others can lead to greater personal balance and less distortion.

Rhonda, the woman who has been described as struggling with an eating disorder, experienced a strong sense of letting go when she chose to express chaotic feelings of anger, hurt, and sadness to other group members. She gave up her distorted sense of responsibility that entailed controlling the image she presented to others. She gained a sense of balance that allowed her to think more clearly about herself and others and to express what she was feeling and observing more honestly.

Stifling feelings is often an irresponsible method of dealing with them because they are never owned. Attempts to overcontrol our feelings result in our feelings dominating us (Perls, Hefferline

& Goodman, 1951/1980; Polster & Polster, 1973). When people try to contain, deny, and overcontrol feelings, the result is tension. This tension can exert a perpetual influence on the quality of a person's relationships and process of being. Letting go of resistance to feelings can help a person to move toward a more relaxed and integrated process of being. Letting go of feelings responsibly, as opposed to destructively, requires awareness. If individuals are in a situation where they can receive support for letting go (for example, in a therapy group), they can use the resulting experience to enhance their learning about who they are. If individuals let go of feelings in an inappropriate context, they may lose a job, may escalate an explosive situation, or may precipitate a destructive interaction with a person who is unprepared to deal with strong feelings.

From a therapeutic perspective, it can be less than helpful to communicate to certain clients that they should control their own destiny. People who are already feeling a great deal of stress can feel overburdened and even act in self-destructive ways if they start to blame themselves for everything that has gone wrong in their lives. People who feel stress and anxiety often blame themselves for problems and suffer because they feel guilty about them. Such members benefit from receiving assistance to acknowledge and work through feelings of guilt and self-hatred. They are less likely to express these negative feelings if they expect to be judged for their attitudes. Part of effective therapy for these people involves an idea of responsibility that does not include efforts to exert control over uncontrollable life events and that does not lead to self-blame. If people can perceive responsibility as an openness that increases integrity and authenticity, their ideas about control are likely to become less constraining. Actual control of their perceptions and life events is likely to increase because they can stop wasting energy and resources fighting and blaming themselves.

Responsibility as Cocreation

Black-and-white thinking leads to the conclusion that either people are viewed as responsible for what happens in their lives or as victims of events beyond their control. Beyond black-and-white categorizations is the view that individuals cocreate their lives through transactions with others and the world. As cocreators, people can be seen as being affected and even formed by external circumstances and events. Individuals often perceive themselves as having been deeply influenced by malicious or random events. However, no matter how random these events, a person's creativity is still involved in how these are understood and interpreted. Individuals' perceptions of events create their meaning. From these meanings, people generate their sense of self and their life goals. Their sense of self influences the relationships that individuals develop and the fulfillment experienced in their lives.

People cocreate their lives with many other individuals as well as with the nonhuman environment. People are unlikely to be effective in cocreating their lives if they disregard social, environmental, or historical realities that also contribute to who they are and who they become. Creativity is most effective when it is integrated with a comprehensive awareness of context. The world forms the person as much as the person forms the world. Individuals often see themselves as cocreators with the world at those moments when they give up attempts to control it.

Contact with the ground of being is necessary for cocreation to be an experiential reality. As a person recognizes those events that are beyond control and is willing to let go of attempts to control feelings, thoughts, and other people, she or he becomes more open to experiences. These experiences are essentially creative, capable of forming novel configurations in awareness (Perls, Hefferline & Goodman, 1951/1980).

If individuals become open to the ground of being, they recognize their potential for communion with others on a basis of equality. This type of experiential learning provides a basis for greater control within relationships. When others perceive a person as able to interact on a basis of equality, they are much more likely to give to that person. If the atmosphere is supportive of members who allow themselves to let go, the movement toward groundedness for these individuals is facilitated. The creativity of group members' responses allows awareness of cocreativity to become part of the atmosphere.

All the aspects of existence that are perceived as outside individual control are interconnected within the ground of being. In a group context, contact with the ground of being often emerges through those experiences that help a participant to learn that there are limits to the power that any individual can exert upon a group. Members then become more free to cocreate their group because they recognize that no one person will direct this creation.

Moving Toward a Center Within Experience

Distorted patterns of self-actualization generally form their center around images that provide a sense of control. Thus, projected and internalized self-images can become important anchors for distorted patterns of being. The projected self-image can support illusions of self-control and control of others, and the internalized self-image can support illusions of continuity and permanence.

As members release illusions of control and permanence based on self-images, they become more open to experience as flux and change. They become more open to freedom as a reality because they are seeking less to control others and experience and more to learn from others and experience. As authentic self-actualization is perceived to be possible, members ground themselves in what they experience rather than what they wish they were experiencing. A present-centered focus emerges within awareness and communication. Members learn that responsibility is based on a center within experience rather than on a center that enhances illusory perceptions of control. If participants can view themselves as responsible without requiring themselves to control everything that happens, they can enjoy freedom rather than perceiving it as threatening.

Members can perceive themselves as responsible for formulating perceptions, values, and goals from within their experience. They can feel free to create meaning and direction. As members become centered within the experience of freedom, they gain a sense of groundedness within their group. This perception in an interpersonal context gives members a foundation from which to work toward integration.

Freedom can provide a basis for the growth and development of perceptions, life goals, skills related to goals, emotional maturity, empathic ability, value systems, interpersonal relationships, and an overall sense of comprehensive awareness. It would be difficult to overemphasize the importance of perceiving the reality of freedom as a basis for growth and development. If freedom is continually seen as anxiety provoking and groundless, a person will have no basis for making life choices that enhance self-actualization.

Members of unstructured therapy groups or personal growth groups may feel deeply meaningful connectedness if they begin to center awareness within the flow of group interactions. At times, members may report feelings of communion or unity with others and become aware of deeper levels of their own experiencing (McClure, 1990; O'Hara & Wood, 1983; Rogers, 1980). These events are evidence of the potential that unstructured groups have, at least for some individuals, to increase a sense of groundedness in a shared field of awareness.

Connecting Self with Others

Members can use their center in experience to connect with the centers of others. This natural movement of connection between self and others may be evidence of a universal center that becomes accessible through dialogue (Arnett, 1989; Friedman, 1986). Within the unique and individual aspects of experience, members find ways to universalize their perceptions and connect with others. For example, as one person acknowledges a need to mourn a loss, others will find corresponding aspects of their own experiences. As members communicate these and center within them, they simultaneously connect with one another in a manner that evidences the universality of loss and grief. Members may then find that freedom can enhance rather than threaten their sense of meaning in life.

Participants in an unstructured therapy group are likely to find that the group process tends to challenge self-centered perspectives and modes of relationship. Because a group's process should serve all who are present, members learn that they must share time and attention with others. They must learn to give to other people, who are unlikely to meet their need to maintain a certain self-image. If members are able to give and receive honest feedback, they learn that others can see through the illusions that they try to maintain. They also learn that others can be effective at pointing out aspects of behavior that are inconsistent with projected self-images. Successful therapy moves the person's center away from restrictive self-images and away from assumptions about reality that unnecessarily constrict freedom and relatedness.

The concept of centering is related to an understanding of meaning as a creation within, rather than an imposition upon, experience. The center is a point of contact between the individual and the universal, between the uniquely personal and the shared ground of being. This point of contact allows experience to be organized meaningfully and permits individual experience to find relationship with the life events of others. As they share their experiences, members affect one another's lives on an ongoing basis.

If members accept the challenge of centering themselves within experience, they tend to create four types of changes within ongoing encounters. (1) Group participants become willing to "own" aspects of experience that they have previously denied or projected. (2) They discover new meanings in situations and interactions, meanings of which they were previously unaware. More comprehensive awareness of experience forms the foundation from which members can create new perceptions of meaning. (3) Members recognize decisions and choices that influence present situations. They recognize interactions as cocreative processes. (4) Group participants are willing to initiate changes that alter levels of exploration and communication. These changes tend to move from lesser to greater openness and contact.

Members may choose to extend their personal center to include more of others and their group as a whole. The unstructured group is an ideal setting for members to realize potentials for extending the individual center to include more of others and the world. These members can then learn how to create win-win situations rather than win-lose situations based on aggrandizement, control, or denial. Win-win situations allow members to feel greater personal power (Rogers, 1977). Creation of a center within experience provides a foundation for movement toward a balanced and creatively integrated expression of love, power, and justice in relationships.

Chapter Five

The Dynamics of
Love, Power, and Justice

Human awareness can be understood consistently to operate within a relational context. Therefore, we can make the assumption that the individual creates and integrates splits in awareness within a field of relationship and that relationships affect the formation and healing of splits. Integration is simultaneously an intrapersonal and an interpersonal event. Members' sense of self moves from enclosed or rigidly bounded to one that functions in the "between." What happens within persons influences what happens between them, and what happens in the between influences what happens within.

If group members are to integrate awareness and extend it to include others, they open themselves to relations that are based on mutual caring and responsibility. This extension of self to include others can be viewed as the operation of love between persons. An atmosphere of freedom in a group can support mutual care between the persons involved. If group members are willing to use their freedom in their group to be aware of what another experiences and to respond with openness and acceptance, then they move toward love. If they sense the potential of a group's atmosphere to support loving interactions, members may feel encouraged to choose the openness that allows the self to include others.

Universal Dynamics of the Interpersonal Field

One way to explain the tendency of the self to move toward inclusion of others is to postulate universal dynamics in the between that can bring people into integrated forms of relationship. Simultaneously, these universal dynamics encourage and support the integration of individuals.

An individual who experiences contact with the ground of being comes into relation with universal aspects of being. This contact with the ground of being opens the individual to the potential for love, to the possibility of including others in the person's process of being. Individuals define and influence their relationships; yet at the same time, those relationships reveal the nature of self to individuals. A person learns about his or her ability to integrate from participating in integrated relationship dynamics. These allow for the expression of love. Therefore, actualizing the potential for love within relationship can provide a basis for the grounding of individual participants' awareness, just as the grounding of the individual in awareness can lead to actualization of potentials for love.

Because awareness and relationship imply one another, it is possible to conceptualize universal dynamics for healing, growth, and development. Universal dynamics for healing and growth can exist within human relationships because all people need relationships to express awareness and all human relationships can enhance awareness. Those dynamics that integrate awareness within relationship provide a universal basis for growth and development— that is, for self-actualization.

The elements of love, power, and justice can be understood as aspects of the process of being. Tillich (1954) views love, power, and justice as central and universal elements that emerge within an ontological analysis, an examination of what it means to be. For Tillich (1954), ontology is "the elaboration of the *logos* of the *on* . . . the 'rational work' that grasps 'being as such' . . . being-insofar-as-it-is-being" (p. 18). Tillich's attempt to grasp being as such leads him to conceptualize the functioning of individuals as an expression of universal dynamics. Tillich states that if we can understand the universal dynamic structures that are presupposed in all real human encounters, we can then comprehend how individuals establish relatedness to each other, to nature, to their cultures, and to their world. According to Tillich, awareness of universal dynamics in no way minimizes the importance of individuality or diminishes the importance of the individual's encounter with meaninglessness and nonbeing. Rather, the operation of universal dynamics helps to explain commonalities that emerge among different individuals and cultures as people attempt to live meaningful lives.

Love, power, and justice are said by Tillich to possess "ontological dignity" (1954, p. 21). They are terms adequate for a discussion about universal aspects of relationship because they reflect core ideas that have shown themselves to be relevant in diverse cultures as well as in contemporary Western culture. Love, power, and justice have played a role in various political systems, philosophical systems, religions, and mythologies that have been created as expressions of human attempts to comprehend a universal reality. Thus, these core elements reflect an ongoing dynamic that is essentially universal within the field of interpersonal interaction. Although it is universal, this dynamic develops through different formulations that arise within various situations, group settings, and cultures.

Analysis of Interpersonal Dynamics

Cultures that do not encourage their members to see universal aspects of human beings may believe that members of other cultures are alien and bizarre or exist as objects to be exploited or removed. Like individuals, cultures can refuse to learn from, can interfere with, and can disrespect one another. One motive that frequently leads cultures, groups, or individuals to create interpersonal barriers is the need for power based on control of resources. People may seek this kind of power to protect themselves, to feel secure, or to dominate others. As we will see, the integration of self with others is blocked or distorted whenever power operates separately from love—that is, when the need for power functions without care for the being of others. Similarly, love that operates separately from power can distort relationships by refusing to acknowledge differences or boundaries. However, if love and power can be integrated, an interpersonal ethic of justice can become the basis for interpersonal and between-culture interactions.

In an unstructured therapy group, an ethic of justice operating within an atmosphere of freedom supports members' cocreation of shared experience and enables participants to achieve integrated love and power. People who are aware of and care about each other can create dynamics of justice that function with flexibility. A flexible justice can meet the demands of changing situations and changing needs of individuals within those situations. The universal healing dynamics that promote the growth and development of group members are those that function as an integrated gestalt of love, power, and justice.

The analysis of the dynamics of relationships in a therapy group might be compared to analysis of a chemical reaction. One could isolate the components of a relationship, figure out how these components are interacting, and formulate a strategy to combine them in a new way. For example, a person could be helped to see how certain needs for security are interfering with meeting other needs for affection. The person could be assisted to understand how to express love more clearly and to act more assertively to meet needs. However, this kind of analysis will not necessarily help a person to learn how to reassess situations on an ongoing basis. Therefore, a more constructive analysis of relationship dynamics would help a person to learn about self as a dynamic process that creates and adapts to changes within various contexts. Useful assessment of interpersonal interactions is likely to involve human emotional resonance and intuitive forms of awareness that would not be necessary for analyzing chemical reactions.

Real change occurs within the present; there is an alteration in the pattern of ongoing interaction. Therefore, constructive analysis of patterns in relationship does not remove individuals experientially from continuing awareness of interactions. Useful observations about relational processes provide a way to become more alive to what occurs within the present. Lengthy verbal analyses are often far less useful or productive than simple invitations to observe clearly what is happening. Members of therapeutic groups can help each other to see the challenges that are occurring within the present, challenges that may require a new integration of love, power, and justice. These kinds of challenges arise frequently because the dynamics of relationships evolve as members reveal themselves to each other.

Love

The longing for love is a recurrent theme in individual and group therapy. Many people have obviously been hurt because they did not receive love that they wanted or needed. Many people are in pain because they see themselves as essentially unlovable. Some individuals are afraid to love or to be loved by others. People sometimes know that they wish to have the feeling of love, but they are uncertain what it involves. People can have stereotypical ideas about or highly idiosyncratic definitions of love. Very different actions can cause people to feel loved by another. In spite of these different perceptions and divergent ways of expressing love, there is something universal about the longing for love. This universality is evident in the key role that love has in the problems and in the fulfillment that people experience.

Tillich (1954) defines love as the "reunification of the separated." He writes, "Reunion presupposes separation of that which belongs essentially together . . . separation presupposes an original unity" (p. 25). Tillich views love as a kind of force that reaffirms unity after it has been broken. In this view, a person could never feel love unless the person has felt separation. Tillich (1954) presents this observation, as he does his other ontological analyses of the human condition, as assertions validated by what can be determined experientially. Love, in this view, is essentially not quantifiable. Love cannot be reduced to the operation of other elements, such as instincts or desires to gain rewards. Its effects can be observed, but love itself must be felt to be understood, as opposed to being observed from outside. The healing effect of love comes through its experience.

Love as a Dynamic Element in
Unstructured Group Therapy

The development of group process often demonstrates members' longing to make open and caring contact with others and to feel that they can be understood and accepted by others. Thus, love plays an important role in the dynamics of healing and growth that occur in therapy groups. Individuals' desires to experience love are often present from the beginning of an unstructured group since it is not uncommon for members to join with the hope of finding acceptance, openness, and caring. Members may have experienced separation from others with whom they were once unified. If they feel unified with others in their group, some of their wounds may be healed. Group members can also often provide useful feedback about other members' longing for reunification with significant others in their lives. Such feedback can help members to learn how to ask for love or how to deal with situations when love is not being offered.

As their problems are frequently associated with their difficulties in giving and receiving love, members may be concerned about issues such as self-esteem, feelings of inadequacy, and difficulties achieving certain life goals. These issues are often closely related to the self-image created by relationships in which there were difficulties in expressing love. With the acceptance and understanding of their group, members' self-esteem can improve. Positive self-esteem decreases feelings of inadequacy and makes it more likely that individuals can set and achieve life goals. Love alone is not the only element involved in successful therapy. However, experiences of love can play a significant role in many therapeutic encounters. For example, members can be affected by perceptions that others care about them or understand them and may gain self-esteem when they express their own caring toward others. The presence of the experience of love—if love is considered broadly—is a fundamental element in therapy.

Another theorist who may be viewed as having presented an ontological analysis of love is Carl Rogers. Rogers (1967a) delineates congruence, unconditional positive regard, and empathy as three necessary and sufficient conditions that promote therapeutic personality change. These three core conditions are central in Rogers's lifelong work (see Rogers, 1980). The conditions of congruence, unconditional positive regard, and empathy can readily be understood as aspects of love. When love is expressed from one person to another, this expression must be authentic (in other words, congruent with experience), if therapy is to heal rather than manipulate. Expressions of love that are genuine are likely to promote well-being whereas expressions of love that are inauthentic are likely to contribute to mistrust and estrangement. Unconditional positive regard, the second core condition, represents the expression of love as respect, caring, and involvement. Empathy, the third of Rogers's conditions, can also be understood as an important aspect of love; empathy is necessary to understand how the other person feels. An individual must be able to assess how the other feels if love is to be communicated and demonstrated in a manner that the other can appreciate. The absence of any of these conditions weakens the ability both to love and to express it.

Referring to empathic understanding, respect, genuineness, and specificity, Patterson (1985) writes, "The essence of these conditions is love, in the sense of the Greek *agape* . . . love is the most effective agent for change that we know" (p. 8). Defining conditions that are conducive for therapeutic change, according to Patterson, is equivalent to analyzing the components of a loving relationship. If Patterson's premise is valid, then therapy heals through the experience of love. However, love cannot simply be provided by one person (the therapist) to another (the client). Love implies a dialogue, and persons who participate in dialogue can experience a loving relationship only if they create one together (Arnett, 1989; O'Hara, 1984).

The therapist and group members may work together to create a climate wherein members can congruently express thoughts and feelings, respect and value each other without placing conditions on their mutual acceptance, and can form empathic relations with one another. Participants may also choose to work against the creation of a loving group climate (McClure, 1990). One frequently cited barrier to such a climate can be the maintenance of fear and resentment as a reaction to participants who express negative feelings toward other members (Gans, 1989). Another barrier can arise if members communicate their lack of respect or valuing of certain other members (Unger, 1990). A third barrier can be the difficulties that members can experience if attempts to communicate lead to misunderstandings or misinterpretations (Leszcz, 1992).

The creation of a loving group atmosphere can only occur if members are willing to acknowledge the barriers to mutual caring that exist and are willing to work on them (McClure, 1990). A loving atmosphere in a group is not created simply by believing that it would be a nice thing to have. The group needs to struggle with doubts, self-esteem problems, the need to maintain roles, and various other impediments. The creation of a loving environment requires awareness and commitment as well as good intentions.

Aspects of Love

Love can be viewed as an expression of the fundamental integrative principle of relationship, just as awareness is the activity of this fundamental integrative principle within experience. The basis for claiming awareness and love as expressions of one integrative principle is that experiences are the basis for relationships and relationships are formed within experience. Therefore, the integrative principles of love and awareness are very closely aligned. Love allows individuals to feel integrated with other specific individuals, with the human community, and with the world of nature. Love is the basis of a shared relational context that can be experienced as benevolent rather than neutral or harmful. Therapy groups seek to establish a shared relational context that is benevolent and that can ideally include all members. Love is therefore a basis for an effective therapeutic atmosphere. Freedom is closely aligned with love because an optimum group atmosphere supports freedom and love. Both need to be experienced to be understood, and both allow a person to extend the self to include others.

Participants in unstructured therapy groups are very likely to be consciously or unconsciously wishing for exposure to unifying love in the group. Members would like to be accepted by others and would like to extend acceptance to others. As we have seen, the reason that groups do not automatically blossom into loving environments is that participants carry with them all the obstacles to love that they have experienced in the past.

Although members wish for the experience of love, they may find ways to undermine love through mistrust, aggression, or self-protection (Agazarian, 1992; Gans, 1989; Yalom, 1975). Mary, the client described in Chapter Four, demonstrated with one of the authors this tendency to seek love and acceptance while undermining her own efforts. Mary let the therapist who was conducting the unstructured group know that she wanted his affection and respect; at the same time, she attempted to become extremely dependent on her facilitator. She had a previous history of trying to develop close relationships with other counselors and then becoming overly dependent in these relationships. Once Mary became involved in therapy, she never wanted it to end. Mary was able to avoid assuming responsibility for her own actions in this manner. This facilitator encouraged the other members to provide Mary with feedback in the group when they observed her being too dependent on others, including the facilitator, and gradually she was able to develop more self-confidence and greater ability to function independently.

Love can be characterized as having four basic aspects: *agape* (or universality), *epithymia* (or desire), *eros* (or life-enhancing values), and *philia* (or friendship) (Tillich, 1954). Tillich (1954) thought that although love has been treated traditionally as a fragmented process by various religious and secular institutions, love actually operates without fragmentation if it is accepted as a whole or totality. If, as Tillich (1954) suggests, the different aspects of love are all expressions of integration in human relations, it would therefore be incorrect to regard the expression of one aspect of love as being more valuable or worthy than another.

Patterson (1985) has noted the connection between agape and therapy. Agape is selfless caring for others and represents a willingness to give to others. A person who expresses agape is not concerned about whether others reciprocate love or give something in return. Because it does not favor one person over another, agape is considered to be the universal form of love. Yet it would be a mistake to equate the growth of group members in therapy only with the experience of agape. Agape arises from the awareness of a shared context for all beings. Perhaps the experience of agape is always present to some extent whenever members feel that they are part of a caring group atmosphere. However, members also move toward mutual acceptance by finding ways to enjoy one another's presence in the group and by experiencing a bond that is established when intimate aspects of oneself are shared with others. Members extend their centers to include others not only because they sense a universality with others but because they enjoy talking to specific individuals and because they have confided in them.

Thus, love also has an individual aspect—one that joins specific people for particular interpersonal aims. In unstructured therapy groups, members generally move to accept and include specific others. The individual center of one member can be extended to include another member because of shared values, because of attraction or desire, or because of the potential for friendship. The more that two members are willing to include each other, the closer their personal relationship comes to the I-thou form of encounter. Although the joining together of individuals can sometimes create discomfort for other members who feel left out, it can also be a positive experience for the group. The joining of two members who experience a bond can be helpful if other participants feel gratified to observe that two members have connected on a meaningful level. Jealousy or feelings of rejection may surface as barriers that must be acknowledged and experienced before the group can move to acceptance of this bond.

As we saw earlier, Tillich (1954) has written that different forms of love are expressions of one force in human affairs. The apparently selfless agape aspect of love is not, in reality, separated from the *epithymia* aspect of love, which is expressed as the seeking of pleasure and self-fulfillment. Groups become more cohesive (that is, participants experience more mutual acceptance) if members can accept the various expressions of love that can be important to individuals. If a male member strives for selfless love and denies his selfish side, he may not connect fully with others. If a female member denies her more selfless or universal feelings because she thinks she will be taken advantage of by others, she may also limit her fulfillment in the group and in life. Any one-sided approach may be limiting.

Some people, including Freud (1930/1961), have viewed the

foundation of all love as a drive for pleasure. At the other extreme are people who believe that love is a spiritual reality which sometimes may contradict the self-centered tendencies of sensuality and desire (Maslow, 1964; Vaughan, 1986). *Epithymia* has traditionally been treated by many religions as the lowest form of love. Yet *epithymia* is present in all desires whose fulfillment brings pleasure, including eating, movement, sexuality, or participation in a group. These activities provide pleasure as they unite the person with the environment and the person with others. Pleasure is the by-product of integration with the world, with individual others, and with the human community.

If pleasure is sought as an end in itself, the integration of the person with the world becomes limited. In therapy groups, members who have tried to live only for the experience of pleasure often express a confrontation with meaninglessness in life and in relationships. Groups can provide environments where members learn that integration within relationships includes pleasure but that fulfillment through relationship may be limited if pleasure is seen as the only goal.

Tillich (1954) relates the movement of human energy toward life-affirming values to eros, the form of love that is expressed as an enhanced experience of life, nature, and culture. He links the movement of human energy toward friendship and personal involvement with the form of love that the Greeks called *philia*. These two aspects of love form a polar relationship, with eros representing a transpersonal aspect of love and *philia* representing a deeply personal aspect of love. *Philia* and eros can be conceptualized as existing in interdependent relationship, and neither aspect would be possible without the existence of the other (Tillich, 1954). People cannot fully appreciate the meaning of nature and beauty if they are unable to personalize feelings in the context of specific encounters and relations. The dynamic relationship between *philia* and eros can be seen in the context of group therapy. As individuals' personal interactions and relationships develop in the group, their values are often affected. As a result of group interactions, members may develop more positive views of society, relationships, certain ethnic or minority groups, males, females, or the potential for beauty and love in life.

At the same time, eros—according to Tillich (1954)—is founded on *epithymia*. Eros can use desire to transform persons who are estranged from the positive possibilities of life. Eros is the attraction that people may feel toward reunification with values that disclose beauty in nature and the potential for meaning and truth in culture. Therapy groups can be considered to begin to work successfully as members become attracted to the group and to each other. This attraction, along with mutual interpersonal acceptance, is a necessary part of the development of cohesion in the group (Yalom, 1975). Members are much more likely to experience a positive transformation of values if they first experience attraction to others in their group and to their group as a whole.

The eros aspect of love may affect members throughout their group participation, whenever they feel the possibility of life-affirming values. Eros can lead members to prize their group experience as a whole for the values that it represents—for example, openness, honesty, and equality.

The *philia* aspect of love is most evident when members disclose and respond to specific others in the group with the understanding that there is a fundamental equality between the individuals. Perceptions of fundamental equality are likely to be more readily available if members see others in their group as coming from shared environments or life experiences. Equality can also be recognized between those from different backgrounds, usually if members come to experience empathy and respect for one another.

The *philia* and agape aspects of love can intertwine in experiences of empathy. Through *philia*, a member can experience a unique kind of bond with another who has shared an empathic encounter. Through agape, a member can experience the potential universality of empathy, the possibility of joining with any other who is willing to be joined. Empathy represents an attitude of openness, and it also represents willingness to learn from the experiences of others. Empathy, like awareness and love, cannot be forced. Empathy can be viewed as awareness and love working together. By relating empathically, a person is able to become aware of the world of another and to care enough about that world to be affected by nuances of the other's perception that are highly personal and subjective.

Therapy groups have the potential to help members learn how to unite aspects of love that may be fragmented in the experience of individuals (for example, *epithymia* and agape). A group can help members to learn that they can care about the group as a whole and can integrate this caring with a special feeling of attraction for one or more members. Members can get feedback from others that helps them to validate all of who they are—their spiritual longings as well as their desires for "earthly" pleasures.

The person who has adapted to an environment where it is emotionally unsafe to express or seek love is likely to repress longings for love. Theorists have had different explanations for difficulties that people have in engaging in loving relationships. Kohut (1971) emphasizes that a person's lack of empathic relations with a significant nurturing figure leads to lack of self-esteem and an emotional emptiness that makes love difficult or impossible. Maslow states that people adapt to emotionally deprived environments by learning a form of love that he terms "deficiency-love" (Goble, 1971). This kind of love attempts to fill a void. A person who experiences self as deficient attempts to take from others to feel better about self. Perls (1971) might say that this kind of person wants to fill self-created holes in the personality by taking from others. Kohut (1971) would probably say that the person only created these kinds of holes because of experiences of deprivation or rejection. Theorists can invest various explanations for experiences of self-deficiency. Each individual's perceptions of past history and ability to draw on esteem-enhancing resources are important aspects of the rationale for negative self-perceptions (Combs & Snygg, 1959). Such a person will have difficulties believing that he or she has anything of self that is worth giving.

Most likely, experiences of a loving nature can help heal the kinds of wounds preserved as negative self-perceptions, whereas experiences of a rejecting nature will maintain or exacerbate these wounds to the sense of self (Bacal, 1985; Kohut, 1971). Although loving relations in therapy can promote healing, therapists are constrained by their roles from engaging in a fully equal and loving relationship in which partners express and meet needs and wishes of the other (Yalom, 1980). Therefore, an advantage of group therapy is that members can learn about love on an equal basis from each other. Members may experience greater benefits from the relations that they form with others whom they perceive as equals than with a group's therapist (Yalom, 1975).

Therapeutic groups provide opportunities to meet the needs that help build self-esteem—the needs with which theorists such as Kohut (1977) and Maslow (1962) have been concerned. A person can find others who are willing to give, but just as important, a person is likely to find others who are willing to receive. A person's belief that she or he has sufficient resources to contribute meaningfully to others and can experience joy within the act of giving is a central aspect of the love that Maslow (1962) calls being-love and Patterson (1985) terms agape. This love is altruistic insofar as the reward of the person giving it is gained by the act of giving; no obligations for reciprocation are involved. When a group is functioning therapeutically, members often give each other verbal and nonverbal messages of caring in which nothing is asked in return. Awareness of nonverbal messages that attend communications is necessary to understand how emotions such as love and hostility are involved in interactions between group members (Applbaum, Bodaken, Sereno & Anatol, 1974).

Members, as they assist each other's self-actualization, help each other perceive that being-love is possible. Although emotions that are traditionally considered negative are often shut out of individuals' awareness (for example, anger, lust, or anxiety), positive feelings may also be experienced as uncomfortable or threatening. People frequently repress awareness of loving feelings, perceptions of competence, and feelings of positive self-esteem as part of their maintenance of negative self-images. People may eliminate opportunities to give and receive affection because they regard love as unreal, phony, or manipulative. If a person eliminates opportunities to experience love, longings for love may be expressed in the form of addictions. Addictions are compulsive and repetitive forms of activity and self-expression. In groups that treat addiction, members often must acknowledge their longings to give and receive love before they are able to give up addictive patterns (George, 1990; Lewis, Dana & Blevins, 1988). One great benefit of Alcoholics Anonymous groups is that members give each other support and other-

wise contribute to one another's experience constructively and on
an equal basis.

Distortions of Love in Therapeutic Relations

To be able to communicate and respond empathically, a person
must be attuned to who the other is and to what the present experience of that other is. At the same time, participants need to have
clear awareness of their own unfinished business. Without this clar-
ity about past relationship patterns, participants can mistake their
own projected feelings or motives for the feelings of the other person (Polster & Polster, 1973). Others can only guess at the extent to
which individuals may take their own perceptions of reality to be
true for other people. Therefore, the most fruitful assessments of
distortion are made by the person creating it.

The gestalt of love, power, and justice within present relationships becomes skewed when participants in relationships deal
with unresolved emotional issues from the past in ways that are
unjust within the context of the present relationship. Whether this
distortion is evaluated in terms of transference dynamics (see Greenson, 1967) or the maintenance of unfinished business (see Polster &
Polster, 1973), therapists seek to use the therapy process to assist
completion and letting go of past dynamics as new present dynamics become possible. Therapists who work in terms of transference
tend to focus on learning about a client's past, whereas work on
unfinished business tends to focus more on here-and-now effects of
communications. In unstructured therapy groups, participants may
be invited to assess how past relationships affect current interactions
(Wolf & Schwartz, 1962; Foulkes, 1975) or may gain potent experiential learning by being invited to communicate within the context
of present dynamics in ways that challenge distorted patterns of
relationship (Leszcz, 1992).

A person who has experienced rejection from a significant
other in the past often rejects the possibility of empathic encounters
in the present. Such a member could be assisted to reconstruct important past events and to be open to experiential aspects of these
that were shut out. Additionally, this individual could be encouraged to be open to empathy offered by another member. A member

will usually provide cues whether an exploration of past or present events is focal in his or her awareness. Others who trust and affirm a person's creation of directions for awareness assist movement toward integrated relationship dynamics.

A client named "James," a member of an unstructured therapy group conducted in a residential drug treatment center, shows how people can benefit from both examining their past and learning about how to relate effectively in the present. James was a black multidrug user who had intimidated many of the staff members and other residents in his program. He had a reputation among them for being dangerous and crazy enough to do about anything. He was also a former Vietnam veteran. James tended to undermine his relationships with other residents by projecting a violent image of himself. During one group session, he described having seen a good friend killed by a policeman for what he thought was no good reason. The policeman was white, and since that time James had developed some highly unfavorable opinions about white people—especially white authority figures.

After a fairly extended interaction with the leader wherein James described his friend's death and his own feelings about the incident, James became more open and honest with the facilitator and the other participants. The leader and James ended up the group by indicating that they liked each other. James was able to describe a tragic incident in group that had affected his attitudes toward white people unfavorably, and he also learned that he could relate in some rewarding ways to an individual whom he considered to be a white authority figure.

If therapists are unaware of their own uncompleted or unacknowledged longing for love, they may create skewed relationships with clients. Such patterns can become overt if a therapist plays the authority role and encourages client dependency, if a therapist demands or manipulates caring from the client, or if the therapist attempts to play an exclusively intellectual role. In a group situation, such a therapist tends to be either under- or overinvolved with the group process. By being overinvolved, the therapist tries to win affection and perceptions of his or her significance from clients. By being underinvolved, the therapist portrays an image of self-sufficiency and emotional distance.

In psychoanalytic psychotherapy, the therapist needs to be aware of any countertransference issues (the therapist's unfinished business projected onto the client) so that he or she can correctly interpret the client's transference (projections onto the therapist) (Greenson, 1967). The central thrust of psychoanalysis is on interpretation of a client's transference. This interpretation helps a client to learn how unfinished themes and relationship patterns are repeating themselves and interfering with present relationships. Gestalt therapy warns that a therapist who has not worked on unfinished business is not likely to function with full effectiveness in assisting clients to work with their own problems.

Centering Therapeutic Relationships in the Present

As we saw in Chapter Three, present-oriented concerns can be assumed to be valid therapeutic issues without necessarily or automatically relating them to past patterns (Perls, Hefferline & Goodman, 1951/1980). Although awareness of unfinished business can be helpful, the present relationship should not be reduced to a vehicle for understanding the impact of past events. Instead, the past can be considered significant insofar as it forms part of the meaning of the present. The unknown aspect of the present, its becoming, can never be sufficiently translated in terms of the past, which is known. Therefore, powerful therapeutic work can be done within the context of the present to assist people in becoming more open to unknown aspects of their own processes of being-becoming.

An ontological perspective of therapy leads us to view being as centered in the present. From this perspective, unfinished business is a kind of resonance of events that is reconstructed within each current moment. If the person is viewed as a creative, present-centered being, then unfinished business is that individual's own construction based on perceived similarities of the past with the present. Unfinished business is a means to learn about how the person is constructing self within the present. Viewing unfinished business in this manner requires a unique view of transference and countertransference issues.

Unfinished business thus reflects commitments, beliefs about self, and goals for relationships. As we have already seen, these can twist current relationship dynamics and limit the atmosphere of love that can be created between participants. Members who work to own feelings within the present and to confront dynamics based on blame and shame will challenge their reconstruction of unfinished business.

Personal Power and Self-Love

The integration of power and love has been seen by many theorists to involve the ability to care for and love one's self in a manner that can include caring for others (for example, see Fromm, 1956; Kohut, 1971, 1977; Rogers, 1977). The more that one can include another, the deeper is the experience of love. The more others that one can include in the experience of life, the more universal is the experience of love. The universality of love is not demonstrated by any quantity of friends and loved ones. Universality is shown in the completeness of love, especially by the quality of openness and acceptance that characterizes relationships. One relationship can be the basis for learning about universal aspects of love. Indeed, a person might withdraw from a relationship that lacks love or one in which love and power are imbalanced in order to learn from a process of self-reflection and contemplation. Of course, the full potential for the integration of love and power is not realized by contemplation alone, especially if it leads to withdrawal or self-absorption. A therapy group can provide opportunities to extend knowledge that has been developed through reflection in a way that includes other people.

If a person's process of self-reflection has been the basis for a constructive process of change, he or she becomes able to engage others more fully and openly. The person also may become more capable of making decisions about when and how and whether to engage others. The ability to make decisions based on one's own experiential process and perceptions of relationships is evidence of an awareness of power (Bugental, 1978; Rogers, 1977). Thus, power can enhance the significance of love. An absence of personal power detracts from the importance of the love that is expressed because it is not grounded in abilities to make firm decisions and choices within relationships. In unstructured groups, members can explore options for integrating love and power in an interpersonal context.

The person who has ambivalent feelings about self is highly likely to develop fragmented relations with others. Fragmented relationships are evidenced by the inability of participants to connect as fully as they would like, to express themselves completely. The price can be a loss of personal integrity, a disassociation of love from power. Love may be withheld in such relationships. If group members risk expressing themselves openly and fully with others in their group, they will experience congruence between the image that they present and their own experience. This congruence ends fragmentation in relationship.

The universality of love can allow individuals' centers to be infinitely extended; but if inclusion of others leads to relationships that deplete energy and enthusiasm, then love has probably become imbalanced with power. A person must be able to take care of self and to meet needs in the world in order to develop in a way that can include others.

Love, viewed as the extension of the center to include others, requires self-love as a foundation. At the same time, self-love must include others because one cannot have a self without other people. This kind of self-love is very different from obsession with one's own image, or destructive narcissism, which blocks relatedness. A healthy kind of narcissism, used in the construction of self-esteem, plays an important part in love (Kohut, 1977).

Clients involved in therapy often complain of low self-esteem or a poor self-image. These clients can be taught new ways to think about themselves; but if they lack the experience of self-love, their new thinking is unlikely to have much of an impact. Defenses against extending love to include others, or against receiving love from others, often reflect fears that to love means to lose power in some way. The therapeutic group is one that is able to provide an atmosphere where members experience a love that enhances their power, competence, and strength, and authentic self-love.

Participants who strongly value independence may hold themselves apart from others in the group. If these members feel free and accepted, they may find that they can be interdependent without losing their independence. They may find that their independence gives them something to offer others and their ability to depend on others gives them an opportunity to experience mutual caring. They can give and receive appreciation and expressions of caring and still can say no to interactions in which they do not want to participate. They do not have to pretend to feel something that they are not feeling. Love that is empowering to individuals never robs them of the chance to think or express themselves differently or to experience events uniquely.

Power

As a basic element of anything that exists, power is the identity and coherence of that thing (see Tillich, 1954). In human life, power is demonstrated by a coherent awareness of self and by the ability to use that sense of self as a basis for formulating directions and influencing events.

Power as an Integral Element in Therapeutic Process

Powerlessness can be the result of environmental factors or social prejudices as well as self-perceptions. Environmental factors and self-perceptions interact in ways that either contribute to or detract from awareness of personal power. A therapy group can create an environment that assists empowerment by providing open and honest feedback about how a person is experienced by others (Leszcz, 1992). This feedback can contribute to development and maintenance of a coherent sense of self. The environment in a therapy group can also free participants from reliance on limiting social stereotypes that diminish awareness of power. In addition, members become empowered when they see that they influence others in their group.

If love is the inherent movement of reunification that connects a thing with everything else, power is the inherent movement toward distinction that differentiates a thing from everything else. If love and power are integrated, a person experiences her or his distinctiveness as a way to connect to others. If love and power are functioning in an imbalanced manner, people feel that they need to avoid connecting with others to maintain their distinctiveness or need to merge with others in a manner that denies their individuality.

Power is an assertion of distinctiveness associated with knowing what one wants and needs, expressing these wishes or needs, and acting to move toward what is desired. Thus, personal power is evidenced by the person's willingness to function as an active agent (see May, 1972; Yalom, 1980). If power is integrated with love, a person is able to express wants and needs in a manner that is considerate of the feelings of others and that respects their integrity. If power is expressed in a manner that is disconnected from love, others are likely to feel imposed upon, coerced, or manipulated in a dishonest manner. Therefore, integrating power with love usually helps people to meet needs in interpersonal situations more effectively. A group member who is willing to express needs or wants toward other group members usually contributes to the development of a therapeutic (that is, integrative) group atmosphere. Power and love are intrinsically unified, and their separation in interpersonal dynamics diminishes the ability of either of these elements to function fully and effectively.

A person's sense of agency can be actualized in many ways. Agency can involve the construction of perceptions, the recognition of potentials, the achievement of goals in the environment through exerting energy, and influencing of others through relationship processes. Power must be aligned with awareness in order for individuals' influence over events to be congruent with individuals' actual needs, feelings, and values. For power to be used responsibly, the freedom of others must be recognized and respected. Thus, the element of power interacts with the gestalt of awareness, freedom, and responsibility. Awareness assists the integration of power with love; through awareness, a person can recognize the needs of others and can also understand the destructive consequences of power that acts without love.

Power and Choice

The initiation of interaction may involve risk for the initiator, particularly if this action upsets the status quo in a group. Yet a person can also take a risk by *not* initiating an action that others expect or require. Personal power may be expressed by not moving or not reacting to a stimulus as well as by initiating something. For example, a group leader who does not provide an answer to a question may assist others to construct their own responses. A participant who listens or asks a simple question about what is occurring in the group may be showing personal power in a situation where others are excessively concerned with asserting the significance of their opinions. A group member who does not respond to name calling from another member may also be showing personal power. Thus, personal power is expressed as the ability to make choices how and when to engage others within ongoing interactions. Power allows a person to maintain a centered presence with others and to choose how to react to situations. Lack of power means a loss of center when interacting with others and leads to habitual reactions to situations. Whether automatic reactions are emotionally or cognitively based, they can impair the development of power integrated with awareness.

People generally feel powerless if they have no other options for response except to hurt others or themselves. In a trusting interpersonal atmosphere, members may tentatively discuss feelings of powerlessness and related perceptions of their own incompetence, inadequacy, and passivity.

One theorist who notes the prevalence of the theme of power in human relationships is Alfred Adler. Adler has observed that a central motivation for the achievement of power is the individual's perception of insignificance (Mosak, 1984). Adler also believed that people become healthier as they learn that they make choices that alter events. They can then learn to be creative in their approach to life and others and can gain significance without damaging themselves or others. People may often wound themselves and others by attempts to overcompensate for feelings of insecurity, by trying to demonstrate their superiority to others, and by trying to control situations and people (Adler, 1972).

Tillich (1954) takes a broad view of the theme of power. He postulates that individuals are motivated toward power in an attempt to attain victory over nonbeing. The threat of nonbeing is a general category that can encompass feelings of guilt, perceptions of one's own inadequacy and insignificance, experience of life as meaningless, or awareness of death. People sometimes assert their power over perceived threats through behavior that is self-destructive.

Fromm (1964) and Perls, Hefferline, and Goodman (1951/1980) have asserted that the threats that people perceive may be projections of disowned aspects of their own experience. If this assertion is true, people are trying to overcome an externalized aspect of their own experience when they act against these threats. No amount of external victory will be able to alleviate their own awareness of themselves. They may be driven toward increasingly extreme measures until their actions have self-destructive effects. Therapy groups act as social microcosms (Leszcz, 1992). Thus, as members interact they reveal patterns of perceptions that they use in other social settings and have opportunities to gain immediate feedback about these perceptual schema.

An authentic victory over nonbeing can only come as a result of owning the nonbeing within oneself. Owning projections can involve the group as a whole as well as individual members. Just as individual members grow through working to acknowledge their "shadows" or negative aspects of self, groups can acknowledge hurtful tendencies of the collective gestalt (McClure, 1990). Group members can help each other to gain more power and choice in their lives by giving each other feedback about the feelings and behaviors that they are disowning as they interact and self-disclose.

According to Tillich (1952), courage is an essential characteristic of people who are able to act in spite of perceptions of the threat of nonbeing. It is this willingness to risk that can lead to greater fulfillment and self-respect. Group members often help each other to take risks that require courage. A participant can sometimes be comfortable initiating actions that others see as risky and dangerous but will be afraid to acknowledge feelings of vulnerability. Feedback from group members can assist participants to clarify perceptions about those areas of life—including feelings of vulnerability—that are personally challenging and that require courage. Courage is always an individual matter because actions that require bravery for one person may be habitual for another person, and vice versa. By helping each other to take risks in what is owned and what is expressed, members help each other to see that they have more choices within interpersonal interactions.

Developing an Empowering Group Atmosphere

Power generally involves a coherent sense of self that includes trust in one's perceptions, a belief in adequate resources to meet needs, a sense of one's adequacy to deal with challenges, awareness of the capability to affirm self and others, and the ability to initiate changes in situations. Members can assist each other's empowerment if they are able to give each other feedback about perceived strengths. If they are unable to discuss weaknesses, members' reactions about strengths are likely to be viewed as insincere or superficial. Members must be able to discuss weaknesses and strengths, perceived threats and successes. By being open with each other about who they are and who they are becoming, members can create opportunities to affirm one another. Affirmation is expressed within a process of open interaction, empathic responding, and appreciative feelings about others. Affirmation is not avoidance of conflicts; rather, it allows members to see themselves as worthy contributors to group process, including their willingness to engage conflicts constructively.

Members need to create an inclusive atmosphere so that all members feel that they have access to the attention of others. If members avoid disclosure of perceived threats and experiences of nonbeing, work toward empowerment and self-actualization will be inhibited. Members may shy away from an atmosphere that encourages the discussion of perceived threats. Participants may experience anxiety about the potential for conflict between participants and also about some of the subjects that may be discussed. Disclosure of personal anxieties is usually considered an intimate form of communication. Members may need to develop a strong sense that their group is trustworthy before they acknowledge perceived threats of nonbeing. Aspects of being that are not usually part of social discussions (sexuality, aggression, history of physical or sexual abuse, or adjustment to disturbed dynamics in the family of origin) may emerge as members confront perceived threats.

As participants learn how to use their group therapeutically, they tend to move away from unnecessary politeness in their interactions. Yet some members may continue to resort to modes of communication that express needs for power indirectly and covertly. As a group becomes a safe place to work on issues of personal power, members tend to confront each other about interactions that they perceive as manipulative or dishonest. A central way that a group can empower members is by helping members to become aware of covert activities designed to influence others and by creating norms that validate directly asking others for what is desired or needed (Leszcz, 1992).

The group atmosphere that promotes empowerment is one that encourages members to feel acceptable, even when they deviate from previous patterns in their own lives or in their group. Members feel safe to express being different from both others and their own previous self-image. Such a group environment is approving of diversity and allows members to share in making decisions that influence the direction of the group. Although the optimal group atmosphere balances the power needs of members, members often engage in imbalanced power dynamics before a constructive distribution is attained.

Norms and Roles in Power Relations

In therapy groups, the group process evolves as members (1) form perceptions of their own power in their group, (2) form perceptions of the power of others, (3) find ways to relate their own sense of power with others', and (4) gain an understanding of the power of the group's leader. These four aspects of members' perceptions of power can change throughout a group, depending on the course of interactions. Members gain or lose status in their group depending on a general, often subtly formed consensus based on members' understanding of norms and of each other's personal power in relation to these (Napier & Gershenfeld, 1987). Determining which people have power requires careful assessment because members who are not overtly controlling can sometimes have a great deal of power in determining values or directions for the group as a whole.

Those who have more power generally command more attention from others when they speak (Napier & Gershenfeld, 1987). They may be allowed to take more of the group's time without being interrupted. Other members respond more frequently to the contributions of those who are powerful and orient the focus of the group more often to issues important to powerful members. One value to developing an awareness of how a group shares power is to determine if all members have access to attention from the group as a whole. A group leader may wish to draw attention to the dynamics of power in a group to assist participants in taking responsibility for the way they are choosing to spend time and energy. However, if a leader is too assertive about the importance of his or her observations or comments, that person may assume a dominant position in group process that interferes with the opportunities for others to feel that their observations count.

Power struggles can become overt at certain times in a group's process. These struggles may express one or more members' rebellion against dynamics that seem unfair. A power struggle can also represent an attempt to control the direction of a group or to determine the values and beliefs that will guide decisions that influence directions (Gans, 1989). At the same time, struggles for power often are engaged in covertly. A member may direct comments only toward certain other members. If one subgroup dominates by directing comments and eye contact toward one another, it may be demonstrating a shared awareness of events, and other members may feel excluded (Agazarian, 1992). The kind of connections that form subgroups become intertwined with individuals' attempts to influence group process.

Relationships can be based on a pattern that prohibits the sharing of power, that sets and maintains unequal power between participants. These relationships by definition are those wherein the purposes of power are separated from the purposes of love. Love is oriented toward inclusion of the other; if power is used in ways that exclude or diminish the other, then it operates in a manner divorced from love. Power becomes divorced from love when the power of the other is perceived as a threat.

As members make contact with each other, they seek to establish norms that help them to feel secure and safe with the expression of power within relationships (Napier & Gershenfeld, 1987; Vander Kolk, 1985). The norms that people tend to establish are usually not consciously thought out but relate to past group structures that have assisted survival (Napier & Gershenfeld, 1987; Yalom, 1975). The establishment of norms for power in a group can lead participants to follow behavioral cues or verbal directions from the leader or to impose their values or preferred patterns of relating as norms that others should adopt.

Participants may generate conflicts in which other members take sides or may seek to establish exclusive relationships with the leader or others. Group members may seek to establish a role that allows them to gratify needs for attention because they are anxious about a situation wherein their functions have not been defined beforehand. Members may, for example, define for themselves such roles as caretaker, complainer, challenger, mediator, victim, commentator, comedian, and so on (Vander Kolk, 1985). If they can explore feelings of anxiety and uncertainty, members may then learn how they use roles as a way to diminish uncomfortable feelings such as uncertainty, insignificance, or powerlessness (Vander Kolk, 1985).

Changing Established Roles

Strategies that lessen opportunities for fulfillment through interaction may be attempts to maintain power while avoiding the discomfort of enhanced awareness. Enhanced awareness could bring a realization of imperfections in oneself and others that might increase perceptions of vulnerability and decrease illusions of security or superiority. Enhanced awareness can reawaken experiences of anxiety that have been sealed off by stereotypical structures for perception and relationship. Unstructured therapy groups can support participants who are willing to experience anxiety as they confront self-limiting patterns or previously denied perception.

As we have seen, members' experiences of anxiety can be viewed as opportunities for growth, learning, and actualization of possibilities. If members become more open toward the experience of anxiety, they are more likely to be able to do the work on the self-confrontation involved in changing patterns that have separated the goals of power from those of love (see McClure, 1990; Yalom, 1975).

Patterns that have separated the goals of power from the goals of love serve the purpose of preventing experiences of anxiety. When power is aligned with love, people allow themselves more vulnerability with each other. Vulnerability associated with caring for someone can lead to joy and fulfillment but also entails some uncertainty and anxiety as part of establishing and maintaining intimacy. Power can be expressed in a context of love by learning how to give and receive and by becoming more open to the uncertainty of an evolving relationship.

People separate power from love because they would like to believe that they can be strong by eliminating uncertainty and vulnerability, by controlling as much of life as possible, and by controlling their forms of self-expression and relationship. Conversely, people who perceive themselves as inadequate to gain this kind of control but who also want to eliminate uncertainty and anxiety may have fantasies of being controlled. Change is a journey into unknown aspects of self and relationship. Members can learn that there is a kind of power that comes from entering and sharing experiences of anxiety and intimacy with others, power that is not based on maintaining a projected self-image (Gemmill & Wynkoop, 1991).

Personal Boundaries and Interpersonal Justice

As group participants let go of attempts to defend a self-image, they release their defensive interpersonal strategies (Leszcz, 1992). Although members become open to being influenced by others, they may also become more definite about setting limits for their own participation and communication. Self-definition within a relational context can be described as a formation of boundaries (for example, see Agazarian, 1992; Perls, Hefferline & Goodman, 1951/1980).

The ways that individual boundaries are formed in overlapping patterns with others' boundaries result in bounded subsystems for interaction within the overall group system (Agazarian, 1992). Boundaries define where one's perception of "self" ends and of "other" begins and how different from self another is perceived to be. These feelings about inclusion and exclusion influence how close a person is willing to become to specific others and to the group as a whole. Boundaries, along with norms, help define how much time and attention is given to individuals. Nonverbal expression of boundaries can be exhibited by physical distancing, seating arrangements, and attentional cues (see Applbaum, Bodaken, Sereno & Anatol, 1974). Perception is the basis of boundary formation. Persons may perceive certain others as included (or partially included within the self at one time in a relationship) and may exclude those same people at another time. Thus, boundaries of selves and subsystems of selves shift throughout the life of a group.

As power aligns with love, boundaries can become firm yet permeable. Members will then neither seek contact compulsively nor compulsively refuse it. They will allow sufficient openness to acknowledge if and how they are influenced by the people with whom they interact. In a group that functions therapeutically, members tend to learn from and with each other how to move toward flexibility in interpersonal boundaries (Agazarian, 1992). They will feel able to choose vulnerability and will recognize that they can grow through allowing themselves to be affected by the experiences of others.

For example, a young graduate student named "Paul" attended an unstructured therapy group for college students. Many of Paul's difficulties had surfaced in sexual relationships in which he would back off quickly before emotional intimacy could develop. Paul was able to talk openly about his difficulties in relationships and felt free to explore the impact of childhood sexual abuse that involved his mother. However, Paul always carefully maintained a barrier to others' feedback by maintaining a "storytelling" presence in which he commented about himself as if he were an objective observer, thus limiting how much of his vulnerability he exposed.

Later in the life of the group, Paul began to feel confident of his ability to maintain boundaries. He could then relax from the stress and let others into more of his experience. He was then able to respond to feedback more immediately and emotionally. At this time, he also began to respond with emotion to others' revelations of problems and difficulties in their lives. Members began to express appreciation of Paul's perceptiveness and ability to demonstrate understanding of others. Paul's attempts to carry these newfound patterns of communication into his relationships outside of group proved to be difficult when romantic feelings were involved; yet he made slow but steady changes in his willingness to let the woman he was dating into his emotional life.

Shared risk taking occurs as interpersonal connections and trust develop. The atmosphere of love in a group can support and assist members' empowerment as they risk new ways of experiencing and interacting. These risks can further intimacy, facilitate centering within ongoing experience, and encourage a person's self-confidence in abilities to initiate changes in relational patterns. Thus, the processes of growth and healing in a group form interpersonal patterns that unite the purposes of love with the purposes of power.

Justice

The patterns of an individual's interpersonal relationships, as well as interpersonal patterns in groups and societies, can be considered as embodiments of forms of justice (Tillich, 1954). Forms of justice mediate the integration of love and power by determining how needs, demands, expectations, and wishes are expressed and met in interactions.

Changes in Modes of Justice

As members experience increased permeability of boundaries, they change the form of interpersonal justice that mediates their transactions and interactions. Members can move toward a more dynamic and creative form of justice if they (1) support an open atmosphere in which everyone can freely express individual modes of caring and personal power, (2) develop awareness of others through actively listening to that which is expressed and revealed, (3) develop sufficient caring for others to value their work on personal and interpersonal problems, and (4) view others' self-revelations as potentially important contributions to interpersonal learning. Thus, justice includes the dynamics of awareness, freedom, and responsibility, as well as connections between power and love in interpersonal interactions.

If members perceive that each participant has opportunities to contribute and receive, they will perceive that their group is just.

Justice supports new learning because members become willing to express more completely whom they experience themselves being with others and others being with them. Creative justice allows members to respond spontaneously and openly to novel challenges in group interactions. Group norms, the quality of communication between members, and structures of power and authority that members create reflect forms of justice. The form of justice of a group determines who gets heard if there are competing needs for attention. Justice is also involved in how members are heard and responded to and how judgmental or nonjudgmental group members are. Each person has needs for love and power that the group can potentially meet. Members' individual perceptions of their abilities to satisfy their needs for love and power form the basis for their sense of personal boundary in the group.

The Challenge of Creative Justice in Group Therapy

Forms of justice are created by people through an interactive process and provide the structures through which people make sense of their feelings, needs, and desires. Any ongoing interaction evolves a form of justice because participants constantly make choices about what to offer and what to withhold, how much to care about the experience of the other, what to request or demand from the other, how to assert self in relation to the other, and how to respond to assertions made by the other. Forms of justice exist along a continuum. At one extreme of the continuum are rigid forms of justice that attempt to predict and regulate exactly what will transpire during the course and outcome of interactions. At the other extreme are kinds of justice that attempt to be totally adaptable and flexible to constantly changing interpersonal dynamics.

In practice, interpersonal justice lies somewhere between these two hypothetical extremes. Even the most rigid forms of human justice need to allow for some accommodation to unpredictability because of interactions that break with predetermination and predictions. Nevertheless, even the most fluid forms of justice must maintain some structure that regulates behavior because a degree of continuity and predictability is necessary as a basis for human communication and relationship.

Creative justice arises as participants ask something of each other, hear each other, become aware of each other, and respond spontaneously without preconceptions about who the other is capable of becoming. The unstructured therapy group is an environment that can challenge members to develop forms of creative justice within ongoing encounters. The unstructured group is never without form but makes demands on all the participants involved to form structures within interactions that meet everyone's changing needs.

In the unstructured group mentioned earlier in this chapter, for example, Paul's willingness to reveal aspects of his emotional and sexual life formed a challenge for other members who had not broached such intimate material. His tendency to back away as others got closer led to some confusion about how they could best help Paul as well as learn from interacting with him. Members had to create a structure of justice that was new for their group. This allowed Paul flexibility in asking for help or retreating from exposure and also permitted members to express their reactions to Paul's maneuvers honestly. The basis of this new mode of justice was a willingness to give and receive at a new level of intimacy, along with respect for individuals' abilities to regulate their own exposure of thoughts and feelings to others.

The determination of forms of justice for relationships and communities is potentially a creative activity. Justice has a creative element that emerges as individuals perceive themselves as adequate authorities for determining the forms for their relationships. Justice lacks creativity if participants simply accept a predetermined form of justice from an authority figure or social institution. If people are willing to repeat unquestioningly the forms of interaction that have become habitual and comfortable, they are avoiding the anxiety of a creative encounter with life and other people.

Self-actualization requires a creative form of justice that is adequate to the demands of changes in situations and environmental realities and to shifts in personal and interpersonal needs and wishes. If members are able to question their stereotypical responses to others and their predetermined structures for interacting with their own experiences and with others, they can engage in a process that moves toward a mutual creation of an adequate form of justice.

If the challenge of constructing this kind of justice is avoided, then members may continue to feel isolated, and their potential to become a group may not be realized.

Members will not function fully as a group until they are able to recognize a mutual purpose that can align individual desires for love with those for power. This unifying purpose is the recognition that each person is responsible within each interaction to participate in a manner that is creatively just. Of course, this kind of responsibility is seldom addressed specifically and cognitively. To address it overtly may defeat the very process that moves toward this form of justice. If members become self-conscious about the mode of justice that they are forming, they are likely to develop an excessively cognitive approach to being together and may miss learning opportunities that arise spontaneously.

Creative Justice as Mutual Awareness of Significance

Members reflect a concern for justice when they interact with the unspoken recognition that participants each have the right to ask something from their group. In Tillich's (1954) view, each member has an equally valid claim for justice from the group. Participants move toward creative justice if they begin to understand each person's claim on the group from the perspective of that person. If a member makes a claim that is perceived to be unfair or illegitimate, the others should be willing to investigate and understand that person's point of view. They will assert their own reactions in terms that acknowledge the humanity of the other, even if the claims seem unfair. Thus, their response will not be designed to humiliate, stereotype, or reject. A creatively just group will help members to understand how others are seeing them and why certain demands seem unrealistic or unfair.

Unjust claims are often based on unfinished business (for example, see Johnson, 1963). A person may demand something based on unmet needs in other relationships or may think of and relate to others based on previous relationship patterns (Johnson, 1963; Wolf & Schwartz, 1962). A group can become a setting where members can confront each other's unjust claims, can learn about each others' unfinished business, and can give and receive honest feedback concerning how members are establishing relationships with others.

Of course, participants often feel uncomfortable making *just* claims on their group. Effective group therapy generally focuses on assisting members to recognize the value of their authentic claims for justice. Members are not assisted to feel self-righteous or to expect that life can be expected to be fair to everyone. Instead, they are taught to recognize and value their own need for justice, one that may have been disowned due to powerful and unjust relationship patterns with others.

Just as life is imperfect, no group can create an environment that meets all members' needs or even all of any one member's. A creative mode of justice encourages members to listen, to ask, and to respond. This form of justice empowers people to act on the world, to be receptive to the world, and to recognize the power of acceptance. Although creative justice does not guarantee that all needs will be met, it does optimize potentials for a group or community to meet as many needs as possible of as many members as possible.

Creative justice can beneficially be applied by a person to himself or herself, as well as to others. The person who is creatively just toward self will not impose "shoulds" that require maintenance of a facade. Rigid forms of justice result in self-imposed perfectionism for a person who strives always to be reasonable and always to account for every action. Members in a group encourage each other's self-actualization by creating an atmosphere wherein members can be heard and can receive open and honest responses, not wherein members strive to show how just they can be. Creative justice thrives on mutual caring, commitment, and honesty rather than on perfectionism, legalism, and self-consciousness.

Because it is always based on the dynamic flux of present experience and interpersonal encounters of power with power, creative justice cannot be determined *a priori* or from a formula of what is loving or just (Tillich, 1954). Creative justice can, however, be recognized by certain qualities that appear in members' interactions as they move toward it. These qualities are listening, giving, and acceptance (see Tillich, 1954).

Creative Justice as New Organization

Members who have split off and disowned feelings and experiences have been influenced by experiences and patterns in relationship that were perceived by the person as being unjust. The split is evidence of a mode of justice that is punitive and rejecting toward the self. To create order (justice) within a disorderly (unjust) life experience, people disown aspects of self that they associate with negative experiences. In the example given earlier, Paul was dealing with a past mode of justice within his family that allowed his boundaries to be disregarded. As he discovered his feelings about times when his mother had made sexual remarks and used seductive behaviors, Paul recognized that he had cut off his feelings to allow himself to survive and maintain a relationship with his mother. He began to acknowledge feelings of hurt and self-negation, and this acknowledgment preceded his willingness to allow himself to be more affected by others in the group.

An interpersonal dynamic is often involved in the process by which a person disowns experience. This dynamic is based on rejection (for example, humiliation, hostility, or neglect) as a consequence for unacceptable thoughts, feelings, or behaviors. Rejection is used to punish a participant for acknowledging certain feelings, thoughts, or experiences. Participants who feel rejected for certain feelings have usually learned self-rejection. In an effort to create an illusion of perfection, a person can become more rejecting toward self than others have been. People who lack the acceptance of others usually reject aspects of self and are accepting of others when they approve of self (Perls, Hefferline & Goodman, 1951/1980). However, people who are approving of others can sometimes be unduly harsh and rejecting toward aspects of themselves. They expect themselves to achieve a moral superiority that they do not demand from others. Thus, individuals can engage in distortions of self-actualization in which they increase the rigidity and harshness of values that they have adopted to feel significant or powerful. If members are genuinely accepting and provide feedback about a participant's self-rejecting behavior, they may assist that person to reevaluate rigid forms of justice used toward the self.

Reclaiming disowned aspects of self forms new relationships

within experiencing and can establish a new self-organization (Mahoney, 1990). A new self-organization is a form of justice within awareness of relationship; it allows what was previously rejected to be accepted. Because denial and projection are no longer useful, this form of justice encourages acceptance and contact. Likewise, if members can create forms of relationship that negate denial and projection, they can assist each other to internalize new interpersonal forms of justice as self-acceptance.

As group members become willing to experience pain that has been disowned, they often must reevaluate relationships with others in the present, as well as their interpretation of the meaning of past relationships. Creative justice, experientially understood, is a willingness to include within one's sense of order more of what has been rejected as disorderly. Therefore, a more comprehensive sense of wholeness and integrity arises for participants as they move toward creatively just interactions.

The position of the leader changes during this movement toward mutual acceptance and responsibility. Members have less of a need for an authority figure to ensure that they do not lose control or "get out of hand." Creative justice moves the leader from a position of special authority or power to an equal footing with other members. This justice can be recognized when members are willing to maintain different values from each other and the leader and are comfortable and appreciative of these differences. Creatively just norms allow members to learn how their needs and perceptions differ. They may then attempt to give what they perceive that each needs and what they feel can be legitimately given. One person may need attention, another may need to be comforted, another may require space, and yet another may desire confrontation. If members intend to balance and meet each others' needs, they must develop a sensitive and comprehensive awareness of one another.

The Gestalt of Love, Power, and Justice

The unified functioning of love, power, and justice as a gestalt within relationship is similar to the Chinese Taoist's thinking of the unified movement of Tao, the way of life. Tao was said to move without resistance or fragmentation, to nurture strength when strength is appropriate, and to be able to yield when flexibility is appropriate (see Fung, 1948; Lao Tzu, 600 B.C./1963). If love, power, and justice are integrated, people are able to respond assertively or receptively according to the dynamics of a specific encounter. They are open to the possibilities of becoming and are receptive to their own and others' experiencing within an ongoing encounter. If this relational gestalt is integrated, people experience a unification of thinking, feeling, intuition, and acting.

Inferred in the operation of the gestalt of love, power, and justice is the relatedness of each individual to a larger whole or totality. Individuals have different ways of thinking about this larger whole within which they define relationships. However, people tend to find the functional meaning of this whole through the context of ongoing encounters and relationships. Participants can move closer toward each other as they experience increased integration. At other times, a person may move away from others as a way to feel increased integration. Individuals may also experience a kind of connection with others that does not require immediate contact or expression of feelings. Connecting with a larger totality can include accepting and appreciating the space that mediates encounters.

Taoists say that Tao is essentially beyond definition (Fung, 1948; Lao Tzu, 600 B.C./1963). Similarly, the dynamic functioning of love, power, and justice evades full description. The purpose of delineating these elements of relationship is not to propose a complete definition of love, power, and justice. Rather, we seek to understand how denial or distortion of one element leads to imbalanced expression of the other elements. In the same way, we find that an overemphasis of one element leads to neglect of at least one of the others. Integrated relationship is therefore understood as balance within an ever-changing dynamic. In therapeutic groups, members are assisted to find their own balance within the context of changing interpersonal dynamics that occur in their group.

Because the integration of love, power, and justice is centered in the present, this gestalt cannot be used as a formula for predicting how a person should grow or how the developmental stages of relationships and groups should be formed. The functioning of this gestalt is not a way to dictate the course of events that will lead a person to a balanced life. Love, power, and justice interact continually through the process of self coming to be. The essential unity of the gestalt allows participants in relationships to construct their being together in ways that promote their own healing and growth according to their own experience.

Each individual should be viewed as a potential initiator of integrated love, power, and justice. Therefore, individuals can look at which of their decisions within relationship process have contributed to their own disintegration of love, power, and justice. Many of these may have reflected messages from significant others, but some decisions reflect self-initiated messages. Individuals have made a choice to distort relationship process by learning how to avoid awareness (usually while experiencing significant distress), how to ensure survival, how to maintain a sense of security, and how to avoid hurt. Members of unstructured therapy groups can grow by doing work with others to reclaim themselves and their experience and by learning through this work to make new decisions that move toward greater awareness.

The reunification of love, power, and justice for a group member often occurs through a spontaneous experience that allows her or him to express and trust perceptions, to be open to feelings, and to trust in the process of sharing with others. Members can also learn from the experience of not trusting the interpersonal process of a group. They may learn that relying on their own perceptions involves refraining from sharing with people not viewed as receptive or trustworthy. A member's awareness of personal power might be enhanced in these situations by making a statement about his or her perceptions. Essentially, however, members grow by learning that they have an awareness of timing that allows them to sense when to share with others and when to abstain. This awareness of timing is an awareness of relatedness.

Integration of love, power, and justice cannot be defined as any type of final goal because the dynamics of relationships always require reintegration as contexts and forms of interactions change. The integration of this gestalt should therefore be viewed in terms of process and dynamics, as a movement that deepens awareness and experience and helps direct choices and decisions. Movement toward an integrated dynamic of love, power, and justice can help group members develop their motivation to initiate changes in relationships and can encourage their confidence to give voice to new expressions of self. Finding and creating a balance within the gestalt of love, power, and justice can empower a person to regard self as an initiator of change. In unstructured therapy groups, members learn about their abilities to initiate change as they receive feedback from others about how they affect them.

As members develop relationships in their group, they learn that relationship has continuous and discontinuous aspects. Some aspects of relationship are developed continuously over time, as members share, disclose, react, and elaborate themes. Through prolonged interaction, members can develop increasingly rich and complex perceptions of who others are and are capable of being. The discontinuous aspect of relationship occurs through immediacy of encounter. People are who they were not and are not who they were. Each moment offers a fresh opportunity for discovery. Often people learn through spontaneous self-expression that they are not limited to being who they have been. Thus, the gestalt of love, power, and justice functions continuously and discontinuously.

Through continuous and discontinuous development of relationship, members learn to recognize each other's power and ability to care, develop trust in each other's use of power, and move toward integration of love with power. This movement requires awareness because members only gain this integration if they are willing to invest themselves in a shared process and if they are open to learning from one another. The gestalt of love, power, and justice functions, not as a machine functions, but as an organism functions. This gestalt is given form by human awareness and human spirit. Through dynamics created by feelings and perceptions in moment-to-moment encounters, the gestalt then functions to give form to human relationships.

Chapter Six

The Development of
Therapeutic Group Process

An integrated dynamic of love, power, and justice allows participants to express individuality and to experience communality and universality. Therefore, an optimally therapeutic group encourages the development of cohesion between individuals while also supporting them to be free to reveal (and even celebrate) their differences from others. In an effective therapeutic group, an ensemble of individuals moves from an initial awareness of separation to an increasing awareness of being connected. As connections form, members can learn about their distinctiveness as well as discovering their universality.

If a group functions countertherapeutically, individuals may feel required to surrender their individuality for the sake of establishing a group. As we saw in Chapter Two, members may feel pressure to conform to "groupthink"; they may perceive that others find ways to penalize those who offer discrepant views and that others expect members to avoid disagreements (Janis, 1982). Another countertherapeutic development occurs if members emphasize individualism, if they behave like a collection of disconnected and separated entities who happen to be in the same location.

Group Development and Individual Development

The attempt by members and leaders in therapeutic groups to create a "we" through an interpersonal process that discourages individual choice and freedom is related to interpersonal dynamics that create authoritarian social and political groups (Wolf & Schwartz, 1962). An unstructured therapy group can offer members opportunities to examine the motives, beliefs, and expectations they bring to encounters when they meet others who may become "we." Members can learn through experience about their tendencies to surrender their individuality in a group, to become an observer or follower, or to become an engaged and individuated participant. Members can encounter basic human emotions and choices that are involved in the creation and use of collective realities.

Tillich (1954) has observed that people often relate to the groups they create as if these groups were organisms or beings. Tillich also points out that members of a group are free to come and go, whereas constituent parts of an organism are not. This freedom of movement represents a significant difference between organisms and groups. If people reject their own freedom of movement because they feel responsible to a group that is an entity, they deny the value of their own individualism. A more useful motive for remaining within a group is the recognition by an individual that caring and responsibility mutually involve him or her and others.

An individual involved in a dyad—a close relationship with another person—makes choices concerning how a "we" will be formed. Some dyads require one or both partners to sacrifice their individuality, whereas other dyads accept and support individuality. Other people have found that the closeness of a relationship has been used as the basis for hurting or manipulating them and may have learned to minimize those encounters. Learning about the meaning of joining with others begins at birth in the family of origin and is influenced by various important groups throughout the life of individuals.

Groups and individuals mutually define each other and therefore exist as a dynamic transaction. Therefore, individuals can be considered as creative agents who form boundaries but who are never completely self-contained or fully autonomous in their self-definitions. People are defined within the context of relationships. Thus, though individuals define themselves, they are never able to do so completely. Effectively therapeutic group work can use this relationship of self and group to assist members in forming new meanings in the process of being a self with others.

Foulkes (1957) has written that groups exist as matrices for interpersonal communication. This matrix is seen as the necessary basis for communication between individuals, a view implying that a person cannot truly become who he or she is capable of being without the existence of groups. If groups are matrices for communication, individuals can become different people in different groups, depending on how each group influences modes of communication, interaction, and experiencing. Each group has a different atmosphere based on the unique dynamic gestalt of interpersonal process. The meanings of individual interactions occur within this context. Interaction between participants in a group simultaneously influences and is affected by the group matrix.

Although group dynamics affect who the person becomes within a relational process, individuals affect how this process is created, maintained, and acknowledged. Therefore, groups can be understood as transactions through which part-whole relationships arise along with ongoing individual ones. The group's relational gestalt can be understood as a collective awareness of expressions of love, power, and justice between individuals. These three ontological elements are alive *within* each individual, *as* each individual, and exist as forces that receive form in relations *between* individuals. Each interpersonal interaction contributes to the ongoing group integration (or disintegration) of love, power, and justice. As members interact, they help create and maintain the group gestalt. This gestalt can assist them to work constructively with perceptions of self and relationships if members create a context wherein they connect meaningfully with others and can communicate authentically and openly.

Paradoxically, participation in a collective reality can enrich the unique world of the individual's perception and experience. A person becomes more aware of his or her distinctive perceptions of the world through the process of receiving from others and sharing perceptions with them. A growth-enhancing interpersonal process enhances an individual's strength of self through an opening of self to others, reception of others within self, and sharing one's self with others. This somewhat paradoxical transaction raises the question of who is responsible for the growth of the individual. Is the individual alone answerable for her or his growth, or are others and groups of others also responsible? If others and groups of others must also play a part, how can we assert meaning to individual responsibility? The answer to these questions does not lie in either-or, black-and-white thinking. Individuals and groups are simultaneously responsible for growth, and the reality of each incorporates the other.

Individual and Collective Transactions

Awareness and acknowledgment of individual and collective responsibility for growth are basic for the construction of an effective therapeutic group process. One way to imagine this responsibility is to view growth as a movement that evolves through specific actions and events. If we can find specific ways in which individuals can contribute, we can then understand how growth as a principle of group development operates. Group members can be assisted to understand specific aspects of their interactions with others and may also be helped to appreciate more general principles of interpersonal functioning. Members may move from specific encounters to general and abstract awareness and back to the specific again. However, if generalities become an early and ongoing focus for discussions, members may escape into intellectualizing to avoid awareness of uncomfortable feelings or to put off anxiety about getting to know each other. Generalities that are derived from awareness of each other and from specific aspects of encounter can be used as a context to initiate new encounters and to enrich awareness of ongoing encounters.

A group cannot force an individual to choose actions that foster healing and growth, although it can provide a context that encourages caring and authentic modes of participation. Groups that assist members to escape from the anxiety of choice and awareness are likely to use unconscious or semiconscious collective decision-making processes that place an unnecessarily great degree of authority in the leader or that lead to members' perceptions of their group as an entity. Members then seek to conform to the demands of the leader or the larger entity (or both) and may lose their sense of individuality in the group. In a group that encourages individuation, members recognize themselves as collectively responsible for the group's process and as individually responsible for forming their own contributions and directions within that process.

The self that is actualized through participation in a group interaction is at once a uniquely formed individual gestalt and one formed collectively through interpersonal dynamics. Self-actualization therefore does not occur only through an individual's perceptions and conscious choices. Self-actualization is influenced by the quality of relationships that people form through transactions. Transactions can be considered as interactions that affect participants across boundaries, not merely at boundaries. If an interaction is an effect of one entity upon another, a self-actualizing transaction can be understood as an effect between entities in which they function synergistically. Through these transactions, each participant allows self to change by accepting the other into self.

Much of the impact of transactions appears to occur outside individuals' conscious awareness. Group therapy can help members to recognize how these transactions alter a person's sense of self. Members can learn how specific encounters can influence them and how mutuality between members can alter the group gestalt. Individuals may perceive themselves being affected by transactions, and at times they may experience that their group as a whole has been affected.

The Nature of Group Process

Theorists such as Bonney (1974), Corey and Corey (1987), Page (1983a, 1984), Rogers (1970), Vander Kolk (1985), and Yalom (1975) have used a model of stages to describe the sequential progression of therapy group members' interrelatedness. Though these theorists' definitions vary, all serve as a basis to discuss perceptions that change occurs predictably within group process, that temporal as well as interpersonal effects exist, and that alterations take place in meaningful patterns between individuals who relate over time.

Each stage develops from what went before and in some cases is described in relationship to what is expected to come after. Stages consistently represent a sequential ordering of interactions related to changes in gestalts of meaning for individuals and the group as a whole. The stages represent a syntax that gives overall meaning to the specific and individual interactions of participants.

Stages or Phases in Group Process?

One potential limitation of defining sequential group stages is that a leader can impose his or her idea of stages on the process. A leader who wants to "progress" to the next group stage may begin to steer the group in that direction. The group members might sense, however, that they would benefit from working at their present level of exploration. Thus, a leader who insists on moving on can create unnecessary resistance and impede the therapeutic movement of the group. If a group leader recognizes that the conceptualization of stages simply provides a convenient framework for the theoretical analysis of process, she or he will allow each group to find unique paths that fit individual members' movements toward integration of love, power, and justice within relationships.

Although unstructured group therapy is based on the assumption that structure does not need to be imposed, this theory acknowledges inherent form in the development of any group. The theory also recognizes that structures are created as leaders and members respond to their perceptions of their own and others' needs and wants. Thus, groups can be considered in terms of imposed, inherent, and created structures. Unstructured group therapy attempts to minimize imposed structures. Phases in unstructured therapy groups reflect members coming to terms with a lack of imposed structure, their growing awareness of inherent structure, and their growing assumption of responsibility for creation of structure.

Love, power, and justice are inherent forces that interact to form structures within each group phase. Awareness, freedom, and responsibility are factors that also influence the development of modes of communication and interaction. As we have seen, these forces have a degree of predictability in their impact on the evolution of human groups because there is a universal aspect to how people interact. At the same time, there is a degree of unpredictability to the interaction of these forces because each group is unique and formed through the specific interactions of the distinct individuals who compose the group. We can talk in a general way about the interaction of several factors. Even these general trends sometimes develop in an unusual sequential order. In fact, if we look at groups' phases rather than stages, we can infer that sequential ordering is relative rather than absolute, and reversible rather than irreversible.

Specific interactions are the product of the unique individuals who engage in them, and their results could not be meaningfully predicted without a deep personal understanding of those individuals. Even with a personal understanding of participants, prediction would be difficult, except in a general manner. Each person represents a unique and constantly changing gestalt constructed from a present perspective and experience, personal history, physiology, goals, desires, and so on. Not only do complex factors influence interactions, some of these factors may change unpredictably within the present. The course and outcome for a group as a whole or for an individual in a group can thus never be considered as predetermined at the beginning of the group. Our purpose in discussing group phases should be considered less important for comprehensively predicting group behavior and more important for understanding ongoing behavior, appreciating how the forces in a group can lead to its constructive evolution, and for setting goals within a present moment of interaction.

The Evolution of Group Process

All groups deal with achieving the degree of cohesion that the members perceive as necessary to gain what they need or want from their participation. For cohesion to develop, members must create structures in the form of norms and themes that affect communication between participants. Certain norms (for example, nonviolence) and themes (for example, interpersonal healing and growth) are inherent in the situation and influence process from the initiation of a therapy group. Additionally, all groups deal with the temporal structure that forms during the beginning, middle, and ending of relationships. These three basic stages tend to evoke basic human feelings associated with beginning an association with others, working together with others, and ending those ties.

A stage-oriented model of group therapy presupposes that there is an evolutionary aspect to the development of a group. Cohen and Smith (1976) view "evolution in the group" as an "unfolding" and a "development" that occurs in a process of "gradual, orderly change from one stage to the next." Evolution implies the existence of "progressive states" that are expected to lead to "improvement in group and individual effectiveness" (pp. 160–161). The idea of evolution, according to Cohen and Smith, has a Darwinian connotation that implies that effective behaviors are born and survive, whereas ineffective behaviors are extinguished. Members may learn through experience that trust, self-disclosure, and cooperation help them to use the group effectively, whereas mistrust, denial, and competition limit their ability to receive what they need and want from others.

However, the metaphor of evolution may be extended too far if we forget that individuals and groups can benefit from relaxation and free play, from temporarily abandoning concerns with survival and progress. As members move toward acceptance and freedom, they become less defensive, less concerned with how to survive in their group, and less vigilant about which behaviors should be extinguished. Therefore, if we discuss the evolution of group process, we need to examine the playful development of themes and relationships, as well as the serious work on problems that members do. Phases can shift according to the current mood. Members can constructively move from serious work to a playful or relaxed phase to another period of work.

A theme may develop and prevail throughout the life of a group or may appear at a particular phase. A theme may be general (for example, the importance of trust in relationships) or specific (for example, what Mary and Mark can learn from each other). Themes serve as focal points for members' awareness and conversation. Maintaining a focus on an individual's, a dyad's, or a group's theme promotes the theme's evolution. Examples of group themes that tend to develop are the group's purpose, reactions to leadership and authority, questions about personal responsibility, issues of control and security, intimacy issues, and feelings about termination. These themes are not always addressed directly; members' communications about them can be metaphorical, can be presented in the form of humor, or can be expressed through actions and tones rather than words (McClure, 1987; Roller, 1989; Rossel, 1981).

Themes change as members develop more trust and openness in each other and in the process of the group as a whole. For example, members often need to develop much interpersonal trust before they are willing to expose and explore their intimacy issues. Cohen and Smith (1976), as well as Rogers (1970) and Yalom (1975), have examined how groups generally evolve from relatively low levels to deeper levels of interpersonal trust and understanding. These authors also agree that a shift of power and responsibility moves from the leader to members as the group evolves, a finding that is consistent with the observations of psychoanalytic group therapists such as Foulkes (1975) and Wolf and Schwartz (1962).

As members' perceptions of personal power and responsibility change, the themes that they discuss usually alter. Members become more willing to confront and discuss each other's needs for control and power in interpersonal relationships. As members become more comfortable in asserting themselves, they often discuss interpersonal issues related to themes of justice. Members assert themselves in ways that reveal their perceived closeness to others. Group phases evolve through movements between and within central themes (for example, between separation and relatedness or within increasing recognition of the reality of termination).

Group phases thus develop in a manner that might be imagined as a spiral rather than as a line. Members may leave a theme, become involved in a new meaning-orientation, and then return to the first theme. When members return to a theme, they often address it with different attitudes or feelings than they previously had. For example, group members may shift from an apparently consistent atmosphere of mutuality to repeat an earlier phase of mistrust or conflict. However, their new discussion about mistrust may demonstrate enhanced knowledge of each other's issues. Group phases can also be altered unpredictably by specific events. An unexpected conflict between two members who had previously agreed can alter the themes and dynamics about which members are concerned. If a new member enters a group or a participant decides to leave, the process will be influenced (Yalom, 1975). In spite of various unpredictable occurrences, certain trends occur that represent the beginning, progression, and termination of a collective human encounter. Group members tend to deal with issues of trust at the beginning of a group, themes related to disclosure and intimacy toward the middle phase, and feelings about ending relationships toward the termination phase of a group (for example, see Bonney, 1974; Vander Kolk, 1985). Of course, the issues involved are not truly discrete. For example, members are aware of the reality of termination from the onset of a group; they are likely to be dealing with this reality, perhaps unconsciously, from the very beginning. Similarly, issues of trust may dominate early on, but it is likely to remain a concern, to some extent, throughout a group.

Defining Group Phases

Using the Hill Interaction Matrix (HIM-G) as a measure of types and levels of interaction, we have analyzed the phases of a sixteen-hour-long marathon group conducted with illicit drug users (Page, Davis, Berkow & O'Leary, 1989). The results of this analysis showed that various levels and types of interaction occurred in any given phase of the group. Whereas many types and qualities of interaction occurred during any phase, the types and qualities of interaction considered most therapeutic by the HIM-G occurred most frequently during the middle eight hours of the group, rather than during the initial or termination phases. This information supports the findings of previous research conducted with unstructured marathon groups composed of illicit drug users (Page, 1982; Page & Bridges, 1983; Page & Wills, 1983).

These collective results indicate that although unstructured groups that were studied did not have distinct phases, they did exhibit an overall tendency to work toward the establishment of trust, then intimacy, and then toward mutual disengagement. These studies confirmed our experiential learning from participation in personal growth groups and from facilitation of various groups with physically disabled individuals, psychiatric clients of various ages and differing levels of impairment, secondary school students, and college students in Ireland (Page & O'Leary, 1992) and the United States.

We have thus defined five group phases that serve as a framework to explore the dynamics that form members' movements toward and through trust, intimacy, and disengagement. We have drawn no firm lines that separate portions of group members' ongoing interpersonal experiences; phases are merely convenient constructs useful for discussing the development of a rational process. Practitioners of therapy should be able to orient themselves toward group phases as a way to enhance their awareness of certain key themes and messages. This awareness should not distract a practitioner from any idiosyncratic theme that emerges in the context of a specific group, however.

An orientation toward the recognition of phases in a group's life could, of course, lead practitioners to react stereotypically. Therapists must be watchful not to become habituated to reacting to their own expectations concerning group process. They should become attuned to the continuing (and sometimes idiosyncratic) themes of each unique group and participant. Because phases do not inevitably continue in invariable sequences and are not irreversible, therapists and other members enhance the available meaning in interpersonal process by attending to specific present dynamics.

The five phases that we will describe are based on frequently occurring themes in groups we have led, in which we have participated, or which we have observed. Although these phases are relatively consistent with the developmental themes that stage-oriented theorists have generally observed (for example, Bonney, 1974; Yalom, 1975), we will review how key interpersonal aspects of self-actualization influence this development. For example, we note the interaction between individual awareness of freedom, mutual willingness to assume responsibility, and development of relationship between participants. We also assess how members can generate a shared movement toward integration of love and power through creative justice.

Phases of Unstructured Therapy Groups

The following phases are relevant either to single-session marathon groups or to ongoing unstructured therapy and personal growth

groups that last more than ten sessions: (1) preliminary socialization, (2) ambivalence toward authority, (3) exploration and self-
revelation, (4) mutuality, and (5) ending. These phases can be
viewed as constructs around which themes and potential knowledge
gained from the group can be organized. As previously noted,
themes may build on each other sequentially or may appear and
reappear throughout the life of a group.

Preliminary Socialization

As participants first enter a group, they understandably tend to feel
anxious about what is about to happen. They are often unsure of
the degree to which they can have confidence in the leader and the
other members. Although some may be ready to have trust in others,
most members must build toward it. Many members find that they
need to interact with others before they have a basis for trusting
them. Other participants must experience feelings of trust before
they are willing to interact in ways that are personally meaningful
and revealing. These members may feel anxious because they hope
to establish meaningful relationships with others but are uncertain
about how safe it will be to do so. Such people may believe that if
they ask for something from the group, they will become vulnerable
and might be hurt or manipulated by others.

  The anxieties that members initially experience are frequently based on past experiences with the process of gaining membership in a group of people. On the basis of previous experiences
in social groups, members may believe that they need to find out
with whom they are interacting and what consequences will follow
from membership before they commit themselves to an interactive
process. Some members may apparently express themselves openly
and freely. However, they may not trust others fully and may be
interacting in a pattern that is (for them) stereotypical.

  By contrast, other individuals may disclose their feelings and
needs prematurely. Such members may trust naively; they may initially idealize their group and believe that it is a place where people
will not be hurt. Some participants, who are less initially trusting,
may rebuff or hurt a member whom they consider to be naive. These
themes can be disguised by a process through which members feel

each other out by interacting in stereotypical ways. Later in the life of a group, the importance of interpersonal trust is often addressed more directly and openly than in the initial group phase.

Group participants may try to find common ground with others by talking about themselves as they would at a cocktail party (Rogers, 1970). They may discuss sporting events, the political situation in the world, or may seek out information about others' occupations and domestic situations. Discussing safe topics affords participants some protection while they investigate whether others in the group are approachable or are worth approaching. As members learn more about each other, they can process the ways in which they are different and similar. As their awareness of each other's lives increases, they learn which experiences are shared and which may not be.

The leader of a group may experience a sense of effort in remaining attentive to these apparently meaningless and superficial discussions. Yet hidden within these apparently superficial exchanges are clues about who each person is and who they may become. If the group leader disregards early exchanges as meaningless chatter, he or she will lose the opportunity to begin forming an understanding of these individuals.

Rossel (1981) observes that a useful therapeutic approach is to view all communication in a group as meaningful and significant. The themes upon which individuals choose to focus for a discussion of current events may later emerge in a different form as an immediate personal concern. For example, a member who discusses protest marches early in the life of a group may later express rebellion toward group norms or may question the authority of the leader or other members. If participants project a great deal of emotion or animation about an apparently innocuous theme or humorous exchange, they are probably communicating around a metaphorical message or theme (Rossel, 1981). Unstructured groups may provoke anxiety about ambiguity, and members may use fantasy to explore possible goals in an ambiguous situation. Humor may represent an attempt to gain acceptance or partnership or may be used indirectly to reveal aspects of who members are if they perceive threats of rejection.

Many people have learned from past teaching and experience

that "otherness" is a dangerous aspect of interpersonal encounter. Otherness can be associated with possible threats from others who are perceived as harboring negative intentions toward oneself or whose goals and desires are thought to be incompatible with one's own goals. It is impossible for group members to move toward creative forms of justice if they do not come to terms with their perceptions of otherness. Coming to terms with otherness requires members to acknowledge aspects of being different as these influence communication and relationship (for example, differences in perceptions, attitudes, past experiences, desires, opinions, goals, economic status, appearance, culture, and so forth).

In the initial phase of a group, members are often reluctant to learn about those aspects of the other that are truly different and unique. Many members attempt to establish ways in which they are the same as others or can share with them before they feel sufficient safety to explore otherness. Members have generally learned that awareness of differences can lead to conflict. Some may believe that conflict is a way to feel out one's own strength. The manner in which members develop the theme of contact with otherness helps determine whether an atmosphere of interpersonal trust is established. If members can accept, perhaps even enjoy, the otherness that they experience, an atmosphere of trust is likely to develop. If they cannot accept aspects of others' lives and experiences that are different from their own, interpersonal trust will be blocked or inhibited.

The first phase is therefore exploratory in nature. Members may first seek to discover where and how they are similar to one another before they can feel safe to explore the extent of their mutual estrangement. It is unlikely that participants will begin to experience their estrangement until they feel and acknowledge that they want or need something from one another. People establish how much closeness seems to be possible and desirable and how much distance may be necessary. Some members take risks that help them to establish whether one can give something worthwhile to another, such as honest feedback or open revelations of self.

Members who initiate personal contact and self-disclosure early in the life of the group may find themselves accepted and cared about. They may initiate a change in the group atmosphere that leads to more disclosure and to work on personal issues. However, if their timing is off, such members may be rebuffed or disregarded. This experience can be hurtful to their self-esteem and self-image and can damage their sense of confidence in relating to others. They may be confirming their own negative expectations that others will be untrustworthy and unaccepting. Although such interactions may cause pain, they can also lead to learning about being with others and can be viewed as part of the process by which interpersonal distance is established. A member who has taken a risk with others and been rebuffed may learn about her or his own courage and willingness to follow through on intentions. Members can benefit from learning that they can survive rejection from others without catastrophic consequences.

Members typically look toward their group leader to set the tone of the group (Napier & Gershenfeld, 1987; Yalom, 1975). As we have already seen, body language and other nonverbal aspects of communication play an important role in whether members decide that they can trust in the group's members and leader (Applbaum, Bodaken, Sereno & Anatol, 1974). Theorists who have written about unstructured group encounters, including Rogers (1970) and Yalom (1985), have indicated that verbal and nonverbal behaviors of the leader influence the other members' perceptions of the safety and trustworthiness of the therapeutic group environment.

The atmosphere early in the life of a group can be constricted simply because members are uncomfortable and uncertain in the group therapy setting. These members may experience stress if they perceive themselves as being expected to take the risks that promote contact with others. Some participants may want to make a point of expressing their independence from group norms or indifference to demands for sharing. As a group evolves toward creative justice, such members may become more comfortable in their interactions. If they have successfully established comfortable boundaries, they may subsequently relax and decrease defensiveness. The healing group does not force members to make certain choices through peer pressure or the imposition of norms by the leader; rather, it provides the opportunity for people to experience freedom to choose how to interact with one another.

In unstructured group therapy, members may test their freedom by expressing their resistance to the goals that they believe that the leader seems to have. They may express negative feelings about their leader if that person has presented himself or herself authoritatively or in an aloof manner. Members may show mistrust toward other members or the group as a whole. If participants feel free to resist possible impositions from the leader or to express doubts or anxieties about group process, their openness can usefully lay a foundation for later perceptions of mutual responsibility. If members do not feel able to express doubts or resistance, they may never perceive themselves as being responsible for determining group norms and as being free to reveal negative feelings and attitudes.

Ambivalence Toward Authority

This phase of the group generally evolves from a previous one in which members tend covertly or unconsciously to form impressions of the leader's persona and character. Members develop a sense of the degree to which they can trust both their leader and by extension the group that the leader has organized. On the one hand, members are likely to feel frustrated if their leader is too distant, aloof, or analytical about group events (Leszcz, 1992). A leader who is experienced as consistently maintaining an emotionally distant position is also likely to seem uncaring, self-protective, or unapproachable. On the other hand, a leader who establishes a powerful presence that demands attention from members may be perceived as imposing, intimidating, or superior. Such leaders tend to elicit cult-like responses from group members in therapy settings (McClure, 1990; Yalom, 1975).

Participants may be concerned if they perceive the group's leader as being too powerful because they are likely to be aware that this power could be used to negate, hurt, or manipulate members. Members may perceive a leader as powerful because of his or her personal characteristics or because there are situational factors that give the leader real power outside the group setting. The leader may be in a hospital setting wherein he or she can make recommendations that alter the course of treatment or the rewarding of privileges. The leader in a mental health clinic may be required to report to judges if members are receiving treatment as the result of legal proceedings or have been mandated to receive treatment by the court. In prison or in other treatment settings, there may be concern that the leader cannot be trusted to maintain confidentiality.

Members may resent a leader for being powerful, but they can also refuse to work on problems if they perceive the leader as powerless or ineffective. Gemmill and Wynkoop (1991) refer to a group's "aura" as positive emotions and potentials that tend to be collectively disowned and projected onto the leader or one member. Members may be influenced by the images and wishes that they project onto the leader because of their past experiences with figures of authority. Psychoanalytic theorists such as Wolf and Schwartz (1962) have emphasized this transference aspect. Transference theory indicates that members are likely to establish again their past patterns of relating to important authority figures in ongoing relationships (Greenson, 1967; Wolf & Schwartz, 1962). Transference is likely to show itself through ambivalence feelings of attraction and anxiety that are expressed toward authority.

Individuals may seek to view another as an omnipotent rescuer. They may long for this impossibility and might also resent or hate the other for being unwilling to provide rescue from life's anxieties (Yalom, 1980). Following this logic, a member could experience love and hate for a leader who is longed for as a rescuer and hated as a withholder of rescue. In particular, members who were affected by abusive relationships with significant others in childhood may continue to hold deep feelings of mistrust and anxiety toward authority, coupled with a desire to receive love from a powerful other. In psychoanalytic terms, these members are likely to be perceived as "difficult patients" who tend to exhibit "hostile transference" (Ganzarain, 1992, p. 219). A phase in which members express anger and ambivalence toward the leader can set the stage for learning whether the group can function as an environment that contains feelings of anger and creates the freedom that allows constructive work on these feelings. This freedom allows members to begin to reveal problems and concerns on which they want to work. As they recognize that their leader will not be able to rescue them or make them feel significant, members may reveal dilemmas they have with the goal of receiving support and feedback from other members. Of course, they may need to contend with the realization that support and comments from others will not serve as a rescue either.

Some groups may not involve a phase in which angry feelings are expressed. Although such groups may function effectively, they may lack opportunities for work on anger. Effective group work can be conducted without giving overt attention to these kinds of issues, and many individuals may not see work on anger as a focus for their growth. However, anger is a socially dangerous emotion, and members are not likely to propose that their group atmosphere shift so that individuals have opportunities to work on anger. Participants may not recognize the usefulness of working to integrate angry feelings until they have been expressed in their group.

If members feel free to express anger or lack of cooperation, their awareness of personal responsibility is likely to be enhanced. Members may see themselves as helpless or as victims if their expressions of anger do not lead to recognition of responsibility. A group setting can be an exceptionally useful environment for participants to deal with and present situations in which they have felt abused or frustrated. Other members can help a participant to look at options, to recognize strengths, and to process the experience and meaning of feelings.

The phase in which members deal with ambivalent or angry feelings toward a leader or others is thus likely to lay the groundwork for constructive interactions between members. Participants may learn about their own power to assist one another as they recognize the futility of excessive dependence and magical thinking about how the leader can protect them from having to face life's problems. As group process develops, the group's leader is likely to move increasingly toward an equal position in terms of interpersonal power and responsibility for determining directions. This movement is relative because members will still recognize their leader as such throughout the life of a group.

Although members may rebel against their leader or may refuse to cooperate with her or his suggestions, they may also expect this person to provide directions or to clarify issues. Thus, members are often ambivalent about the position in which they want their leader to function.

Thus, if a group's leader is attacked by one member, another member may defend the leader or may launch a counterattack against the first member. A member who confronts the leader may back down if he or she perceives the leader as vulnerable. Members may not only question the leader but may begin to ask this person for help on different issues at this point. A member's ambivalence may then continue to be expressed in the form of difficulty accepting the help that has been requested, responses that demonstrate a lack of listening, or dissatisfaction that the problem is not adequately "solved" by the leader and the group.

Because their leader is viewed as the organizer of their group, members who criticize or express frustration with their group are indirectly expressing frustration with the leader. Additionally, members may express frustration and resentment toward another member even though some or all of this anger is related to leadership in their group (Gans, 1989). For example, if a member is attacked for talking too much, the others may also resent their leader for failing to restrain this person's actions or failing to provide direction and structure. As their group is increasingly experienced as safe, these members may become willing to express feelings directly toward their leader. Their leader can then work with them to understand how members can become responsible for generating their own directions and structures.

Members may also express anger toward the therapist as a kind of test. This test may help members to discover whether there are unspoken limits that regulate authentic expressions of self. Members typically regulate how they demonstrate anger without the imposition of external controls if they perceive their environment and their group leader as being trustworthy. Although members may experience anger toward the leader, they also tend unconsciously to wish for this person to withstand their anger and to help them move toward a balanced and mutually responsible dynamic. Members usually want opportunities to move toward creative justice and will spontaneously create these if given the chance.

Members of groups in specific settings may have similar backgrounds that create common assumptions about authority figures. Illicit drug abusers, for instance, often exhibit overt or covert discomfort or hostility when they approach authority figures in a therapy situation. Unstructured therapy with illicit drug users often brings anger to the surface, anger that often seems disproportionate to the present situation (Page, 1979). Members may attack the personality or capability of their group leader. They may pointedly discuss the unfairness of authorities or society, and they may focus on incidents in which they received unfair treatment from authority figures who are not present. If a leader clearly makes an effort to listen and to understand, the participants may begin to reevaluate how they perceive authority in this particular situation. The expression of anger is often an opportunity to begin to address the dynamics of group relationships within the therapeutic setting. Anger within the therapy setting can often be interpreted as the expression of a legitimate claim for justice from the group.

Like certain other forms of communication (for example, being too demanding or feigning helplessness), anger can be used as a manipulative strategy to gain attention, significance, or dominance. Games that manipulate others unjustly to gain attention or dominance are likely to be confronted by other group members. Such confrontations can play an important part in a group's movement toward creative justice.

The group benefits if the leader can intuit the function that a particular expression of anger serves for a group. If a leader prematurely confronts a member's apparent game playing, this action will have implications for the role that other members will come to expect the leader to play. The leader may be seen as expressing his or her perception that other members need to be taken care of or protected; a leader who protects members will influence the formation of group norms concerning responsibility. Creative justice can also be impaired if a group leader is perceived as someone who takes sides or who is highly evaluative.

Members may allow or encourage one member to express anger because they can allow this person to be their spokesperson and thus can avoid responsibility. Members can avoid responsibility by directing anger toward a safe target (for example, "the system," by using another member as a scape goat, or by encouraging one person to act out the angry feelings shared by others). They can also resort to labeling or blaming angry persons (Gans, 1989; Unger, 1990). If anger is dealt with covertly and indirectly by one or more members, this manipulative behavior can lead to passive-aggressive interactions. Passive-aggressive strategies allow members to withhold feelings and can have a detrimental impact on the group norms concerning honesty and openness. Of course, members would not be withholding feelings if they experienced their group as safe and accepting. Therefore, during the phase of ambivalence toward the leader, members are working to establish norms that permit safe expression of feeling. As members establish interpersonal freedom, passive-aggressive strategies become increasingly unnecessary and are perceived as counterproductive by members.

Members who are addicted to rage may feel very comfortable expressing anger although they have blocked awareness of what it is about (unfinished business). A therapy group can provide such persons with a setting where they learn that it can be safe to explore submerged feelings of hurt and vulnerability that are intertwined with compulsive expressions of anger. Once anger or frustration has been expressed, members can deal with the issue of how they can most effectively and constructively use these feelings.

Many people in our culture have problems learning to use anger constructively (Rubin, 1969; Travis, 1982). For example, people may ignore or stifle angry feelings, may displace these onto inappropriate targets, or may demonstrate anger in hostile ways instead of ones that invite communication. Participants may have learned in their families or peer groups to avoid anger or other strong feelings or to use anger to control others. Moreover, men and women often learn different rules for dealing with certain emotions. Men may feel that anger is acceptable but sadness or vulnerability is not. Women may have learned that expressions of vulnerability are appropriate but anger is not. As members begin to express anger or other strong feelings, they can experience their group as a place where they do not have to limit themselves to stereotypical reactions and interactions.

People can express anger in a blaming manner that stifles dialogue and perpetuates struggles for control. Individuals who express this kind of controlling and blaming anger are usually using it in the service of power detached from love. If power and love are integrated, people express angry feelings in a manner that leads to meaningful contact and that increases interpersonal openness. Often, if their anger is not expressed with the intention of blaming others, individuals recognize other feelings associated with anger. Feelings of having been hurt by others or having been let down by them are often associated with an initial reaction of anger. If expressions of anger lead to increased openness in expressing feelings, then a movement toward integrated relationship can occur (Travis, 1982). Members may then learn new patterns of relationship in which expressions of anger can be used to generate beneficial change and enhanced intimacy.

If members express anger, frustration, or mistrust about their group's leader or their group's process, they may be reacting to aspects of learning of which they are not consciously aware. Members may feel uncomfortable about demands being made on them that are not overt or that are experienced emotionally more than cognitively. For example, a member may feel that a demand is being made to cooperate, to belong, to contribute, to reveal, to assert, or to formulate directions. These demands may seem unfair or uncomfortable, although the member may not be fully conscious about the meaning of the discomfort. As members discuss negative feelings, they often become more consciously aware of choices they are making and the meaning of various feelings that they are experiencing. They may learn that negative feelings represent opportunities to learn about justice (by learning about perceived injustice), power (as members make themselves known to others), and love (as members give and receive acceptance and caring about the pain of others). Therefore, dealing with ambivalent reactions to authority and to group process is an important foundation for moving toward integrated interpersonal dynamics in a group situation.

Members' basic ambivalence is based on a wish to be included in the group coupled with anxiety about being dominated or smothered by it. This anxiety may be expressed by demonstrations that one can exclude oneself from the group, such as withdrawal from others or attempts to control others. In the phase of ambivalence, members are often unsure of their motives. They may express anger although they also feel a desire to join or may attempt to join in ways that also demonstrate a desire for control.

The phase of ambivalence toward authority is thus one of membership versus self-exclusion. Members learn from their interpersonal process as they work together to determine a direction for their process in spite of equivocal feelings about belonging in their group. They learn how and when each participant seeks inclusion or self-exclusion. This knowledge helps to determine the closeness and independence that members seek. Some participants may want to belong and be accepted, but they may not want to be constrained by the expectations and demands that a group can make on them.

A leader can react effectively in these challenging situations by remaining aware that ambivalence and attacks from group members may have a constructive purpose in the group's dynamics (Gans, 1989). If the leader responds to expressions of anger defensively, this reaction will have effects on the group's perception of the leader's power and perhaps on how involved the members are willing to become in the group. If ambivalence and overt or covert expressions of anger can be treated by the therapist as meaningful communications of emotion rather than as a threat to his or her control of the group, interpersonal dynamics in the group are more likely to move toward listening, giving, and acceptance.

If members are accepting of a complacent atmosphere wherein risks of self-disclosure are avoided, a group leader may wish to challenge others by expressing her or his awareness of the superficiality of the communication or by discussing specific aspects of this that she or he perceives as not being genuine. This kind of challenge can stimulate members to respond by expressing their dissatisfaction with the leader or by taking risks to reveal self to others.

Although at least some of a group's members are likely to experience a period of ambivalence or anger toward the leader, many people may go through this phase largely by confronting their own ambivalence about joining with others. If members work through their feelings about joining with others and accepting others, they can facilitate an open atmosphere for discussions and expressions of feeling. Confrontation and questioning that moves members toward greater responsibility can grow from challenges to the leader, challenges between members, or self-confrontation that members disclose to others. As members decide to work through their ambivalent or negative feelings, they may develop trust through a process of shared experiencing and are likely increasingly to facilitate mutual self-revelation.

Exploration and Self-Revelation

The assessment that members make about the trustworthiness of their group may be cognitive and may reflect judgments about how accepting group members have overtly shown themselves to be. Additionally, members' sense of the trustworthiness of the group is influenced by unspoken norms that regulate self-disclosure and by intuitive awareness of emotional safety (Napier & Gershenfeld, 1987).

As some members reveal more of their thoughts and feelings, others become more aware of these members as people who are present with them. If members value the interpersonal learning that begins to occur, they can help each other to explore individual's experiences and concerns and the meanings of ongoing interactions. Mutual assistance in exploration requires members to become sensitive to the issue of imposition of values and directions. As members learn how they can facilitate each other's exploration of self and experience, they also learn to be aware of each other's defenses and vulnerabilities. This awareness can help them to move toward just norms to regulate exploration and revelation and toward an acceptance of the various ways that individuals define and maintain interpersonal boundaries.

The interpersonal dynamics of love, power, and justice evolve toward integration in a spiraling manner. As one member risks exposing a vulnerable area and is heard and accepted, other participants often spontaneously begin to do the same. Members' desires to move toward more personal levels of relationship are "triggered" by one individual who shares at a personal level at the right time in a group's process. The timing is right for this triggering if other members have sensed that they would benefit from sharing personal feelings and perceptions but have not yet acted on this intuition.

The interpersonal dynamics that assist integration can also be sidetracked, can be interrupted, or can dissipate due to lack of involvement (Gemmill & Wynkoop, 1991). Interruptions and other shifts away from a meaningful focus can occur if interpersonal events have been experienced as unusually intense, demanding, or chaotic (Gemmill & Wynkoop, 1991). These shifts provide a method to avoid a challenge or growing conflict but can also serve to regulate interactions so that members maintain a comfortable sense of distance and safety. Interruptions can occur in the form of humor, abrupt shifts in topics, or assertions of self that ignore the current interpersonal process. Dissipation can occur if members transform an experience of threat into boredom and thus avoid learning more about each other.

Members' assertion of who they are in the group can be viewed as an expression of personal power. Power can be asserted with awareness of the interpersonal process or with a lack of awareness. During the phase of exploration, members learn how their assertions of self can facilitate learning or can interrupt it. Members are also likely to encounter their desires to be approved of and understood during this phase. Their motivation toward love influences the level of closeness that participants seek with each other, and their fears of closeness affect how much they are willing to disclose and express. Members learn that they must find a workable balance between a need for safety and a motivation to take interpersonal risks. If interpersonal safety occurs that allows risk taking, individuals are likely to experience excitement rather than boredom (Perls, Hefferline & Goodman, 1951/1980). Members assist each other in creating this awareness of safety by confronting their experiencing of relationships within and outside the group without unnecessary intrusions, judgments, or interruptions. Their mutual exploration can facilitate the beginnings of a movement toward creative justice.

At times, the power of the group dynamic and the influence of the group atmosphere have a noticeable impact on individual members (Korda & Pancrazio, 1989). A member may suddenly share a problem or concern that she or he has not confided in others outside the group. Members may have the experience of disclosing at a level of intimacy that is unusual and unexpected for them. For example, in a therapy group conducted by one of the authors with prison inmates, a member disclosed obviously deep and uncomfortable feelings of rage at his father, who had sexually abused his sister.

This individual had not intended to share these feelings when he joined the group and did not appear to have been consciously aware of how deep and disturbing they were. Because there was a level of mutual acceptance and concern established in the group, his feelings spontaneously "came to the surface." The unconscious desire of this member for reunification, his need to assert his own perceptions, and the current level of creative justice in the group were all contributing elements. In turn, this member's self-exploration and disclosure led to the same from another person dealing with similar problems.

As support and mutuality develop between members, the scope of personal disclosures tends to increase. Participants express aspects of who they are aware of being, who they are aware of having been, who they see themselves becoming, and their current problems or concerns. Members may experience their ongoing relationships with each other as increasingly meaningful. They discover both their similarities and their differences. Their similarities are likely to include shared emotions, such as love, sorrow, or fear; perspectives; and life experiences. Members may find that they have similar problems in dealing with relationships, self-assertion, and anger, in developing self-esteem, or in coping with depression. Differences that may surface can be related to individuals' backgrounds and living environments, to socioeconomic and class distinctions, to unique ways of perceiving events, or to idiosyncratic patterns in relationships.

Although various levels of sympathy and empathy can develop around members' shared concerns and feelings, members may not fully encourage each other's actualization of self if support is limited to those aspects of others' experiencing that are like their own. Self-actualization involves acceptance and development of unique aspects of being in the world, as well as universal and shared aspects. The phase of exploration and self-revelation inevitably increases members' awareness of their differences as well as their similarities. Although people generally feel comfortable approving of those who seem similar, their developing awareness of differences creates important opportunities to move toward integrated and open relationship dynamics. The integration of love, power, and justice develops as members respond to the challenge of accepting and caring about others while respecting and acknowledging those aspects of others' lives and selves that are different from themselves. This challenge can provide a central focus for interactions during the phase of exploration and self-revelation.

If group members overemphasize similarities in beliefs and experiences, they may avoid the difficult work of exploration in an atmosphere of freedom. Group members can collude to maintain an artificial atmosphere of homogeneity (a distorted form of love), may adopt limiting norms (a restrictive form of justice), and may create subtle or overt penalties for those whose perceptions or experiences are too divergent (a misuse of power). During this phase of a group, a group's leader can assist the development of integrated relationships by supporting those who question norms, by assisting those who wish to express what they are experiencing and observing, and by encouraging those who may feel unsupported or rejected (Gans, 1989).

Besides creating directions that facilitate exploration, members can respond to self-disclosures by providing comments that demonstrate caring and facilitate learning. Empathic responses and absence of pressure, particularly as members reveal their vulnerabilities, are valuable contributions to an atmosphere of safety (Korda & Pancrazio, 1989). These kinds of responses help participants to reveal themselves fully and to receive feedback that might be uncomfortable or disturbing to their preconceived images of self.

During the phase of exploration, some members are likely to experience a contradiction between their desire to belong and their wish to demonstrate their uniqueness. Group cohesion usually begins to develop during this phase, and it can be creative and generative or restrictive and bland. Members may also experience a conflict between their desires to conform to obviously acceptable areas for exploration and their desires to test the boundaries that have developed. This kind of conflict is likely to develop for an individual who has a pressing need to work on a problem or who enjoys the stimulation of emotional openness. Following the phase of ambivalence toward authority, members often feel more free to explore differences and investigate conflicting needs or attitudes. The phase of exploration allows members to develop an atmosphere of freedom wherein spontaneous expressions of thoughts and feelings can enhance interpersonal learning.

Creative cohesion can increase when members deal with a crisis. A crisis may arise if a member presents a problem or mode of relationship that challenges the stereotypes or expectations held by others (Napier & Gershenfeld, 1987). For example, participants may have difficulty accepting feelings or opinions voiced by someone who is in some sense in the minority. Some minorities may be more acceptable in a given group than others. In a group of well-educated college students, for instance, expressions of values associated with African-Americans or lesbians may be more acceptable than those associated with drug addicts or racists. For some members, problems resulting from the experience of sexual abuse from an alcoholic parent could be unfamiliar and difficult to hear. Another kind of group crisis can arise if a member expresses hurt, anger, or caring toward another member who is unable to respond or understand. Creative cohesion can be created in these situations if members learn that their group can grow from dealing with differences and that members can acknowledge and accept differing perspectives, backgrounds, and life experiences.

As members explore and reveal themselves to each other in an unstructured group, one or more themes will usually be developed as the basis for their ongoing interaction. During this phase, themes are oriented to more personal concerns of members and grow out of their need to make sense of their interactions, their desire to communicate meaningfully, and their maintenance of cohesion in the process of discourse. Themes are structures created by members that allow them to relate themselves to each other.

Themes can be categorized in many ways, and a nearly infinite number of potential themes exist. Some questions, however, are typical. What does it mean to care about another person? What is the meaning of my anger? What is the connection between hurt and anger? How can I express myself so that you'll understand? Participants may also state, "Relationships are vital to my life," "I feel hurt when you say no," "Change is possible but scary," "Life is unfair," or "Love is developed through giving." A continuing interaction between two or more members can also form a theme around which others orient their interactions. Other participants may learn from processing their observations about these interactions between specific members and may refer to this knowledge throughout a group.

A group will usually use certain themes as temporary foci and maintain others throughout the life of their group. Group phases are formed by the themes with which members concern themselves. A unified theme can develop in slightly different forms across separate group phases. For example, the theme of questioning authorities may arise during the socialization phase, direct questioning of the leader may occur during the phase of ambivalence, and disclosure of hurt suffered with parents may occur during the phase of exploration. Awareness of patterns developed to deal with feelings of hurt may be understood in terms of ongoing group relationships during the phase of mutuality. These themes develop as members find areas where they have shared problems or concerns.

Structured therapy groups usually provide a predetermined thematic focus, and members of these may work on knowledge and skills that relate to that particular focus. Unstructured therapy groups encourage members to create their own foci. Therefore, members of unstructured groups may need to cope with ambiguity to learn how to assume responsibility for focusing on themes. During the phase of exploration, members begin to develop themes that allow them to deepen their awareness of each other's personality and life experience.

When people who come from diverse life situations realize the extent of their similarity with others, a unique kind of learning about universality takes place (Yalom, 1975). This type of learning is central to the healing power of unstructured therapy groups if it leads to the experience of reunification with others. Members may then perceive value in the uniqueness of each participant within the common experience created by the group. They may also be surprised to learn the extent of common life experiences that members share as they reveal feelings and reactions to various situations.

Certain interpersonal skills can be enhanced through the process of participating in an unstructured therapy group. Essentially, these are relationship abilities associated with the acceptance of differences, the willingness to listen and to share, and a decision to engage in open and authentic communication. These skills are not taught but are learned through a process of participation. As members explore issues with each other, their interest is usually directed to learning about each other's experience, rather than to learning relationship skills. Therefore, unstructured groups facilitate the development of these skills by encouraging the development of relationships. As members become willing to reveal who they are to others, they facilitate the potential development of interpersonal relatedness.

Participants learn that they can work interdependently to further the individuality of each member. Although members may accept interpretations or advice during the phase of exploration, especially if these seem to arise from the concern of others, they predominantly want to be accepted. Members may perceive interpretations or advice as impositions or misunderstanding, especially if simply knowing that they have been heard by others is important. They are likely to diminish their self-exploration and self-revelation unless they feel that they have been heard and accepted. The central interpersonal dynamic that allows members to increase their self-exploration is the experience of reunification with others. Self-exploration assisted by others can align the dynamic of reunification with a sense of personal empowerment that often attends an individual's willingness to be more fully aware.

As members explore their feelings, experiences, and goals, they may feel relief and may become more aware of freedom. This awareness grows as they find that they are able to be honest with others about who they are and what they want. Members often seek and receive feedback from others that can lead to new approaches to situations and relationships both within and outside the group or to increased acceptance of themselves and others. They may encourage each other to explore new patterns of relating to others or to take risks in forming directions or expressing themselves. In the process, a new level of mutuality and involvement is achieved. Transactions that lead to I-thou relationship begin to emerge as possibilities for members who are willing to contact each other openly and fully.

Patterns of Mutual Relationship

A person can be open, can allow self to be influenced, and can resonate with others' experiences. Yet human beings are all limited in the degree to which they can share themselves with others. The ability to share experientially is constrained by time, physical limitations, and the inadequacies of language and nonverbal forms of communication. An individual's interpretation of another person's experiencing is inevitably influenced by that individual's ability to be aware, focus of attention, and perceptual map. No one can know the experience of another the way that the other knows it. In spite of these limitations, people attempt to share aspects of who they are with others and often hope to feel understood and accepted by others for who they are. People seek to learn how others see them, and a great deal of their self-image forms by "internalizing" others' reactions (Combs & Snygg, 1959; Guidano, 1987; Kohut, 1977).

The process of self-formation seems to be an integration of external events and internal aspects of awareness; thus, the total self cannot be properly defined by the categories "internal" versus "external" or "personal" versus "social." The phase of mutuality brings opportunities for members to experience firsthand how different selves intertwine. This experiential knowledge is available when members are willing to allow the type of contact that influences awareness of self and constructions of identity. Useful contact is not necessarily a merging with others or an awareness of shared unity with them, although these kinds of experiences can also facilitate growth. Useful contact can in fact sometimes occur through disclosing differences if individuals gain mutual awareness through these.

People learn about themselves through experiences in which they share their own feelings and perceptions even though these are different from others' (Perls, Hefferline & Goodman, 1951/1980; Yalom, 1980). These feelings and perceptions may not have been formed through interpersonal communication but are just as much "the self" as are interpersonal relationships. The self about which individuals learn in therapy groups therefore can be understood as an integration formed through awareness of one's physical perceptions (for example, sensations and feelings) and psychological perceptions (for example, imagery and cognitions) along with awareness of others' experiences and perceptions. If a member's own view of events and self differs from that of others, that person can learn about power by asserting his or her own awareness. Power becomes united with love as others are able to accept a member's assertions of self and as that member can hear and integrate others' awareness of that person. One important aspect of the learning that occurs through group process is a sharing of experience, and another important aspect is learning to accept differences that limit sharing. Members move toward mutuality as their ability to open to others and to share is enhanced and as their ability to accept differences and limitations is enhanced.

If strong disagreements arise between participants, they can learn from honestly exploring them. They may find a common ground, or they may agree to disagree. Members' learning can grow in areas where they agree, but some areas of difference are inevitable. A primary limitation when people adopt "groupthink" is that they do not explore their differences and they only focus on areas of agreement (Napier & Gershenfeld, 1987). As members move toward mutuality, they tend to question any assumptions of sameness that have previously limited their abilities to learn from each other.

As we have already seen, group participants may hold back aspects of themselves and their experience that they believe to be frightening, undesirable, or harmful. For example, a member who has been taught that it is bad to be selfish may inhibit self-expressions that might appear self-centered to others. A member with a history of abuse may hesitate to explore how these experiences have influenced present reactions to perceived movement toward intimacy. Other members may have convinced themselves that they are not interesting or worth knowing. Individuals often judge themselves more harshly than others have. The phase of mutuality tends to present a challenge to members. During this phase, members can allow boundaries within and between themselves to become more permeable to emotionally meaningful issues and aspects of awareness (Gemmill & Wynkoop, 1991; Yalom, 1975).

Besides safeguarding the comfort achieved with adherence to social roles, people may also keep part of themselves hidden from others (and often from themselves) out of fear of discovering the whole person that they are or may be. This hidden part of self is sometimes termed the *shadow* and exists in groups as an individual and collective psychological aspect of process (Gemmill, 1986). During the phase of mutuality, members experience the quality of interpersonal acceptance that can facilitate work to reclaim the shadow. Individually, this kind of work involves the owning of negative emotions that individuals have previously only seen in others. Collective ownership of a shadow occurs if members acknowledge within their group negative emotional realities previously attributed only to other groups (for example, families or social organizations). Mutuality in relationships facilitates this work to own negative feelings because participants perceive that their vulnerability will not be used against them.

Anxiety about increasing awareness of "negative" aspects of self can form a therapeutic impasse often associated with feelings of shame and self-blame (Korb, Gorrell & Van De Riet, 1989). The phase of mutuality is the time in a group's life when members, individually and collectively, are most likely to confront impasses that they have previously ignored or avoided. Members may review previous events in their group and disclose feelings of discomfort or pain that were previously unacknowledged. This disclosure allows their awareness of who they are with others to become more comprehensive. An impasse generally requires prolonged work in awareness and should not be expected to be fully overcome in a single meeting (see Perls, 1992). Therefore, awareness of an individual or collective impasse should not lead to attempts to manufacture a breakthrough but to attempts to grow through honest self-examination and confrontation (McClure, 1990). Participants in therapy grow if their confrontation with an impasse results in increased energy, awareness, and willingness to live life more fully (Korb, Gorrell & Van De Riet, 1989).

During the phase of mutuality, members can address individual and collective aspects of such an impasse. They can examine individual splits in awareness, splits between subgroups, and ways that the group as a whole has avoided dealing with conflicts or negativity (Agazarian, 1992). Members can also choose to avoid awareness of an impasse and thus avoid anxiety about openness and interdependence. They can, for example, manipulate group process in a manner that allows certain members to dominate and other members to become passive followers or can retreat to an illusion of harmony in sameness (McClure, 1990). Rather than using obviously regressive strategies, a group can stagnate within the phase of mutuality by generating a meandering discussion in which focus is lost

(Gemmill & Wynkoop, 1991). Additionally, participants can undermine trust by voicing judgments of others based on stereotypical views or by ignoring aspects of others' communications that question individual or collective expectations. Members can move from beginnings of mutuality to a phase of superficiality in communication.

As awareness grows, members may risk new forms of relationship and communication. They may experience themselves as more powerful or as more capable of expressing vulnerability or caring toward others. Mutual support for risk taking and spontaneous self-expression often increases during this phase.

The risk involved in exposing one's being to another is that one will be misunderstood, harshly evaluated, rejected, or imposed upon. There is also the risk of exposing one's being in areas in which one perceives oneself to be vulnerable. This risk may involve fears that one will be perceived as weak, antagonistic, frightened, pompous, inadequate, lonely, unlovable, or hurtful. In addition, there is uncertainty in revealing longings for love and justice that have previously been denied or shut out of awareness. By reconnecting with these longings, members allow themselves the opportunity to experience reunification with others. In a therapy group, each member exposes his or her process of being to some degree from the very beginning. However, this exposure may be limited by strategies that diminish self-revelation. Members usually avoid mutual exploration of core concerns until they feel emotionally supported by others.

Individuals subjectively assess certain aspects of their lives and selves as more central to their process of being than other aspects (Combs & Snygg, 1959; Mahoney, 1990). Thus, a discussion of current political events may seem important but may be perceived as more distant from one's immediate process of being than a discussion of how members have expressed caring or anxiety toward each other. Certain areas of experience are more intimately associated with being because they reflect vulnerabilities, needs, desires, and hopes. These aspects of experience are more likely to emerge as basic themes during the phase of mutuality.

Mutuality in relationships can provide the basis for challenges that undermine certain illusions about self and life. These misconceptions normally persist through reliance on relationship patterns that use mechanical, predictable, and "safe" forms of interaction to confirm expectations about who one is with others. During the phase of mutuality, members can learn about stereotypic and repetitious patterns in their relations with others and can learn about new ways of interacting that challenge expectations.

Mutuality that develops in a therapy group intensifies an important group principle: that what goes around comes around. Members may respond quickly and spontaneously to those that they feel are subverting movement toward mutual awareness. For example, those who criticize or label are likely to receive opinions from others about the effects of these actions. Members move toward mutuality by confronting self-created interpersonal barriers to intimacy and freedom. As members move toward intimacy, they also learn about their own resistance to it.

Participants are more likely to confront what they perceive as each other's self-deceptions, games, anxieties, and self-defeating strategies as they become more comfortable with honesty in their group (Berne, 1964; Rogers, 1970; Yalom, 1975). They may give feedback that is subtly blaming or may give responses that are clear and direct. Members may also respond in ways that are imaginative and emotional. Members who feel that others in the group have attempted to impose on them or to manipulate them may learn that they are accepted even if they express perceptions of unjust treatment. If participants have been harboring unexpressed frustrations about their group or about specific members, they are likely to express these during the development of mutuality in relationships.

Members tend to become relatively relaxed and open in their interactions during the mutuality phase. If the leadership style has been democratic and focused on people rather than roles, they will move toward increasing interpersonal cohesion (Vander Kolk, 1985). They are likely then to decrease reliance on their leader for cues on how to create their interpersonal process. As they feel less dependence on a leader, members demonstrate a movement from tributive justice that confers status on those who are powerful toward creative justice. Participants question the imposition of values and do not respect or honor conformity for its own sake. If members express negative feelings during this phase, some of these may represent dissatisfaction with interactions that lack creative justice. For example, members may express dissatisfaction with themselves or others if they perceive responses as highly predictable, inflexible, or incomplete. Participants increasingly display intuitive, spontaneous, and uncensored responses during this phase.

During the phase of mutuality, listening, giving, and accepting are likely to become noticeably and actively employed in members' interactions. Participants have gained experiential learning concerning how to disclose their perceptions of self and others and how to use these disclosures to create interactions in which mutual involvement is demonstrated. At times, the experience of interpersonal acceptance may deepen to the point that members express loving feelings toward others and show that they feel sincerely cared for. The agape form of love may become evident in the group as a deep level of interpersonal acceptance and mutual respect. The *philia* aspect of love also plays an important role in the life of the group during the phase of mutuality as members are increasingly able to acknowledge how specific others in the group have contributed to their experience and understanding.

A majority of group members may sometimes be relating on the level of mutuality although one or two members have not become as involved in the group as the others. The dynamic element of reuniting love is often expressed by members who reach out to those who have distanced themselves, have withdrawn, or have disengaged from contacts that seemed intense or perhaps threatening. Reuniting love is not expressed as a demand or imposition upon reluctant group members. Rather, the possibility of acceptance is extended to those who seem to feel that they have not been included—members extend invitations but they do not demand that others join. Participants can accept differences in each other's need for distance and desire to communicate.

A crisis can occur for the group if a member is so threatened by the growing intimacy in the group that he or she begins to act out this discomfort in ways that interfere with communication. Acting out in a group therapy context involves behaviors that subvert the growing closeness of members (for example, through unjust accusations or through dramatic expressions of feeling that serve to interrupt communication or that distract attention from developing relationships). Yalom (1975) has observed that " 'acting' out as a form of resistance to therapy occurs only when the patient refuses to examine and to allow the group to examine his behavior" (p. 337). (Of course, if a participant *is* willing to examine her or his behavior, it becomes an opportunity for learning.)

Nonverbal expressions of disinterest or boredom, indirectly expressed hostility, withholding of feelings after beginning a confrontation, or resentment expressed toward members who seem to be enjoying acceptance from others may be part of such acting out. Additionally, a member may insist on keeping the group's attention for a prolonged time while she or he discusses an involved issue with very little focus on feelings. This long discussion may serve to interrupt patterns of mutuality that were previously being expressed and worked on.

It is sometimes possible to identify an overt or covert conflict between group members who feel included in the group and those who do not. This conflict can become apparent during the phase of mutuality. Some members may express resentment toward those who they believe are resisting an atmosphere of empathy and support. These members may identify with their group, but they may have feelings of anger or resentment of which they have not become fully aware and that they have not fully integrated. Thus, deviant members serve a function by allowing others to express anger and resentment that does not fit with their image of an empathic group.

Members' images of a worthwhile group can function similarly to self-images that define desirable feelings and behaviors and exclude undesirable ones. Just as effective unstructured group therapy challenges self-images that restrict individual growth, this therapy can challenge images that restrict growth for the group as a whole. The member who confronts the group by taking a deviant stance may therefore be allowing other participants to bring into awareness a conflict in the overall group dynamics of love, power, and justice.

Members are willing to work directly to understand deviance by certain members during the phase of mutuality. They are also willing to discuss how to deal with the reactions that they have experienced as they have tried to gain cohesion and accept divergence. The deviant member may feel uncomfortable with an increasing level of intimacy or may be expressing a sense of uneasiness that others share. If others are trusting of their movement toward increased intimacy, they probably will accept one or two members' discomfort. If they share feelings of mistrust that they have not voiced, they are likely to have a strong emotional reaction to the deviant individual. They may attack this individual as a scapegoat rather than recognize their own fears of interpersonal aggression and their own ambivalence about the direction of their group (Gemmill, 1989). By coming to terms with their own strong feelings, they can extend acceptance toward a member whom they previously wanted to reject. They may agree to examine their uncomfortable feelings about movement toward intimacy and may gain a sense of new meaning by engaging in this uncertain process (Gemmill & Wynkoop, 1991).

During the phase of full mutuality, members develop awareness of a shared and interdependent context for their communications. This context is an optimal environment for the development of I-thou relations between members. Although participants are likely to move toward this form of relationship, they may not fully experience it; after all, it is an ideal state.

Yalom (1980) states that the I-thou relationship "is a wholly mutual relationship involving a full experiencing of the other. It differs from empathy (imaginatively viewing the situation from another person's perspective) because it is more than an "I" attempting to relate to an "other." . . . the "I" appears and is shaped in the context of some relationship. . . . one's whole being is involved; nothing can be held back" (p. 365). Members may hold back some of who they are and yet still be moving toward enhanced mutuality.

Group participants often find that they more easily establish genuine I-thou relatedness with other members than with the leader (Yalom, 1975). If members are able to accept and affirm each other's uniqueness, they are likely to feel that this affirmation is fully genuine. Affirmation from a leader may be experienced as more or less genuine but as conditioned by the role of leadership. Similarly, members are likely to believe that they can give more fully to other participants than to their leader. They are likely to perceive that these others may need something from them, and these people are less restricted than the leader in personally asking for something.

Though members may not see the leader as personally needing something, they recognize that this individual will feel successful if they appear to find ways to generate interpersonal healing and to experience growth. Of course, if participants concern themselves about meeting the leader's wants, they may distort their own directions for growth. Therefore, effective leaders cultivate a willingness to allow mistakes and failure in areas that they might think are important. The less that a leader needs to feel successful, the more she or he can contribute to the atmosphere of freedom that promotes healing and growth.

During the phase of mutuality, the leader is more likely to reveal himself or herself as a person with hopes, needs, and wants than during other phases. This self-revelation should not be made in order to receive therapy from others; attempting to do so would be an abdication of responsibility by the leader. However, appropriate use of self as a more fully interactive participant can serve as a leader's acknowledgment of mutuality and can assist movement toward creative justice. Members may experience some sense of themselves as being able to contribute to the awareness and well-being of their group's leader.

As interactions move toward mutuality, members tend to mirror each other's growing openness and are likely to see themselves as altered by those who have also allowed themselves to be altered. This mirroring effect occurs in individual relationships as well but can be greatly enhanced by the nature of collective participation in an unstructured therapeutic group. One person's affirmation of personal power opens the way for others to assert their power. Potentially, a network of I-thou relatedness can evolve through this process.

Typically, members share most of who they are during the phase when relationships move toward mutuality and begin to withdraw as they deal with termination of the group (Vander Kolk, 1985). The termination phase represents the ending of either the life of the group or the participation of a particular member. Recognition of the therapeutic power of the termination stage of a therapy group arises from our recognition that dealing with endings is an often difficult and meaningful aspect of interpersonal relationships.

Ending

A person who is able to accept and integrate the meaning of loss is often more likely to risk the openness and caring that characterize intimacy and mutuality. People often hold back from the possibilities for I-thou relationship because they fear losing what they have worked to develop. Additionally, many people have unfinished business related to awareness of loss. They may refuse intimacy to avoid experiencing again painful feelings that they have not accepted and integrated. The phase of ending is potentially therapeutic because members may then become more open to integrating experiences of loss.

Although members may distance themselves from others in preparation for leaving, they may retain sufficient contact to exchange feelings of caring and compassion. By dealing with the meaning of loss, members can prepare themselves for openness to new possibilities for relationship that may evolve in their lives after they leave their group. Members may also spend some time reviewing certain meaningful aspects of their group. As they review events, members express awareness of their involvement with others and their feelings about their shared experience.

Corey and Corey (1987) have observed that if expressions of mourning are accepted and mutually validated, members may gain new learning about the value of expressing feelings about a loss. If the leader believes that members can learn from reviewing some of the events in the life of the group or by discussing awareness of ending, she or he may need specifically to encourage members to allow the time and space to address these issues. Additionally, the leader may need to bring these issues to the group's attention and to solicit opinions from the members concerning how they would like to deal with termination (Corey & Corey, 1987).

The ending phase of the group represents a time when the theme of nonbeing is likely to have collective relevance. Members, of course, have some awareness that their group will end from its inception. They may have addressed some termination issues during previous phases of group process. These interactions may have involved certain members' threats to leave the group or expressions of sadness that one will have to let go of relationships that are developing.

In various ways, group members come to terms with a transition through which existence as a group will end. For some people, this transition may be comfortable, but for many others uncomfortable feelings or sad feelings may arise (Vander Kolk, 1985; Yalom, 1975). Some participants may want to review past events; others may want to talk about their future; and still others may want to deal with their present feelings about leaving other members. As members communicate their feelings, reactions, and concerns during this phase, they form an ending process for their group.

Elizabeth Kübler-Ross (1975), who worked extensively with dying patients, calls death "the final stage of growth." She writes, "When it is the evening of our life we will hopefully have a chance to look back and say: 'It was worthwhile because I have really lived'" (p. 126). This hope is also our wish for how participants will experience the termination stage of a therapy group. We hope that members will feel that the group has been a place where they have really lived. If they have been able to choose openness, their group experience will have been therapeutically beneficial. Unstructured group therapy will have been even more effective if members have moved toward an integrated relationship dynamic through the process of opening themselves to others. If members have used their experience to move toward an integrated process of relationship that can be renewed and recreated in ongoing encounters, then the ending phase is a transition that can lead to continued growth in awareness that is self-directed and self-organized.

Ending sometimes brings unfinished business to the surface, particularly if some participants have been "sitting on their feelings" about previous incidents and interactions. Unfinished business can provide a way to hold on to the group at a time when letting go is most appropriate, and it can distract members from dealing with termination. It is also possible that some members with unfinished business may not have opportunities to process these feelings. Most participants will hesitate to bring up emotionally charged personal issues at the time of termination. Someone who expresses such an issue may need a referral to allow continued therapeutic work.

Kübler-Ross (1975) writes that death is avoided as an issue because it "reminds us of our human vulnerability" (p. 5). Similarly, members may be reluctant to address termination as a problem. Perhaps they are uncomfortable with the emotional vulnerability that they may expose if they acknowledge parting with one another as a loss. Some members may want to address the issue because they sense that dealing with it will be a way for them to learn and grow. Other participants may not have developed feelings of closeness that would lead to perceptions of loss with ending. Those who have felt close with others during their group may mourn. They may also feel accepting of this loss if they feel ready to continue their journey apart from their group.

Although members may want to continue their contact and sharing with others, they may also be aware that separating from others creates distance. Members may experience ambivalence between feelings of being connected and separateness. If members have had ambivalence about ending past relationships, an echo of these feelings can arise for them as they terminate with their group. Some may again experience feelings of abandonment. They may try to cling to others or may react by acting aloof and unconcerned. Participants may be maintaining a pattern of dealing with termination that is continued from past relationships.

Thus, the ending phase is likely to generate different perceptions and reactions for participants. Although individual reactions vary, members often use the ending phase of their time together to dissociate from their previous levels of involvement and commitment (see Page, Davis, Berkow & O'Leary, 1989).

Yalom (1975) has stated that different issues are involved in the termination of an unsuccessful client, a successful client, and the group as a whole. The client who perceives herself or himself as unsuccessful may express feelings of demoralization and worthlessness. This client may benefit from scheduling a private talk with the therapist to discuss what has occurred. Although Yalom finds constructive and therapeutic ways to deal with termination issues, he also notes that "termination is the jolting reminder of the inbuilt cruelty of the psychotherapeutic process" (p. 373). Yalom recognizes that members often avoid dealing directly with issues of termination and suggests that the therapist "repeatedly call the members' attention to the impending termination" (p. 374).

Vander Kolk is another group therapy theorist who has connected members' tendencies to avoid dealing with the ending of the group to a wish to avoid the anxiety of separation. Vander Kolk views this avoidance as an expression of members' wishes to remain dependent. He has also observed that "how members handle ending the group may reflect how they handle endings in their lives" (p. 203). Members may be feeling anxiety, disappointment, anger, jealousy, love, or regret (Vander Kolk, 1985).

The theme of ending is present throughout the life of a group and is an essential factor in the potential learning that can facilitate actualization and individuation for participants in therapy. Most theorists who describe the developmental process of unstructured therapy present the most therapeutic time as the phase of mutuality (for example, Rogers, 1970; Yalom, 1975). These theorists rightly view the establishment of trust and the development of potential I-thou relatedness as a central healing dynamic that unstructured therapy has to offer. Because members tend to create interpersonal distance during the ending phase, it can be construed as less than optimal. As we have seen, participants generally disengage with each other, and their interpersonal communication generally becomes less intense and personal. Members may not feel the same quality of contact and being understood by others at this time and may be confused about their own feelings.

Nonetheless, though Rogers (1970) for one does not address growth during termination, it *can* assist therapy. The benefit comes not necessarily through contact or empathic understanding that others express but through the meaning gained by experiencing the process of ending. Termination can open up awareness of the possibilities of transformation for members. Group members can effectively create new awareness of meaning if they accept rather than reject perceptions of uncertainty and chaos that are part of a transitional experience (see Gemmill & Wynkoop, 1991).

During the process of ending a group, members seek less understanding from others and more understanding of their own feelings. Members tend to focus on awareness of what it means to leave others as they terminate within-group relations. Perhaps they sense the beginnings of feelings of isolation, aloneness, or loss. Being able to integrate these feelings (and thus using these to grow in awareness) is an important opportunity. Members can help each other to deal with these feelings if they are able to say good-bye and do not attempt to avoid the experience.

Some members may not gain closure on their experience of ending. Whether a participant will be able to accept lack of closure comfortably is likely to be related to this person's capacity to accept incompleteness as an unavoidable aspect of life experience. Acceptance of incompleteness is a healthy response to termination, insofar as all loose ends cannot be tied up, all possibilities cannot be explored, and movement toward the future opens up unknown territory.

Many people seem more easily to understand that connecting with others can assist growth and healing than to grasp how leaving others can promote these processes. This difficulty is probably associated with awareness that losses are often setbacks for people. Participants in groups often grow as they experience reunification with others. However, members can also grow in awareness of personal power as they meet with individual differences and interpersonal distance as factors that are aspects of their creation of relationship. Distance allows space for members to figure out how and when they wish to create connections with others. Termination is a letting go of the experience of being connected, but this letting go can be part of a process through which members learn that ending creates freedom to form new connections.

Ending one's relationship with others in the context of a group encounter is a unique and personal experience for each person and is not totally predictable. Whereas members, during the phase of mutuality, tend to give clear signals about their emotional reactions to events, clear communication may be less evident in the termination phase. The learning that occurs from the experience of ending is in many ways the most private (and often most ambiguous) learning that occurs from participation in therapy.

If a participant leaves an ongoing group or if it ends, members are likely to experience ending differently than they would if they were terminating a one-day or a weekend marathon group.

One difference is that an ongoing group often comes to represent a stable and continuing source of support and understanding, whereas participants in a onetime group do not develop the same kind of expectations. If a member leaves an ongoing group, he or she may need to deal with the loss of support and concern from the other members. Those who remain must deal with losing someone whose presence and participation have lent a unique quality to their group. Issues of abandonment may arise for some members who remain in the group, and abandonment issues and fears of independence may arise for the one who leaves.

A group may disband because of prearranged time limits, because of a leader's decision to end the group or to change residence, or because of a group decision to terminate. Participants' reactions are likely to differ depending on the meaning that they construe in the process of ending. A group leader can help by attending to meanings that members form. In particular, a leader should act with sensitive awareness to signals that a particular person is experiencing significant difficulty in dealing with an experienced lack of closure. If a participant is feeling unusual levels of anxiety, resentment, depression, or guilt, the leader or others can assist this individual by providing encouragement and possibly references to pursue additional therapy. The group leader may need to schedule time to talk to this member apart. Members sometimes need more time than the group can allow to discuss feelings that have been stirred up during the process of ending.

As participants become able to express how they are feeling about the end of their group, those who are experiencing sorrow, regrets, or hurt at the ending of significant relationships are likely to realize that they are not alone. If members express painful or regretful feelings, others in the group are likely to hear this pain as a reaction that reveals a universal aspect to loss within human experience. By acknowledging that something is being lost, members simultaneously recognize that something is gained or that something worthwhile has been shared. If participants are able to mourn together, they may constructively manage and express the anxiety or sadness that ending relationships can bring.

Along with expressing feelings related to loss, members often discuss the plans that they are making to deal with problems that they have addressed in the group and that remain concerns. Members may use a process of review to clarify their awareness of their experience and to reinforce any learning that has occurred during the group. Individuals may discuss their plans for establishing new relationships or for working on existing relationships.

Members whose awareness is centered in the present may respond to termination without any apparent need or desire to review experiences, gain closure, or formulate plans for the future. These individuals are likely to feel content simply to participate with others in the process of ending their group. There is no one "correct" response to this ending; it is merely hoped that members will feel free to express their reactions in a manner that is congruent with their own experience of events.

Chapter Seven

Responsibilities of Group Membership

We learned in Chapter Four that individual recognition of responsibility is a key factor involved as members learn to use a group
encounter to enhance their own growth and healing. Members
move toward assumption of responsibility as they learn to use their
freedom to explore personal problems, examine their splits or
blocks in awareness, and investigate the patterns that they bring
into their relationships. Especially during the phases of exploration
and mutuality, participants may challenge themselves and others to
assume responsibility for what occurs in their group. However,
members' responsibilities influence each phase of a group.

Responsibility is also a central element of constructive leadership within therapeutic as well as other social groups. Destructive
leaders in various social groups evidence irresponsibility when they
deceive others (and often themselves) about the nature of their actions and motivations, blame others as a result of their perfectionism or as a way to increase power, maintain or manufacture polarities in relationships, and attempt to control the awareness of
others. Responsible leaders are able to be honest with themselves

and others, create win-win situations for the enhancement of power, help to resolve and integrate polarities between people, and enjoy freedom of awareness for themselves and others. Responsible leaders accept their own and others' mistakes as evidence of humanness and as opportunities for learning.

Membership and the Dynamics of Therapeutic Groups

In an ideal therapeutic group, all members would see themselves as equally responsible beings who were constructing a shared experience. They would learn that leadership roles shift as different problems and encounters were explored and that various individuals were capable of assuming responsibility for contributing to the directions and modes of communication most effective within changing situations. Because experiential learning about responsibility is one of the keys to successful therapy, the leader of a therapy group is functioning well if he or she is able to help members assume leadership within their own group experience. Leadership in an effective unstructured therapy group is not associated with the ability to impose values or norms on others. Instead, leadership involves assuming responsibility for one's own communications and expression of self and assisting others to recognize responsibility.

Although an effective group leader is aware of ways in which his or her presence may influence others, she or he also recognizes that the growth of individuals and the group as a whole is facilitated as other members recognize their own abilities to be authorities within group process (Foulkes, 1975; Page, 1983a; Rogers, 1970). Each participant is an authority on his or her own experience and own awareness of events and relationships. Each participant is capable of making effective decisions and choices within ongoing experiences and encounters. Leadership is therefore not a separate role from membership in a therapeutic group. As dynamics shift during therapeutic interactions, a group's leader may temporarily behave more as a coparticipant while another member may function in a more influential manner. Thus, the dynamics of unstructured therapeutic encounters, in both individual and group therapy settings, encourage participants to move toward recognition of themselves as responsible and aware beings.

The role of the group leader has a *difference* in quality from the roles of other members insofar as that person is understood to be the organizer of the group and is expected to assist others to work on personal problems rather than using the group to work on his or her own concerns. The role of the group leader also has a *similarity* in quality to the roles of other members in that the group leader is co-responsible with others for what the group becomes and for the modes of communication that develop there. Since successful therapy leads participants to recognize themselves as cocreators of the process of their group, a successful leader finds ways to use his or her difference and similarity to others as means to facilitate coconstruction of directions in process.

Ontological Infusion and Awareness of Interbeing

As group members move from self-protection to more open sharing of themselves within immediate experience, they move from a position of psychological distance from one another to psychological connectedness. Participants become less concerned with finding safe topics for discussion and more interested in learning how they can create meaning through being with one another (Bozarth, 1981; Foulkes, 1948, 1975; Rogers, 1970). This shift in perspectives can be considered as the formation of an ontological focus for group process. This shift represents movement away from expectations that learning will be conferred or provided toward an understanding that learning can be created together. Members then form a basis for responsible coauthorship of group experience. This all-important shift in the focus of awareness is related to an ontological infusion that occurs if members are willing to use their process of being together to open themselves to their current experience and to increase their awareness of the meaning of relationship.

Ontological infusion is a centering and opening of participants' awareness within their present and ongoing experience. This kind of centering involves awareness of one's own present and continuing experience as interconnected with the present and continuing experience of others. Interconnection is established through interactions and transactions that involve shared aspects of experience and perception, emotional resonance, and communication of empathic understanding.

Mutual influence occurs as a nonlinear and relatively unpredictable process through which members simultaneously affect one another across boundaries. For example, a communication between two members may go on through an exchange of empathic understanding to an impasse. This impasse may reveal differences in perspectives that participants accept and value because they are attuned to each other's emotional responses and world views. However, if one member perceives aspects of this difference as threatening or unfair, relationship may be diminished rather than enhanced. The development of an encounter between participants can also be altered by any number of variables: members' personal histories, emotional states, perceptions of meaning, and spontaneous and intuitive reactions to events.

If members experience congruence between their own dynamics and those of others, ontological infusion has the potential to operate within group process. Being with others may then become in itself therapeutic, and the roles that members play in their group become secondary to the continuing process of relationship. Members' roles become flexible, and participants become willing to relate to each other without imposing their definitions and expectations on each other or on their group.

Members' awareness of interbeing occurs as they recognize responsibilities that link their own process of self-actualization with that of others. Participants will then sense that fulfillment of their own being occurs within a context that includes other individuals who also wish for fulfillment. For example, a college student named "John," who participated in an unstructured therapy group, consistently discounted his own impulses toward more risk taking in relationships. He also minimized the importance of his occasionally expressed wishes to "feel that life could be worth living." However, John frequently assisted others with self-exploration and could be counted on to give feedback that facilitated others' awareness of positive aspects of themselves and their lives. As John observed and participated in the growth of others in the group, he seemed to gain recognition of and confidence in his own wishes to increase self-actualization. At a time near the ending of the yearlong group, John stated, "At first, I didn't feel like I could gain anything from a group like this. It didn't seem to offer much. But now I feel that I did accomplish something important, although it's hard to say exactly what that is. I know I feel better about myself, and part of that is the way we were able to work together here. I know I've tried some new things in my life, although I'm not sure how much of that is because of group work and how much is because of me."

Therapy is created in a process that involves meeting, touching, communicating, and transacting. Personalities interact and create together. Therefore, members must learn to function therapeutically for one another to realize the healing potential of their group. They do not need to learn therapeutic strategies so much as they need to learn how to draw on their own potential to create a balanced interpersonal dynamic. To do this, they must tap their own abilities to facilitate each other's growth toward integration. Effective unstructured group therapy requires the active and responsible cocreation of healing dynamics by aware participants.

Interbeing links observation, participation, and mutual influence within an ongoing dynamic. Interbeing, recognized as such by participants, can function as the primary healing influence in unstructured group therapy. A particular therapeutic approach or device cannot serve as a substitute for recognition of interbeing. A group leader with a relatively integrated personal dynamic of love, power, and justice will use an approach and strategies that reflect and express this integrated dynamic. However, no activity of the group leader can create the recognition of interbeing for participants in a therapeutic process.

As members become aware of interbeing, the connectedness that they establish can enhance their individual power of being. They tend to confront their barriers to intimacy and authenticity as they move toward an understanding of this process that intertwines self and others. Members generally require time, patience, and practice to become comfortable with the experience of interbeing. They need to learn to trust that the interaction of divergent personalities can promote the health and well-being of participants. This trust will develop only if members perceive each other as willing and able to assume responsibility for a healing process. Mutually responsible participation and willingness to move toward integration are necessary for developing a shared awareness of interbeing.

Transferring Leadership

Participants who join therapy groups may wish for the leader or the group itself to provide an answer for their problems, relief from their unhappiness, and success for them in their lives. In spite of this longing for a magical solution, they generally recognize that waiting for magical interventions does not facilitate productive work. Members are aware on some level that what they really need from their group is to find a working relationship with others that can help them to discover and create their own answers and paths to fulfillment. Perhaps their group cannot make pain go away, but it can help them to bear their pain and to explore their options for change. Their group can provide an experience of acceptance that helps them to learn what goals they want to set for themselves.

We have already noted that a therapist is in an influential and powerful leadership position at the initial phase of an unstructured group. At the same time, an effective therapist helps members perceive themselves as leaders and initiators within their own group (Page, 1983b; Rogers, 1970). Group leadership therefore requires an ability to meld the dynamics inherent in the social role of being a leader with those that move a group toward more integrated love, power, and justice. A leader needs to maintain enough of his or her role to mediate both legally and ethically between a therapy group and society. A leader also should share leadership sufficiently that others experience themselves as responsible beings within relationships in their group. As we have seen, a leader can assist participants to recognize the emergent themes that are significant within group process, rather than imposing ideas.

Wu-Wei and the Art of Group Membership

Leadership of unstructured therapy groups can be described as an art of leading *without* leading. A group leader who focuses on facilitating a therapeutic process is likely to become unconcerned with her or his overt role as an authority figure. Members are able to assist each other in working on emergent themes as they learn to encourage each other without attempting to dominate. Group leaders can stimulate this approach by modeling it. Leading without dominating helps integrate the dynamics of love, power, and justice.

The Chinese Taoists developed a concept called *wu-wei*, action that is simultaneously nonaction (Chang, 1963). In application to therapy process, *wu-wei* suggests that individuals heal and grow as they recognize and trust an inherent ordering process that does not need to be controlled or forced and that integrates self and experience with ease and unself-conscious simplicity (Suler, 1991). This idea is also useful in assisting us to understand how leadership in an unstructured group can be highly effective at times when none of the participants feel that they are being led.

Certain theorists have noted that their understanding of healthful functioning and effective therapy has been enhanced by learning about principles that have traditionally been investigated in Eastern philosophy. For example, Meador and Rogers (1984) writes, "It is doubtful that there would be any precursors of person-centered therapy. However, to set the person-centered point of view in historical perspective, person-centered therapy could probably best be traced to some Oriental thinkers" (p. 147). Shostrom's (1976) view of therapy incorporates a Taoist perspective that polarities can function in a unified manner and that persons can grow when they cease struggling against their own natures. Jung (1964) was also influenced by Eastern thought about the human potential to integrate polarities in awareness. Fromm, Suzuki, and De Martino (1960) and Perls (Shepard, 1975) were influenced by Zen Buddhism, a philosophy that emphasizes the centrality of awareness and the power of present experience.

Meador and Rogers (1984) have found that Zen Buddhism corresponds with some of their views, particularly the "Zen tradition of insisting that the person can find the answers within himself" (p. 147). They also mention the importance of *wu-wei*, described as a "Taoist virtue," one basic to "the person that the person centered therapist would like to become" (p. 147). Buber's (1957) explanation of the nature of *wu-wei* influenced the perspectives of Meador and Rogers (1984). Buber describes *wu-wei* as the belief that "to interfere with the life of things means to harm both them and one's self. He who imposes himself has the small, manifest might; he who does not impose himself has the great secret might. . . . The perfected man does not interfere in the life of beings, he does not impose himself on them, but he helps all beings to their freedom" (pp. 54–55).

Attempts to impose directions and values in psychotherapy can interfere with the therapeutic work of assisting participants to reach values based on their own perceptions and interpretations of events (Korda & Pancrazio, 1989). Of course, therapists, like other mortals, are not value-free beings. Attempts to maintain a value-free presence may impair therapeutic effectiveness if clients lack a sense of contact with the therapist as a fully present human being (Cain, 1989). The highest-quality therapeutic assistance is likely to come from individuals who can recognize and clarify their own values, can demonstrate the development of values from experience, can assist others in this work if appropriate, and can accept and respect divergence in experiences and values. A person is least likely to impose values if others are respected as creative beings capable of constructing directions within their own experiential, perceptual, and cultural worlds.

The parallels between the direction of some Western psychotherapists and that of some Taoist philosophers can be clarified by examining the value of assisting people to accept and learn within their own experiential process. The idea of noninterference associated with *wu-wei* should not be misinterpreted as nonparticipation or noninvolvement in the context of therapy. Therapists are more likely to be able to help people learn from within their own experience if they can establish contact, coparticipation, and presence. Therefore, valuing *wu-wei* does not lead to maintenance of an inactive or inert presence in a group, limitation of responses to clarifications and reflections, or failure to acknowledge personal directions and values. Nonimposition does not mean discounting one's ability to influence people. A person's attempt to deny her or his influence will itself influence relationship dynamics, often by distorting this person's ability to be actively present. Nonimposition requires an understanding of how one can most respectfully, coherently, and usefully influence interpersonal situations and address options within them (Cain, 1989).

If presence is itself influential, nonimposition means learning to be as fully present as possible but in a manner that does not interfere with others' abilities to participate. One's presence in itself may encourage and stimulate others to make their presence known. Willingness to support others in this way reflects an openness to the being and choices of others and does not reflect a presumption that a person knows how others should choose to be present. Of course, one person's way of participating should not interfere with others. Thus, a rule of nonviolence is basic to therapeutic group work. To assert that nonviolence is imperative in therapeutic situations seems an imposition on the freedom of individuals to behave violently; yet this rule is not an imposition in the sense that others are more likely to exercise their freedom to be present if they know that they will not be imposed upon violently.

The principle of *wu-wei* has traditionally been applied to martial arts such as T'ai Chi Ch'uan (Cheng and Smith, 1967). Cheng and Smith (1967), in writing of the application of T'ai Chi to martial arts, relate the practice of *wu-wei* to an ability to empty oneself of fear and psychological resistance to pain. Applying the principle of *wu-wei* to group therapy should therefore enable a therapist to proceed without resistance to whatever emotions, tensions, or painful conflicts that may arise.

Cheng and Smith (1967) state that the T'ai Chi Ch'uan classics have advised, "In resting, be still as a mountain; in moving go like the current of a great river" (p. 110). *Wu-wei* can be used as a basis for martial arts because it involves the awareness of knowing when and how to move and when and how to be still. *Wu-wei* is simultaneously nonaction and "effortlessness" (p. 2). The noninterference of *wu-wei* is noninterference with Tao—the essential nature of things or the movement of nature (Watts, 1961). To practice *wu-wei* therefore requires sufficient awareness to grasp the nature of present events and persons from a position fully with and within them, as opposed to a position that is separate or uninvolved.

A group leader who is able to practice *wu-wei* serves as a model for other participants of how they can interact spontaneously and with awareness. Yet the leader serves as more than a model because the integrity of her or his being with others influences them. If group members are able to practice *wu-wei*, their nonimposition on each other occurs, not as a matter of moral principle, but as a natural consequence of their grasp of each other's essential nature and needs. This understanding of each other's nature comes through coparticipation in a mutually shared activity, not from an analysis undertaken from a position of separation.

A person whose awareness is clear and integrated is capable of being fully silent if silence is necessary and can move with great energy if movement is necessary. Applied to group therapy, *wu-wei* does not lead to imposition upon the nature of others, but it often does create spontaneous interactions, high levels of interest and energy, and an intuitive understanding that supplements a cognitive one. Chang (1963) observes that the noninterference of *wu-wei* includes not interfering with one's ordinary mind. Whereas *yu-wei* involves cultivating the mind, *wu-wei* is noncultivation of the mind. Thus, a male leader or group member who practices *wu-wei* does not attempt to make others conform to his expectations, nor does he deny his feelings and intuitions to try to fit his responses to the expectations of the group or his own theoretical model. He does not try to show off to others what he has learned from his group. Rather, this individual comes to feel increasingly free to express his everyday thoughts, feelings, concerns, and honest observations of occurrences both in and outside his group.

Noncultivation allows the emergence of *tzu jan* or "self-so-ness" (Chang, 1963). In self-so-ness, all things are revealed as unique, spontaneous, and natural. The leader and other participants do not see others in terms of how they can help them to improve themselves but in terms of their self-so-ness—their uniqueness and ability to contribute spontaneously. A therapist who values self-so-ness does not check his or her responses against an internalized picture of an "ideal" therapist, and members who learn to appreciate the potential for self-so-ness in their group do not strive to be ideal participants. Uncultivated honesty and openness can then be incorporated into the group atmosphere as healing factors.

Wu-wei is a concept that derives from Taoists' belief that the human experience of freedom arises from the experiential awareness that nature itself is intrinsically free. *Wu-wei* reflects the understanding that freedom is found through learning from and cooperating with it. The principle of freedom within nature represents a "playful freedom beyond human, or even humane, bounds" (Girardot, 1983, p. 269). This freedom is the simultaneously ordered and chaotic movement of nature, of life, and of the universe—a movement that ultimately cannot be constrained by human thought, morals, or imposed values. The group leader who values *wu-wei* believes that members will gain from experiencing themselves precisely as they are and by meeting life exactly as it is. A group therapy experience is not meant to be contrived; it is one that often tests the ability to remain aware as members increasingly come in contact with the reality of who others are.

The sage figure of early Taoism was humorously pictured as muddled, chaotic, and even useless to the world of society (Girardot, 1983). The sage was a leader who did not contend with others and who was not invested in demonstrating power or superiority. People might not be aware of the leadership that the sage was actually demonstrating because the actions of the sage did not necessarily meet social expectations for charisma and authority. If a female group leader is practicing *wu-wei,* she is likely to affect her group constructively without necessarily being seen as impressive. If she is able to be present and aware within the flux of interactions in an unstructured group, her presence itself will affect the process of the group and the quality of communication there. Members will then be likely to notice that their presence also influences their group's process.

Learning from Differences

Members may feel confused, hurt, or resentful because they have different expectations about being together. For example, individuals tend to differ in their perceptions of comfortable or necessary levels of disclosure, empathy, and support. Participants may find that they have differing wishes and hopes. One individual may hope to experience closeness with others, another member may want to learn how to develop a cognitive understanding of relationship issues, and another member may want to relate more assertively to others. Such varying interests and directions can conflict.

At some point in their group process, often during the phase of mutuality, members tend to realize that they have created norms that influence the quality and direction of their communication (Napier & Gershenfeld, 1987; Vander Kolk, 1985). This recognition can lead to questions concerning what members want from their group. If members have different ideas about central values related to group participation, power struggles can develop. For example, people who want to take risks in revealing their feelings may experience conflict with members who find this risk taking uncomfortable, uninteresting, or threatening.

If members desire to create a shared and meaningful experience, they will need to learn how to work with each other to meet each other's needs and desires. Members will sometimes learn to compromise with each other. To negotiate differences requires learning how to listen to one another, to respect others' needs and wishes, and to hear what is being asked for. This learning may then be applied to relationships outside the group in which participants have differing needs, wants, perceptions, and values.

If members examine their reactions to each other, they often find that their authentic wishes and needs are incongruent with their assumptions regarding how a person should behave with others. Because members have different assumptions, they can help each other to examine their reactions from different perspectives. If members draw on the resources available in their group, they often find that rich learning is possible due to the variety of life experiences and perspectives that members bring. Integration of feedback from different sources requires that members learn to rely on their own awareness of events. If others are perceived as contributing meaningfully through their presence and their sharing of perceptions, members may develop confidence in their group's process.

As members learn that they can accept their group's process as a resource for learning, they gain an acceptance for different modes of being. For example, some participants may become more accepting of events and relationships in their lives because of their group participation, whereas others may decide to make radical changes in their life-styles or relationships. As members learn from each other's perceptions and modes of relationship, they become involved in encounters that influence each other in ways that would have been difficult to predict. By reacting to the unexpected, members can learn about aspects of themselves that were previously hidden or unknown.

For example, during a workshop conducted by one of the authors with university students, a woman named "Janet" revealed that she had had an affair with someone who was not her husband; she had not told her husband or anyone else about having this affair. She discussed her affair at length during this group and the reasons that it had occurred. Janet expressed her guilt about what had happened and explored different ways she might deal with it. When Janet discussed her affair, several of the other group members were able to empathize with Janet even though they initially expressed strong disapproval about what had occurred. These members were able to become more tolerant toward people who have had an affair because they sympathized with Janet's specific situation.

Friendships and Romantic Involvements

Through empathic engagement with others, members develop connections that may deepen into caring and friendship. In ongoing unstructured therapy groups, members may decide to extend the intimacy and contact of their relationship by meeting outside the group. They may then face ethical dilemmas, the basis of which is that participation with others *in* their group may be influenced by relationships with certain members *outside* the group.

Some theorists have taken the position that members should not have relationships with each other outside of their group (Bion, 1959; Yalom, 1975). Other theorists, such as Perls (Shepard, 1975) and Rogers (1970), do not discourage these because feelings of closeness and bonding can often arise naturally and can often be a source of growth for clients. Members of ongoing therapy groups may decide to meet each other outside to extend their ability to provide friendship and mutual support. This decision is often an indication that members have moved from experiencing themselves as observers to seeing themselves as authentic participants in each other's lives. This form of meeting can be a way to extend the development of relationships that begin when they are together within a group.

At other times, these relationships may represent expressions of anxiety about initiating involvement with "strangers." If a group's cohesion leads members to perceive outsiders as untrustworthy or unapproachable, it may be fostering an unhealthy form of dependency. If two members foster their mutual dependency, their involvement outside their group may negatively affect their relationship with others in their group. They may form a separate subgroup that interrupts or distracts from the development of contact between others. Members can grow by exploring their feelings of anxiety and mistrust and by accepting responsibility for learning how to bring into their group aspects of an external relationship that is affecting other members.

Another drawback of these kinds of relationships can be that certain members can feel excluded. A member who becomes aware that others meet for coffee or a movie may feel inadequate or hurt because he or she has been left out. Members are likely to feel uncomfortable about raising these kinds of issues in their group because excluded individuals hesitate to trust others with their feelings of isolation, loneliness, and rejection. Members may also be concerned that others will feel pity or will extend themselves simply to appear "fair." Participants may also want to avoid disrupting an illusion of togetherness that has become a shared assumption.

The issues of freedom and responsibility are likely to become a focus for a group that is dealing with subgroups. Members may question whether their freedom should mean that they are free to focus attention on those about whom they most care and to spend less time and attention on those in whom they are not interested. If participants are willing to address these issues, they may learn something new about the feelings of those who experience themselves as separated observers. Dealing with such issues exposes awareness of the operation of love, power, and justice in their group. Members can then address whether each person is simply responsible for self and her or his own participation or whether each is responsible to extend opportunities to those who feel they have been separated. People can move from thinking of responsibility as a function of isolated and autonomous selves to perceiving themselves as having interconnected responsibilities (McClure, 1990; O'Hara, 1984).

Additionally, those who feel separated from others can be

helped to look at how they have influenced others and contributed to events. They may be able to see that they have in some instances moved toward a distanced perspective through choices that altered their responses and interaction. Members who have formed subgroups can be helped to look at how their decision to form exclusive groupings has affected others.

Members are often able to maintain supportive relationships outside that do not impinge negatively on their group. To suggest that they avoid such relationships would compartmentalize lives and would separate the integration of love, power, and justice within the group from relational dynamics outside of it. Learning can be more comprehensive if members recognize that no separation exists between the relational processes they explore in their group and those in life outside the group.

Typically, members do not choose to pursue friendships outside the group with other participants because they value a chance to explore feelings and awareness with individuals who do not play other roles in their lives. If friendly supportive relationships grow between certain members, other members usually understand their value and can learn from their growth. Members involved in friendships outside their group are likely to communicate with others in such a manner that others do not feel excluded. Of course, some participants may feel annoyed if two members frequently use group time to discuss issues between them outside the group. This kind of conflict can be explored like any other conflict involving subgroups and can lead to greater learning about love, power, and justice.

Members of unstructured therapy groups sometimes become romantically involved. This involvement can develop from a sexual or romantic attraction experienced in the group or from a friendship outside the group that becomes a sexual or romantic relationship. A romantic linking between members can raise concerns that are similar to those surrounding the development of an external friendship. However, with sexual and romantic involvement, the emotionalism associated with these concerns is often intensified. As other members become aware of this sexual activity, interactions are likely to be altered. If some participants see their group as a family, they may experience feelings related to incestuous themes in their

family of origin. Other members may be jealous. Still other members may have questions about the dynamics between these two
people. If a romantic dyad becomes the center of emotion and attention in a group, some participants may feel left out. A romantically
linked couple that has problems may want to use their group to help
them work these out. Other participants may feel that this use of the
resources of the group is not fair to those who want to explore their
own issues and problems.

Although a group's leader will probably find it impossible
to prevent romantic and sexual involvement between members, he
or she would obviously be making a mistake to encourage the development of such relationships or to encourage extended work on
these in the group. Other members are likely to perceive the leader
as misusing her or his position of authority if this occurs. The
leader can assist her or his group by facilitating discussions of how
a romantically involved couple is influencing the group, if an impact is observed. Members can grow by assuming responsibility for
working through the various emotions and misgivings that may be
stirred up by the development of a romance between members. Although such romances or sexual liaisons can be disruptive for a
group, these situations also can provide a focus for learning about
interpersonal justice. Any aspect of individual and relational experience can be grist for the mill of awareness if participants use their
group as a vehicle to enhance learning.

The Extension of New Learning

Members of unstructured therapy groups learn vicariously and
through direct experience (Yalom, 1975). As an ongoing therapy
group develops and when members terminate their involvement,
they are faced with the question of how to apply what they have
learned. If participants have experienced a new integration of the
dynamics of love, power, and justice, this learning may be perceived
as potentially altering their future process of being with others. If
members have moved toward enhanced responsibility, increased
empowerment, and a more integrated mode of relationship, we
might even assume that a dramatic change in a particular life
should be observable as a direct result of his or her participation in

a therapeutic group. Dramatic observable changes in outside relationships are not always appropriate criteria for evaluating the
significance of a group experience, of course. Participants may
change overtly, or they may move toward more satisfying forms of
relationship as they alter their perceptions and interpretations without creating any obvious forms of change. In any event, members
often learn that their own recognition of responsibility is a central
factor in guiding changes within their relationships (Perls, 1969;
Yalom, 1975). Members may feel more satisfaction, value, and
meaning within an existing relationship as they perceive themselves
more fully as responsible cocreators in that relationship.

Freedom as a grounding for life experience and for the creation of relationships would be negated by proposing that members
should have improved relationships or are *expected* to experience
certain predictable alterations in dynamics. The specification of
changes identified as beneficial for members or the suggestion that
these are causally produced by participation in a therapeutic group
would undermine members' own awareness and potential for creative justice. Participants can determine directions for growth that
are meaningful for them, directions that are appropriate to changing circumstances within their unique life circumstances. The
manner in which new knowledge is extended is a personal choice
made by a member within that person's experience of sometimes
unpredictable events and encounters.

Some members benefit from therapy groups by developing a
greater willingness to initiate and experience change whereas others
profit from their greater acceptance of themselves and others as they
are. Members tend to vary greatly in their perceptions of what can
and should be changed versus what can and should be accepted.
Some participants learn that they have the courage to create changes
in situations that they perceive as having existed far too long in a
static form. They may make decisions to develop new interests,
initiate new relationships, work on their physical well-being, pursue risks in careers, or develop unused talents. Others may learn that
they were in a rush to alter something because they were unwilling
to accept what they were experiencing. For example, a person who
has been sexually abused may work in a therapeutic group to acknowledge this reality and accept associated feelings and percep-

tions. She or he may then learn that perfectionistic attempts to change self were a form of denial toward feelings of anger and hurt. By doing *less* to change self, this member may experience greater happiness and fulfillment.

Persons' abilities to identify directions, make choices, define self, and construct forms for relationship are directly a function of awareness. Although enhancement of awareness is a major source of growth that can arise from participation in unstructured therapy groups, it can lead to new struggles and anxiety as well as new confidence and initiative. Awareness is analogous in some ways to eyesight. We use vision as a metaphor for awareness in statements such as "I see what you mean" or "I had a sudden insight." Vision can bring both joy or pain and can reveal beauty or ugliness. Members in a group may enthusiastically extend new knowledge about strengths and abilities. However, they may experience anxiety as they continue to deal with new perceptions of their limitations or blind spots. They may have gained new awareness of beauty, but they may also have encountered ugly aspects of their experience that they had previously been successful in denying. The fruits of new awareness may be immediately apparent through decisions and actions, or new awareness may take time to process and be enacted.

Exploration of perceptions and feelings that bring pain or discomfort can eventually lead to changes that enhance self-acceptance and interpersonal effectiveness (Perls, Hefferline & Goodman, 1951/1980; Rogers, 1951; Yalom, 1975). A person may become more effective personally and interpersonally by becoming more aware. At the same time, becoming more aware may bring a loss of certain illusions and beliefs that were comforting and reassuring at the same time that they limited full acceptance and effectiveness. Individuals tend to perceive their losses of illusions of security as irrevocable. New options may appear but the very perception of these may destroy former perceptions of certainty.

The unstructured nature of these therapy groups allows members the freedom to move in directions that arise spontaneously through the process of interacting. Members can learn to trust the process of spontaneous interactions between people, which is also an important element in establishing friendships and intimate relationships. The lack of a predetermined or universal goal for learning in these groups makes it necessary for members to cooperate in establishing norms and directions. Participants therefore have opportunities to learn about many aspects of social situations, including initiation of social interaction, use of various modes of communication, the reaching of agreements and compromises, ambiguity and uncertainty, cooperative decision-making processes, value formation, conformity, independence, dependence, interdependence, acceptance, and mutual responsibility.

Members' sense of renewal and empowerment has an experiential reality that is unique for each person. The uniqueness of each individual and the subjectivity involved in interpreting events leads many researchers to prefer members' self-reports as evidence of effectively therapeutic group work (Vander Kolk, 1985). Of course, self-reports may be slanted toward socially desirable responses or wishful thinking. Individuals may also vary in their perceptions, in their use of language, and in the degree to which the immediate impact of a group continues to make an impact over time. Members' renewal and empowerment occur through attending to others and involving themselves with them. Self-conscious focusing on how to renew and empower oneself can be less useful than an emphasis on participation in relationship that includes listening, giving, and accepting (see Tillich, 1954; Yalom, 1980).

Members are most likely to generalize changes in relationship dynamics that they have established in their group if these changes have led to an experience that is perceived as rich and to communication that is viewed as involving. Experiences of fulfillment, meaningfulness, and beauty serve as reinforcers that induce people to maintain newly established patterns of love, power, and justice and to extend these to other situations. The ideal situation in group therapy is therefore for members to have a shared experience that is fulfilling or one in which they recognize that beauty and joy can evolve through participation in the process of human interaction.

There can be, of course, no guarantee that members will have such an experience. Self-conscious attempts to create a sense of fulfillment are likely (paradoxically) to destroy the possibility that it will occur because it usually arises spontaneously at times when attention is not focused on oneself (Frankl, 1963, 1969; Maslow, 1962, 1964; Yalom, 1980). Additionally, aiming toward one's own happiness decreases the ability simply to listen to others with open-ness. This kind of listening is necessary as a prerequisite for experiences of genuine interpersonal communion. Therapy groups aim toward relationship dynamics that make possible such experiences.

These groups can also assist people to find meaning in shar-ing feelings of hurt or sorrow. The experience of sharing difficult or painful experiences with people who hear and are accepting has its own kind of beauty. Members can extend this learning by allow-ing themselves to be more fully present with others, regardless of the kinds of feelings being expressed.

Ethics and Responsibility

If unstructured therapy groups address and promote responsibility, awareness, freedom, creativity, power, justice, and love, they also reflect ethical considerations. These groups promote an ethic that encourages perceptions of freedom and personal power; that recog-nizes individuals as unique and as potentially just and responsible; and that values the ability of human beings to create beauty and love in their interactions.

The ethics that underlie unstructured therapy groups cannot be fully actualized unless members can own these ethics. Of course, the leader of an unstructured therapy group does not attempt orally to instruct members in the appropriate ethics for human interac-tions in groups. The leader should embody these ethics in his or her interpersonal behaviors in the group and can hope to impart them in this way. The leader certainly does not suggest that anyone im-itate her or his behavior.

Therapy develops through the power of the group process to draw from members their abilities to create just forms of relation-ship and to learn from each other as movement toward integrated relationships occurs. The leader may often voice a perspective on what is occurring in the group's process or may ask others to notice what is going on. This emphasis on interpersonal process repre-sents a kind of faith that if people become aware of what is trans-piring between them, they can then move toward creatively just modes of interaction. Without at least some belief in the creative potential of individuals, there would be no purpose in conducting unstructured therapy groups.

Individual's creative potential is stifled if the group takes responsibility for the individual. In such groups, the collective reality functions as an entity that controls each member's individual reality. The collective reality necessarily maintains itself by constructing a rigidly hierarchical power structure in which individual responsibility and awareness are minimized. In fact, they can be viewed as a threat to the collective reality. Of course, this dynamic becomes active in any system that uses authoritarian measures to enforce obedience to collectively assumed beliefs.

Every human group makes ethical decisions concerning the value that is given to self-determination or conformity, the merit of a judgmental versus a more accepting atmosphere, and the value of trusting and accepting oneself and one's feelings versus mistrusting oneself and accepting the group's right to dictate. Each therapist and each group member who intends to behave therapeutically would benefit from clarifying her or his awareness of values that relate to freedom, autonomy, interdependence, and issues of individual and collective responsibility. These values are implied by the very enterprise of group therapy, and their form is inevitably communicated and constructed during therapy.

Group norms can be established that subtly or overtly value conformity as a necessary price for admission to membership. Because many social groups directly require that members adhere to behavioral and attitudinal norms, the tendency for therapy groups to create pressure to conform is understandable. To some extent, a degree of pressure toward conformity occurs in any group.

The purpose of unstructured therapy groups is not to eliminate any pressure toward conformity but to allow sufficient freedom for members to experiment creatively within group norms and consciously to participate in the construction of these. The group leader's initial attitudes about the desirability of conformity influence the development of a group's interpersonal process. For example, if a leader verbally or nonverbally strongly communicates the importance of establishing certain norms, members may agree because of their social conditioning. If, however, they have a strong negative reaction to their leader, they may act in ways that contradict the leader's norms.

Members of long-term groups can themselves promote conformity by creating norms that maintain the experience of being an "in-group." An in-group environment allows members to feel special in some way and to gain an identity based on thinking alike and being a part of the whole (Bacal, 1985). Although a leader may not have intended to construct this kind of norm, an in-group atmosphere would be difficult for members to maintain without her or his collusion. In-group status is diminished by anyone who brings attention to differences between members and notices similarities between those inside the group and those outside. Supporting conformity and adherence to in-group identities can lead to stagnation, to limitations placed on self-exploration, and to the maintenance of relationship patterns based on insecurity rather than personal power.

The unstructured group therapist who values the integration of love, power, and justice is likely to view group pressure and the promotion of conformity as generally counterproductive forms of interaction. Nonetheless, a certain degree of conformity is necessary and desirable. Freedom does not occur because people have no limits but because they define limits in ways that allow the development of creativity (May, 1981). The group as a whole and the individual always influence each other's norms and always maintain some degree of tension due to the testing that occurs between one perspective and the other.

The ethics that underlie unstructured therapy reflect respect for the feelings of individuals and their own ability to know how to best approach and express these feelings. On the one hand, maneuvers that assist members to deny their feelings or to invalidate their own perceptions of their experience are therefore unethical. On the other, techniques that create pressure to expose feelings can also be unethical. Members can be harmed if others insist that they interpret their experiences in a particular manner or if others demand a certain degree of self-exposure (Korda & Pancrazio, 1989). This kind of insistence can recapitulate a pattern of injustice that has previously led people to develop imbalanced patterns of relationship. If a group is functioning ethically, members are viewed as responsible for constructing and revealing (or choosing not to reveal) their perceptions, reactions, and feelings within group process. Participants are free to explore whatever past and present experiences are perceived as important by each individual.

Therapist Responsibility and Ethical Guidelines

Ethical guidelines have been established by the American Psychological Association (1990) and the American Counseling Association (formerly American Association for Counseling and Development, 1988); specific guidelines for group counseling have also been established by the Association for Specialists in Group Work (1989). All of these indicate the essential importance of valuing clients as persons and understanding what will benefit and what will harm them. The spirit behind these guidelines indicates that the therapist's own awareness is an indispensable factor for determining appropriate actions in ambiguous situations. Although guidelines attempt to prescribe and proscribe certain actions in well-defined situations, they cannot successfully serve as a substitute for therapists' own judgments and awareness of contexts within which actions are taken.

As indicated by these guidelines, therapists should beware of potentials for their misuse of power to manipulate clients, who can be hurt or disillusioned or whose self-esteem can be damaged. Clients are often suffering because of the long-term effect of imbalanced love, power, and justice in relationships. Therapy may be viewed with some hope by these clients as an opportunity to experience how a healthy or caring relationship can unfold. If a therapist uses a position of power to manipulate clients, she or he may be confirming their worst expectations about the nature of human relationships. In a worst-case scenario, clients may give up any hope of reaching a harmonious integration of love, power, and justice in human relationships. Such people may drop out of therapy permanently, may judge themselves unworthy of a caring relationship, or may even give up their belief that life is worth living.

Clients who have adjusted to imbalanced love, power, and justice in relationships are likely to reinstate these dynamics by attempting to manipulate their therapist (or other members) or may unconsciously encourage the therapist (or others) to manipulate them. This enactment of imbalanced ontological dynamics can occur through actions that are controlling, self-deprecating, domineering, antagonistic, demeaning, or seductive. Members may also pose as more weak and helpless than they really feel to get others to play the role of helper and caretaker. The efficacious group leader will recognize such games and avoid repeating the distorted forms of relationship that may have previously harmed clients. The leader and other members can learn to trust their intuitive responses to others in a group if a safe atmosphere for communication and exploration is developed. This trust in one's own perceptions is necessary to differentiate between the genuine desire for help and manipulative role playing, and between authentic distress and attention seeking.

No code or guideline can guard against all the subtle ways in which power can be misused (Kitchener & Harding, 1990). At the same time, if a therapist (or other participant) becomes too cautious and careful about using power and influence, she or he may repress those spontaneous responses to situations that are most valuable therapeutically (Polster & Polster, 1973). This kind of overconcern can also lead to a constrained approach to relationships in which therapists withhold themselves from others and are unable to model freedom (Cain, 1989). Members learn the importance of ethical behavior experientially, by becoming aware of the consequences of their patterns of behavior as they interact with others in their group.

The experience of caring about and respecting others is basic to genuinely ethical behavior. Without this experience, no guidelines will suffice to direct a therapist toward effective group leadership, nor will members learn what it means to interact with others beneficially. If a group leader is capable of care and respect, he or she will be able to deal with interpersonal conflicts that arise during a group, even if their solution cannot be clearly defined by the broad recommendations of codes and guidelines.

A fine line sometimes seems to separate constructive and destructive aspects of human relationships. For example, therapists or members may sometimes be unclear whether an interaction represents a personal attack that is unnecessarily hurtful or whether the pain of this confrontation can lead to empowerment and increased awareness for the parties involved. This question can best be answered by a person who is involved in a relationship with those concerned. A group leader may be called on to assess whether members are using personal power to undermine the confidence of those who are weaker and to evaluate whether a participant is behaving in a self-aggrandizing or sadistic manner (Gans, 1989). The integration (or lack thereof) among the elements of love, power, and justice can be intuitively sensed by a person who is attuned with empathy with others in a group.

Assessment of the dynamics of relationships can be useful for dealing with members involved in potential or present ethical problems, such as how to deal with those who breach confidentiality. At other times, a leader may feel that he or she should breach confidentiality due to threats a client has made to harm self or others. Although guidelines address the issue of confidentiality, in some situations no clearly defined laws pertain. Therapists will then have to weigh for themselves how to resolve ethical commitments to the group as a whole versus the needs of one member or to the larger society versus one individual. Therapists vary in their responses to ethical dilemmas. Evidence suggests that individual awareness, perceptions of threat, settings for group practice, and theoretical training all influence therapists' responses to confidentiality dilemmas (Roback, Purdon, Ochoa & Bloch, 1992).

Other ethical dilemmas can arise as group leaders meet with unexpected emotional pressure and confrontation, sometimes including the potential for threats of violence (Gans, 1989; Korda & Pancrazio, 1989). In most cases, members respect each other's integrity and are able to concur early in the group process on the ethical standards that they will agree to uphold. A leader may assist participants to develop a consensus agreement on ground rules as part of their group's process and may also promote an ethic that allows members flexibility as interpersonal situations change. Therapists' awareness of ongoing interpersonal dynamics is essential for helping members to deal flexibly with ethical concerns and for evaluating options for responding to these dilemmas if they arise.

If a leader demonstrates an attitude of commitment and investment in the process of therapy, members generally sense this attitude and respect it. Members are more likely to experience group therapy as effective if they perceive their leader as caring and as willing to help them make sense out of interpersonal events (Yalom, 1975). Interactions between members are influenced by a leader's ability to convey respect in her or his communications and an awareness of the needs and feelings of others. Thus, the leader's responsibility for behaving and communicating ethically can be clarified if ethics are viewed as values based on awareness of and respect for each member's humanity and potential for wholeness.

Leaders and members share responsibility for supporting an atmosphere that encourages ethical interactions. The role of leader obviously involves social and professional expectations for ethical behavior. What is more important, the leader's commitment to an ethical process of therapy will be reflected in his or her support and enhancement of the element of justice throughout interactions with members. Group members come to appreciate the importance of just interactions as they experientially learn about the rewards of forming an ethical interpersonal dynamic.

Creative Justice and Ethical Relationships

Creative justice uses awareness within the experience of freedom as the basis for ethical choices in ongoing interactions. Members who choose to participate in unstructured therapy groups and who are aware of their nature are likely to place some intuitive value on the ethical implications of creative justice. These include valuing personal responsibility, individual awareness, and freedom. However, a person who does not attend voluntarily or who does not know what therapy groups are like may experience incongruence between personal values and the values that tend to become prominent in an unstructured setting. Even individuals who attend voluntarily may find that their value system has been challenged or threatened by the norms adopted by others or their group as a whole.

The unstructured group therapist is well advised, if possible, to conduct groups wherein participation is voluntary. Clients are more likely to engage in productive and meaningful work in that event (Patterson, 1985). If members have the option of participating or not participating, a therapist's advocacy of an ethic based on personal responsibility will support the group's initial organization and ground rules. Group members whose participation is voluntary are also more likely to respect concerns of confidentiality than those who are forced to attend.

A therapist's perception of responsibility based on an ethic of creative justice can sometimes place him or her in a confrontational position with respect to other group members. This kind of challenge can occur if a leader decides to bring to members' attention his or her perceptions and feelings about dynamics in the group, particularly if unjust attitudes are regulating an encounter. For example, members may decide that they want to expel a participant who has broken confidentiality for the first time. If the leader reviews events and points out the value of extending acceptance, members may change their decision. A group leader might also insist on the importance of allowing participants to learn from mistakes. Of course, if someone repeatedly breaks confidentiality, that person's intention to participate on an equal basis with others can be questioned. Awareness of creative justice could lead members to acknowledge their own wishes to feel approved of and to examine how repeated breaches of confidentiality can create an atmosphere of mistrust that interferes with acceptance.

Ethical guidelines warn therapists to be aware of situations in which dual roles (for example, friend and therapist) interfere with efficacious therapy (American Association for Counseling and Development, 1988; American Psychological Association, 1990; Association for Specialists in Group Work, 1989). Dual role relationships interfere if therapists are unaware of, or deny the impact of, their implicit power over clients. Because they often seek assistance from therapists and counselors at times in their lives when they feel vulnerable, clients may be seeking to be influenced through the therapeutic relationship. Therapists therefore need to be aware of how they are influencing clients and must be clear about the intentions that direct this therapeutic influence.

An ethic based on creative justice leads therapists to view clients as persons who deserve to be heard and accepted and who can potentially move toward I-thou forms of relationship. A therapist who sees a client as a source of gratification runs the risk of using an I-it form of relationship in which she or he is manipulated into meeting needs of the therapist. Therapists, of course, can appropriately feel happy or satisfied by successful work with clients. However, this happiness or satisfaction is therapeutic only if movement toward an I-thou direction in relatedness is concomitant.

Therapists who lack awareness of themselves in relation to clients may also allow themselves to be manipulated into a relationship that blurs boundaries between therapy and romance or other forms of intense attraction. Both clients and therapists may use therapy to express seductiveness or destructive manipulations that were the basis of hurtful previous relationships. Clients cannot be expected to avoid I-it forms of relationship, because these forms of relationship are often the reason that clients seek therapy and counseling. However, a therapist can be expected not to exacerbate I-it patterns by reinforcing and extending them.

The implicit power dynamics involved in the role of therapist can be misused to promote one-sided forms of confrontation. These dynamics can also be misused if therapists favor or single out certain group members over others. For example, a group leader may speak in a more supportive way, may take on a seductive demeanor, or may communicate in subtly demeaning or critical ways to particular members. Cultural stereotypes about gender roles or ethnic groups may also play a part in unfair communication patterns.

These unjust patterns of communication are often not conscious; therapists, like most people, want to think of themselves as fair minded and helpful. A participant who notices unjust interpersonal patterns in a therapist's relations with members may hesitate to bring this subject to the group's attention. If the member is perceiving imbalanced interpersonal dynamics, he or she may appropriately fear being rebuffed, discredited, or even attacked by others.

Members generally see their therapist as a presence whose impact on group dynamics is noticeable. They therefore usually want to be liked and supported by their leader and tend to be less directly confronting toward him or her than toward other members (Napier & Gershenfeld, 1987; Yalom, 1975). A group leader who values creative justice will encourage honesty and open disclosure. The atmosphere that evolves from this movement allows the maximum potential for group members to use interactions to enhance awareness. If members notice specific patterns of attraction or antagonism between certain participants, including the therapist, this awareness can then be used productively. Members can then explore how they handle feelings of attraction and anger, how they deal with wanting to be seen as attractive, how they deal with resentment or jealousy toward others, how sexual and romantic feelings influence relationships, and so on.

As members move toward openness in their interactions, they increasingly experience the freedom to examine the dynamics that influence justice in relationships. This examination of the dynamics of justice does not usually focus on attempts to arrive at an intellectual formulation of a moral code of behavior. In therapeutic group settings, members usually reveal how issues of justice affect them on emotional levels of experience. Much of the unfinished business that members confront involves feelings of hurt and anger associated with treatment from others (or life) that was perceived as unfair. Many of the interpersonal events in their group upon which members focus have to do with observing when someone was treated unjustly or learning how to treat each other more fairly (for example, moving toward mutual respect and consideration).

The most powerful impact of a therapy group can occur (1) if the ethical foundation established and promoted by the leader is congruent with that person's own pattern of relationship in therapy; (2) if this ethical basis for interaction encourages members to assume responsibility for affecting the movement of their group; (3) if such a framework is consistent with ethical standards in counseling, psychology, and other associated professions; and (4) if these ethics consistently support and encourage those group dynamics that serve to promote the movement of members toward new learning, enhanced awareness, constructive interpersonal relationships, and the possibility of greater fulfillment in life. Ethics based on creative justice can create a foundation for increasing group members' awareness of differences as well as similarities, experiential learning of responsibility, and growth in an atmosphere of freedom that they construct.

Chapter Eight

Application of Theory

The theory of group therapy that we have presented in this book is intended to provide a basis for conceptualizing and directing therapeutic work. The ideas that we have investigated are applicable to therapeutic groups and indeed to any situation that requires an understanding of relationship dynamics.

Dimensions of a Viable Group Theory

Lieberman, Lakin, and Whitaker (1969) assert that a viable theory of group therapy should meet seven criteria. These can be used to review the theoretical constructs presented in this text. The first of these criteria is that the psychology of group membership needs to be presented from the perspective of the group member.

    The psychological aspects of group membership that we have presented as influencing and being affected by members' perceptions concern (1) presentation of and work on personal problems, (2) the giving and receiving of feedback related to relationships with others who are present, (3) self-actualization within an interpersonal field,

(4) choices to move toward awareness of freedom and responsibility, and (5) participation in the dynamics of love, power, and justice in group relationships. The perspectives of group members affect and are affected by an interpersonal atmosphere that influences who participants become within their relationships with one another. Members' perceptions are the basis for creating directions for interpersonal exploration and development. Members' perceptions of themselves being with others can be used to promote recognition of interbeing and interdependence.

The second criterion for a viable group theory, according to Lieberman, Lakin, and Whitaker (1969), is the provision of an explanation for the function and significance of the therapist's role. We have described the therapist's role in an unstructured setting as influenced by his or her organization and presentation of the group, by his or her theoretical understanding and concerns, by personally and socially influenced ethical responsibilities, by expectations that are held by members, by the institution (if any) that provides the therapeutic setting, and by the larger society and culture. Leadership functions of the therapist are involved in the setting of time limits, selection of members, and establishment of fundamental ethical ground rules. We have shown that this role needs to be integrated with nonrole requirements of group participation. These requirements are ontological in nature and derive from being with other persons, constructing a dialogue, and extending self to include others. The effective therapist can integrate requirements of a role with personal openness and interpersonal presence.

The third criterion proposed by Lieberman, Lakin, and Whitaker (1969) is that the major regulatory factors that affect members— that is, the norms and standards of the group—need to be explained. We have described how group members develop norms and how this development can be influenced by members' perceptions of the values and expectations of the leader and by their own expectations, hopes, demands, and values. If members recognize their mutual responsibility to create norms that express awareness of relationship, they can move from norms that are restrictive to ones based on creative justice.

Norms can support or inhibit members' movements toward creative justice. This understanding of norms permits us to address

the fourth criterion of Lieberman, Lakin, and Whitaker: an explanation of how a group develops into a therapeutic rather than nontherapeutic force. The norms and interpersonal dynamics of therapeutic
group extend acceptance to those who are estranged, enable members
to experience their own power and responsibility more and more,
and increasingly facilitate members' growth through explorations of
self being with others. Participants in an effective therapeutic group
recognize and encourage each other's choices to move toward more
open and comprehensive awareness of self and others. Members use
awareness to integrate ongoing dynamics of love, power, and justice
if they recognize their mutual responsibility to create themes and
meaningful directions. Members can be increasingly open to and can
integrate affective, cognitive, behavioral, and intuitive aspects of being. The development of an integrated ontological dynamic requires
the leader along with other members to be able to listen and hear,
to accept, to be aware, to form directions, to respond honestly and
appropriately, and to interact spontaneously.

The fifth criterion for a viable theory of group therapy is an
examination of changes that occur because of members' participation (Lieberman, Lakin, and Whitaker, 1969). We have indicated
that although many potential benefits can be associated with participation in an unstructured therapy group, the therapy process
tends to frustrate efforts to predict exactly what form these will take.
Additionally, as a group progresses, personal and interpersonal
awareness changes. Thus, during various phases, members may alter their perceptions of needs or wants.

The unique and changing perspectives of participants influence their use of group interactions, their interpretations of interactions, and their integration of experiences. The positive changes
that members experience derive from participation in a mutually
created healing dynamic. This dynamic is based on interactions
wherein members experience love without sacrificing personal
power and wherein a form of justice is created through which participants can express awareness and creative abilities. Additionally,
therapeutic changes generally involve increased recognition of responsibility and increased acceptance of self and others. Changes in
a nontherapeutic direction can result from group interactions
wherein values and perspectives are imposed on others, members

move toward estrangement from their perceptions and interactions, and conformity is rewarded and interpersonal differences are disrespected. Nontherapeutic interactions usually stifle open exploration of experience and form barriers to the enhancement of intensity and extensity of awareness.

The sixth criterion for a viable theory is that it must account for how members generalize what they have learned from participation in a group to their lives outside the group (Lieberman, Lakin, and Whitaker, 1969). We have portrayed members as being responsible for deciding when and how to implement any new learning that may have occurred. Assumptions that members will or should have learned some type of predictable skill or perspective are inherently limited. Similarly, we have recommended caution about predicting how members will typically apply their learning to outside situations. Although participants in effective groups often report that they have changed the qualities of existing relationships or formed new ones, they usually do not perceive their group as having imposed expectations upon them that they "should" change in specific ways (Korda & Pancrazio, 1989). At the same time, members may have difficulties in an ongoing group if they feel that others expect them to report on their "progress" in a given relationship or situation. In our view, therapeutic groups are most beneficial if members perceive that their own perceptions and evaluations of situations form the basis for their decisions to change or accept circumstances or to explore new directions.

Lastly, Lieberman, Lakin, and Whitaker (1969) have stated that group therapy needs to be compared with other forms of treatment, such as behavior modification. We have not spent much time or space dwelling on comparisons with other forms of treatment because we believe that the reader will be able to make comparisons and draw his or her own conclusions from the observations and arguments we have presented. Different assumptions and goals are involved in those treatments that attempt to provide solutions to clients' problems (such as some behavioral and strategic approaches) as compared to treatments that focus on clients' abilities to enhance awareness and construct their own solutions. Moreover, the resources available and the process developed in a group setting create an atmosphere that differs from individual therapy. A major difference in emphasis results from the multiple perspectives and objectives that influence interpersonal process in group therapy settings. A similarity between these treatment settings is that both can assist recognition of responsibility.

Learning for Leadership

We have emphasized the experiential aspects of learning that are important for participants in a therapy group. This experiential emphasis is consistent with a recommendation that potential group leaders also experience group membership. A viable theory of unstructured group therapy does not substitute for experience but guides its initiation and assimilation. Firsthand experience and observation are a necessary basis for understanding how unstructured groups operate and what they can mean for participants. Conclusions developed from actual observation will be more convincing to practitioners than those developed from afar.

Prospective leaders can, of course, benefit from gaining familiarity with the theoretical issues and concerns that influence the organization and interpersonal process of therapeutic groups. However, leaders also need to develop clear awareness of their own experience with interpersonal process in unstructured situations. This awareness allows practitioners to develop and elaborate theories of therapy that can be unique (insofar as they connect with existing theory). Similarly, experienced group leaders can benefit by examination of their own life as a member and leader. Therapists can also profit from training that allows them to test their experiential learning against that of others and to gain an understanding of the perspectives of experienced group leaders about how their presence and manner of interaction alter group process.

Supervision can help therapists to learn how to notice the themes that evolve for members and for the group as a whole in an unstructured situation. Prospective or practicing group leaders can enhance their effectiveness by becoming more fully aware of how they are affecting the openness, content, and direction of other members' participation. Experienced therapists may seek consultation, supervision, and training on an ongoing basis to avoid complacency or stagnation. Supervision and training can stimulate self-observation, which helps to develop greater centeredness and responsibility. Observation by a competent peer, supervisor, or workshop leader tends to intensify self-observation and can provide new information about the effects of one's feelings and attitudes on group process (Korda & Pancrazio, 1989).

The relationship between a group leader and an effective consultant or supervisor is characterized by sufficiently integrated love, power, and justice to promote trust and self-exploration. Trust encourages self-disclosure, openness to constructive criticism, and willingness to risk new behaviors and approaches. A supervisor can create a double-binding situation for a therapist-trainee by instituting an unjust relationship pattern with the trainee while encouraging the trainee to develop integrated relationships with clients. The quality of a relationship between supervisor and trainee is as important to the learning of the latter as any of the verbal observations about a group process that are imparted by the supervisor (Yalom, 1975).

The Application of Unstructured Group Theory in Various Settings

The training received by a prospective leader of unstructured therapy groups can be applied to diverse settings. Such groups are widely appropriate because many settings seek to promote experiential learning about responsibility and balanced relationships. The nature of unstructured therapy varies in different environments because the central concerns of clients may change according to their backgrounds and problems, but the ontological processes of these groups retain a great deal of similarity. This similarity is evident in the universality of persons' wishes for acceptance, desires for personal power and efficacy, and hopes for just relationships.

Over time, the leader of unstructured groups in a particular setting may become familiar with the concerns that members tend to bring to groups. For example, disabled clients in a rehabilitation setting will usually have themes that are distinct from the concerns of emotionally disturbed adolescents. If the leader becomes familiar with certain themes, this familiarity is likely to facilitate his or her ability to notice and focus on specific issues. However, familiarity can also lead to false presuppositions about these themes. Therefore, an effective therapist can gather knowledge and expertise with a specific population but must maintain sufficient openness to recognize the uniqueness of each client's concerns.

Some therapists, due to personality characteristics or individual communication styles, may function more effectively in one setting than in another. Therapists may gravitate toward environments in which they are most comfortable or toward clients with whom they believe they work most effectively. However, therapists' personal and professional growth can be limited by restriction to a specific setting in which particular types of clients (for example, diagnostically or culturally similar clients) are treated in a similar manner. Therapists can challenge their own growth in awareness by seeking a degree of diversity in their work. Workshop or seminar activities can be used to augment learning for a therapist who feels financially or emotionally bound to a particular setting.

Common concerns of members that can be addressed and changed through unstructured group therapy are awareness of responsibility, recognition of patterns of relationship, movement from estrangement to acceptance of self and others, self-expression in social situations, and desire to enhance interpersonal effectiveness and perceptions of personal power. Unstructured therapy groups are environments wherein members can feel interpersonal acceptance leading to personal integration and to integration of self with others. Alienation is reduced by acceptance. Members may grow from experiencing trust or by coping with mistrust. Perceptions of personal power are enhanced through members' acknowledgment and working through of uncomfortable or unsettling experiences and of their anxiety in interpersonal relationships.

These generic problems that members commonly address in unstructured therapy groups never occur in the abstract and are always expressed as particular dynamics of relationships and self-perceptions. Thus, personal and interpersonal events form a context in which these generic kinds of problems take on specific configurations. Certain settings that provide unstructured therapy groups also contribute a context in which problems are expressed and relationships are formed. Settings may be oriented toward a certain population or certain types of presenting problems.

Adolescents and elderly people are two group that may receive unstructured group therapy in settings specifically oriented toward them (for example, see Kwiatkowski, 1987; Leszcz, 1990). The generic problems that we have discussed are likely to be linked to particular behavioral and social concerns that are typical of a given population. An adolescent's problem with responsibility and sense of alienation is likely to be linked specifically to a family environment and peers. These group participants' lack of a sense of personal power is associated with their lack of social and financial autonomy and status. They may be concerned with formation of attitudes toward authority and sexuality and may test these attitudes on a group leader (Kwiatkowski, 1987). Unstructured therapy groups for elderly clients tend to address ways in which perceptions of self have been damaged due to social or physical problems associated with aging (Kapur & Pearce, 1987). Many of these clients suffer from feelings of depression and age-related losses of close relationships (Kapur & Pearce, 1987). Members of these groups can provide mutual support and opportunities to invest in emotional connections. Leszcz (1990) asserts that generally the most successful approach to group therapy is an open one that allows members to draw what they need from their group.

Other specific populations to engage in unstructured group therapy include sex offenders (Aubrey & Dougher, 1990), other offenders (Zimpfer, 1992), and chemically dependent clients (Matano & Yalom, 1991). Each of these populations may receive treatment as a unique population for many reasons, including placements in institutional settings, legal and ethical obligations, and attraction of participants to particular groups. Therapists who become familiar with the concerns of specific populations may develop awareness of therapeutic approaches to responsibility issues that tend to accompany a specific problem or life phase. For example, adult offenders may benefit from learning that they can responsibly express intense emotion in a group setting (Zimpfer, 1992). Chemically dependent clients can gain by learning about their responsibilities for initiating actions that lead to problems in the present (Matano & Yalom, 1991).

Unstructured therapy groups may be conducted in college or university settings at counseling centers, mental health centers, or as experiential workshops for students who plan to work as therapists. If they are part of a university counseling center's services, these groups can be used to provide peer encouragement and support during times when students encounter problems with relationships, school, drugs or alcohol, or self-esteem. If unstructured groups are offered as workshops or seminars for students of counseling, members may discuss universal themes such as desires for support and encouragement or development of personal power. Issues that are of special interest to counseling students as a group or to particular individuals are also likely to arise.

In a prison setting, members of unstructured groups frequently address issues of self-esteem, emotional self-expression, and relatedness to others (Page, 1979; Page, Richmond & DeLaSerna, 1987). As participants develop themes in their interactions, they may emphasize such subjects as dealing with anger and coping with the violence that usually plays a significant role in prison life. Two issues that concern group leaders in a prison setting are whether participation should be voluntary and unrelated to institutional inducements and whether inmates who make incriminating disclosures in their groups should be protected by confidentiality. Although some authors (for example Patterson & Eisenberg, 1975) have advocated forced or rewarded participation in unstructured groups for inmates, this kind of participation generally undermines the principle of freedom and autonomy that is basic to effectiveness in these groups. Page (1980, 1981, 1983b, 1985) has conducted unstructured groups with inmates of correctional institutions; these groups were voluntary and involved no incentives (such as favorable reports to probation or parole boards). The advantages of voluntary participation are evident in the participants' degree of involvement and willingness to form nonmanipulative relationships and to reveal themselves. Voluntary participation can also become an issue for clients in mental health centers or drug rehabilitation programs if the court system is involved in the referral process.

Unstructured therapy groups can be useful in physical disability settings to give clients opportunities to discuss their feelings and concerns, those either related or unrelated to their disability

(Page, 1978). Psychological difficulties that often accompany physical disability are related to unexpected limitations, coping with
pain, changes in self-image and body image, and needs for emotional support. These individuals may also experience difficulties
coping with institutionally generated stress and with attitudes of
family members. Unstructured groups in these situations may be
useful as short-term therapy, but they can also be conducted on a
long-term basis that allows extended exploration of feelings, relationships, and problems. Successful unstructured therapy groups
have met weekly in a rehabilitation setting for as long as two years;
participants were thus able to work on relationship issues that developed and changed over relatively long periods of time (Page,
1978).

   Terminally ill patients may learn in these groups that they
can form empathic and supportive interpersonal relationships that
are mutually empowering (Leszcz, 1990). They may also come to
terms with their awareness of aging and death as inevitable processes. Unstructured therapy can be used to reach closure on unfinished business and to share present experiences. Human contact
that is honest and direct can be a deeply meaningful experience for
these clients.

   If a therapist forms an unstructured group in a private practice setting, he or she has control over who will be admitted. Therapists can then form groups with members of diverse backgrounds
and with somewhat different personal problems. Diversity can help
members to avoid certain potential pitfalls of group therapy, such
as the development of assumptions of sameness and feelings of being special and exclusivity (Wolf & Schwartz, 1962).

   Therapists who are comfortable conducting unstructured
groups (whether in community mental health, hospital, educational, or other settings) find that they are able to meet the needs
of many more clients than would be the case if they restricted themselves to individual therapy. These groups can be effective in encouraging awareness of responsibility and in experientially
validating and improving relationship skills and awareness. Unstructured groups can be useful for dealing with problems associated with self-acceptance, self-esteem, and relatedness to others.

Members also can create opportunities for examination of life-styles that are unnecessarily self-limiting and/or self-destructive.

Internal and External Frames of Reference

An institution in which a therapist practices may provide a frame of reference that is external but that still must be considered; this frame may undermine or invalidate the value system that under-lies unstructured group therapy. Institutions sometimes encourage groupthink and may oppose the therapist's own values. Institutions may lack confidence in these or may believe that certain other (per-haps contrasting) ones are important to the functioning of the institution.

For example, institutions often wish to encourage confor-mity and predictability in the behavior and attitudes of a popula-tion and therefore find that various forms of pressure and coercion are necessary. This use of pressure reflects an ethical system based on tributive justice, which is the rule rather than the exception in institutional settings.

As they apply their theory, group therapy practitioners often need to learn how their perspective integrated with the frames of reference of other professionals. For instance, a therapist who ad-vocates the promotion of awareness and responsibility may have to accommodate others in the institution who believe that clients' problems are completely biologically based and outside the realm of personal responsibility (Malano & Yalom, 1991).

Genetic heritage and neurophysiology certainly may influ-ence an individual's behavior and psychological problems. How-ever, these biological elements do not prevent an individual's movement toward integration in awareness and relationships. Awareness and responsibility function interdependently with phys-ical systems because the person exists as a meaningful whole. Mind and body are in conflict if individuals lack integrated awareness. Thus, mental and physical aspects of functioning can be considered as related dimensions of one process. The concerns of an unstruc-tured group therapist therefore do not necessarily have to conflict with concerns of professionals who investigate specifically biolog-ical aspects of functioning.

Another type of conflict can arise in penal institutions, where the administrators may believe that inmates are immoral and have lost their rights to autonomy, self-determination, and choice. A group leader may be required to report on the progress of group members to these authorities and may be aware that members are not given many opportunities to assume responsibility within the institution. To function as a therapist in such an institution requires an ability to reconcile a therapeutic frame of reference with a relatively authoritarian one. This reconciliation requires an awareness of interacting social systems and an ability to maintain an internal frame of reference even when communicating in a form demanded by an external perspective (see Page, 1981).

A therapist validates certain values simply by choosing to conduct an unstructured group. These values can be viewed as an internal frame of reference, in contrast to the external codes enforced by institutions. The effective application of a theory of group therapy to an actual situation (no matter how viable the theory may be) requires compatibility between these theoretical constructs and the therapist's own awareness and perceptions. If this compatibility does not exist, the therapist's own theory tends to function as an external frame of reference, superimposed upon experience. Ideally, a therapist can accept full responsibility of her or his theoretical stance, in which case the therapist's perceptual and theoretical frames of reference are not separate.

The frames of reference used by individual participants may differ from those of other members and those of their therapist. A leader who has also taken part in groups as a member can use this previous experience to develop a flexible perspective for leading groups and to understand certain difficult aspects of the role of participant, including how individuals may feel if they reveal something difficult or uncomfortable and how a group and a therapist can either facilitate or miss the direction in which a participant is moving.

Personal therapy in an individual or group setting can also help a group leader to become aware of aspects of self that have been outside conscious awareness. These unacknowledged aspects of self can and do influence group process. A therapist's awareness of self evolves in large part through relations with colleagues, friends, lovers, and family members. Personal integration is thus a function of responsibility and roles in many settings and relationships. The integration and sense of responsibility of the therapist affect choices concerning how to apply theory to specific events in the therapeutic setting and how to modify theory to accommodate ongoing events.

As we have seen, integration of theoretical knowledge with experiential knowledge gained in counseling situations assists a therapist to enhance his or her therapeutic effectiveness. However, a therapist lacking awareness and responsibility in relationships is likely to misapply theoretical constructs intended to facilitate these qualities; such a therapist is not usually able to conduct a group intended to assist others to recognize responsibility. In other words, therapists who compartmentalize awareness by keeping one internal frame of reference for relationships outside their work and another for relationships within their groups will not be able to assist members toward comprehensive and integrated awareness.

Political Implications of Therapeutic Practice

The integrated system that is a person includes chemistry, biology, perception, affect, cognition, action, and interactions in social systems and ecological systems. The person is more than a sum of subsystems. A person's unique individuality can only be partly understood by understanding the contexts and systems within which the person forms an identity and contributes behaviorally. Besides systems and subsystems, individuals are formed by their decisions, perceptions, values, and self-definitions.

We have seen how unstructured therapy groups encourage exploration of experience rather than validation of others' rules and predictions about who individuals can be and become. Thus, a therapist may challenge stereotypes that have defined individuals in certain ways, may question values provided by social institutions, or may experience value-oriented conflicts with the institution that provides the therapeutic setting for a group.

The idea that group members are capable of creatively authoring their own lives may conflict with the teachings of their religions or the patterns of relationship in their family. Institutions, organizations, and families may have an investment in maintaining some or all members in positions where they do not have personal power, do not perceive themselves as potentially powerful, and do not recognize their abilities for creativity and self-determination. Thus, the application of a theory of unstructured group therapy inevitably has political overtones.

For example, unstructured therapy groups are unlikely to be sponsored or recommended by a religious institution that encourages its members to view people as sinners, that expects members to unquestioningly accept religious injunctions as a matter of faith, and that reacts with suspicion toward individuals' desires to be self-responsible beings. Similarly, a treatment facility for addiction will not use unstructured therapy if that facility views addicts as people who need to learn how to conform, who need to be taught specific behaviors that will allow them to live in a healthy manner, and who need to be pressured into changing deviant life-styles (Yablonsky, 1965).

The process of unstructured group therapy is not congruent with the process of authoritarian family structures or totalitarian political systems. The process by which members reach decisions and the rules for expressing feelings and ideas differ because the need for authoritarian leadership is questioned by the very format of unstructured therapy. Members of authoritarian families, political parties, or cultural subgroups can benefit from participation in unstructured groups. However, they may need to explain to themselves how they could be helped by an interpersonal experience with norms widely at variance with those used in other interpersonal environments.

As theorists examine aspects of group functioning within therapy, they inevitably examine some aspects of human functioning that are found in all social groups, such as formation of boundaries, values, norms, and use of resources (Snider, 1992). Therapy groups are peculiar in that they exist as experiments designed to create a setting wherein individuals can recognize a form of mutual responsibility that is not based on blame (Rutan & Groves, 1989). This mutual responsibility is aimed toward the creation of a healing environment wherein the group exists for each member just as each member exists for the group (Rutan & Groves, 1989). Because these groups embody ideas that apply to all social groups and because they aim to create a healing and growth-enhancing environment, the dynamics of effectively therapeutic groups have implications for a variety of social groups.

The value system of an unstructured therapy group is generally, if not always, a relatively democratic and nonauthoritarian one. Of course, members are not encouraged to attack or invalidate the experiences of those who rely on authoritarian value systems. Moreover, if members vote to exclude a person who has become a scapegoat, the group leader may override their decision; similar exceptions to democratic process can also occur in regard to threats of violence or suicide. Nonetheless, these settings generally encourage members to recognize themselves as authors of their life meanings, to share power, and to value their ability to be their own authorities for major decisions.

Politics (the form of justice) within an unstructured therapy group may differ from the politics that determine relationships for members in environments outside their group. The application of unstructured therapy theory to actual situations must account for the possibility that participants live in an environment that will resist their recognition of responsibility and their development of a personally valid frame of reference for evaluating experiences. Participants may themselves mistrust an environment that has no rigid rules and regulations. Members may need to use their group as a source of support for reconciliation between what they are learning about themselves within their group with what they need to do to survive outside. Group members can help each other to learn about their experiences within specific social systems and can often provide useful feedback.

As we know, unstructured therapy groups encourage and support individuality. This encouragement is not necessarily an endorsement of rugged individualism. Individuality means different things and is expressed in various ways by people. The essential encouragement of individuality that occurs in unstructured groups reflects an ethic that no one right way to be exists, that no one expression of uniqueness is correct. These groups support the diversity of members, which is evident in the lack of imposed structures and norms.

Awareness of the value of individuality allows us to support the person as a constructor of meanings and goals and yet to recognize that meanings and goals are formed interdependently. Meanings and goals reflect awareness of relationships with others and grow out of interactions with environments and persons. Therefore, effective independent individuality implies responsible interdependence and is linked to interdependence. Individuality can have a synergistic relationship with collectivity (see Sampson, 1988).

Individuals often vary in the degree of self-sufficiency that they choose in an interpersonal situation depending on their evaluation of the requirements of the situation and the perceived trustworthiness of others involved. Unstructured therapy tends to promote flexibility within interactions and encourages choices based on present perceptions. The political implications of this valuing of individuals entail a willingness to find strengths within divergent cultures and allow for the criticism of social and cultural institutions that abuse individuals (according to the perceptions of those individuals).

Unstructured Group Therapy in Cross-Cultural Settings

The concept that human existence involves ontological dynamics inherent in any individual's process of being suggests that unstructured therapy can be useful across cultures. Person-centered theory, which stresses specific conditions involved in individuals' ways of being, has led to formation of unstructured groups in Japan (Murayama, Nojima & Abe, 1988), South Africa (Hill-Hain & Rogers, 1988), South America (Wood, 1982) and to cross-cultural communication groups held annually in Europe (McIlduff & Coghlan, 1989). The dialogues created in these unstructured groups have demonstrated that persons can participate in meaningful interactions that reveal differences and universalities within and across cultures. An unstructured training group for counseling students in Ireland also showed that culture does not interfere with ontologically oriented learning of members (Page & O'Leary, 1992). This learning is not independent of culture, but it potentially applies within any culture constructed by human beings (Page, 1983a).

When members from different cultures meet in an unstructured format, they tend to learn more about each other than they might in a setting that provided more predetermined structuring. Because predetermined structures are not imposed but created, members learn about each other and each other's world views and culture (see McIlduff & Coghlan, 1989).

We can hypothesize that unstructured groups are useful to the degree that human beings are able to use these settings to assist each other to discover how ontological dynamics operate. If group members are unable to share with each other because of cultural barriers, then they will not be able to assist each other's learning. However, if members are willing to learn about and from others with different cultural backgrounds, then unstructured therapy groups can serve a useful purpose. Members can learn that the ability to care and understand has no cultural limit. People can help each other with this discovery, not because they have specialized training, but because they are able to learn from being together. Members assist each other to learn experientially from mutual encounters by influencing each other through encounters and exchanging their perceptions of these encounters.

As we noted earlier in the chapter, learning can be increased by the participation of those with different backgrounds, histories, or socioeconomic circumstances. Divergent perspectives assist learning about ontological dynamics if persons are successful at communicating meaningfully, at building bridges that form connections. No one culture or subculture has the final word about the meaning of human life and human relationships. Individuals can use their group to question their own or others' cultures or to explore what their own culture means to them and others.

Different ethnic and cultural backgrounds serve as effective catalysts for group interactions that lead to acknowledgment and acceptance of differences and uniqueness. In unstructured group process, members often learn that their assumptions and stereotypes about other cultures are not useful for predicting the reactions of their specific representatives. The uniqueness of individuals, as well as the influence of cultures, tends to be expressed during group interactions. Even when participants are all from the same background or culture and assume that all members share the same basic value orientations, they usually turn out to be incorrect if they develop enough trust to share their true feelings about life situations and issues.

Implications of Unstructured Group Theory
for Social Dynamics

The dynamics of unstructured group therapy, as they have been discussed in this book, have implications for patterns of interpersonal relationship in the larger society. The ontological elements of love, power, and justice operate in families, business corporations, schools, and other social institutions. The discussion of how members of a therapy group can evolve toward integrated interpersonal and intrapersonal dynamics demonstrates how relationships in other settings can also move toward creative justice and mutual acceptance and empowerment.

We are all aware that the current historical epoch is a time of rapid change. Some of these changes include the increasing importance of information-processing technology, a more globally integrated economic structure, and worldwide political changes that increasingly emphasize the importance of individuals and of various aspects of freedom (Naisbett & Aburdene, 1990). Human relationships are currently in transition within and across cultures in ways that are effecting rapid changes in political structures, vocational and economic structures, family structures, and ideas of personhood. (Of course, as rapid as these changes are, some people may believe they are occurring too slowly.) To a great extent, these changes associate more power and responsibility with individuals and less power with traditional structures and traditional authorities. Thus, traditional roles for women are changing; minorities are questioning cultural stereotypes that have prevailed in the past; democratic decision making has grown in importance for many families and societies; and some corporations now attempt to allow workers' viewpoints to be included in decision-making processes.

At the same time, of course, many families and societies adhere to rigid roles, many businesses are run autocratically, and many religions and cultures continue to rely on traditional models based on a central authority figure. Although this current time involves transition and questioning for many people, many others wish to resist the uncertainty and ambiguity of change.

The model that we have proposed for unstructured group therapy is one that values the principle of change and accepts uncertainty and ambiguity as part of the process. Predetermined outcomes or goals are less important than is integration within ongoing process. Constructive change can occur in ways that people experience as unexpected, spontaneous, or serendipitous. Although members are responsible for alterations in themselves, they often could not have said beforehand how they would react within a given encounter. Acceptance or creation of change occurs through interactive and self-reflective processes. Recognition of individual responsibility for creating change and determining goals occurs as members support each other's abilities to function responsibly.

Individuals in a successful group are able to treat each other as members of an intrinsically "spiritual democracy" that functions even when overt roles create differences in power. This democracy of the spirit accepts, nurtures, and validates individuals' determination of values based on perceptions and experience. This perspective could be extended to the dynamics of families, businesses, and social institutions. In principle, maximum development of individual potentials and integration of diverse human elements will occur if people in various settings recognize themselves and others as responsible and nonexpendable. The principle that individuals are nonexpendable means that effective social systems accept and encourage the potential ability of each person in the system to contribute constructively. Social systems are most adequate when they provide their members with opportunities to exercise their abilities to learn from experience in an atmosphere of freedom and to be responsible within and for their own awareness of events.

Implications of Unstructured Group Theory
for Families and Other Groups

Family relationships provide a symbolic and emotional foundation for people's later learning about the dynamics of love, power, and justice. For example, the form of justice learned in a family context can later be used by individuals to regulate their conceptualizations of other people and their responses to perceived emotional demands made by others in close relationships. Similar learning occurs about needs, wishes, and expressions of love and power. Some of the problems that members work on in unstructured therapy groups involve recognizing and changing patterns of love, power, and justice that were experienced in their families. Unstructured therapy groups can challenge members to use their growing awareness of the past to experiment with new roles and dynamics.

Through their interbeing, family members influence each other within a dynamic that they are mutually responsible for creating. Members are not likely to have equal power or to express love equivalently or to employ the same mode of justice. Nonetheless, each participant has an influence on the total gestalt of love, power, and justice within ongoing relations. The impact of this gestalt will have a continuing effect on each of the family's members and can influence how they unconsciously and consciously create future relationships. Family members are not victims of this dynamic, not choiceless automatons mindlessly repeating patterns from early childhood. As cocreators of dynamics in a family situation, family members are responsible for the choices they make to adapt and respond. Members in therapeutic groups often experience growth if they are able to acknowledge decisions to create spits in awareness, for example, or to identify with negative self-images. They are more likely to acknowledge their responsibility within painful family dynamics if they feel emotionally supported by others in their group.

One implication of learning about the ways that people use unstructured groups to change interpersonal patterns is that members share responsibility for all the groups that they create. Certain groups are particularly influential in the formation of awareness of responsibility (for example, families, peer groups, and religious groups). Patterns of perception and action are deeply influenced by how individuals first experienced themselves and others as powerful, as well as how they have been able to affect perceptions of power and experiences of being loved, giving love, and revealing needs for love. Initial reactions from significant others to demands for respect and nurturance and their ongoing reactions have helped form individuals' perceptions of the possibilities for interpersonal justice. The most basic structures of an individual's ontological dynamics tend to be maintained and enacted outside conscious awareness. By becoming aware of how others perceive them and how others are affected by them, individuals can become aware of choices that they make within relationships. The connection of dysfunctional aspects of present dynamics often has clear associations with dysfunctional aspects of past dynamics.

Creatively Just Social Systems

Businesses, religious organizations, and political parties operate according to principles that can acknowledge, distort, or deny interbeing. The structures that people create within organizations reflect their decisions concerning how responsible and interconnected individuals will be within that environment. Individuals create power hierarchies that help determine the form of justice that regulates interaction. Love may be permissible as an expression only within particular situations and following specific limits and guidelines.

Decision making can be regulated to occur in a strictly "top-down" fashion. Those who are at the bottom of a social hierarchy will have little or no decision-making power and will be expected to abide by the decisions of others. Responsibility is only associated with those at the top of the hierarchy. Systems that allow input from those who have less financial or physical power generally function as more open structures with more flexible forms of justice. If "ground-up" decision making is acknowledged as valuable in a family or business, the social structure will allow for greater awareness of mutual responsibility. Flexible structures may be able to organize influence from the top down and the bottom up simultaneously. Members in these types of families or social organizations may need to learn to respond to interactions with creative forms of justice that do not follow predetermined structures.

Both families and businesses generally require some kind of power hierarchy based on divisions of labor, access to resources, and abilities to influence events. The power hierarchy is always associated with the form of justice being employed. One means to gain awareness of the form of justice in a family or business is to examine how influential decisions are made and how key policies are determined and implemented. If coercion and threats are commonly used to implement decisions, a "disintegrated" system is evidenced, and love then functions separately from power. If people who are affected by decisions are involved in making them, love is more likely to function in alignment with power.

Integration of love, power, and justice involves understanding the unique needs of individuals and accommodating those needs in as equitable a manner as possible while also responding to others involved. If social systems function according to the perception that their welfare is supported by maximizing the potential empowerment and awareness of each member, then they move toward creative justice. Such systems function to make the most of possibilities for learning and growth. Members within such systems are expected to contribute constructively to others, not out of fear, but out of awareness of mutual benefit and responsibility. Love is assumed to be just as important a motivation as power in creatively just systems.

As it moves toward creative justice, a social system places less reliance on rigid patterns of response to individuals' needs. The system is increasingly able to accommodate and to respond to changing needs and goals of members and subgroups. Novel challenges are addressed in an atmosphere that fosters full and open communication and an assessment of resources. A creatively just system is not designed to perpetuate itself beyond its usefulness or to maintain its norms by avoiding or repressing evidence that does not fit its norms.

At the time of this writing, the creatively just society is a direction toward which we can move, rather than a reality that we have established. It is beyond the scope of this book to examine specific social and cultural events that have marked movement toward or away from creative justice. For the present, we can simply observe that individuals and nations have struggled historically with themes of fragmentation and reunification, empowerment of certain groups and individuals that opposed empowerment of others, and changes in forms of justice that regulate decision making and allocation of resources.

These ontological themes have reflected a continuing process of relationship developed at collective and individual levels. Balance in social, cultural, and familial groups has grown or decreased based on collective and individual use of awareness and responsibility. Interpersonal forms of relationship and relationships with nature have been defined according to ontological dynamics that have characterized individuals and groups in particular social and historical contexts. In no society has ontological integration successfully been imposed upon people through political programs based on coercion or manipulation. It is hoped that integration at a social level can evolve from the recognition that social systems can function as environments that reinforce individuals' self-initiated movements toward awareness and responsibility.

The application of a theory to unstructured group therapy is an attempt to describe a microcosmic pattern of relationship that can potentially be created at a societal level. Members of a therapy group can successfully create an environment wherein people learn from each other without imposing on each other. They can learn to acknowledge and express conflict constructively and can choose to accept differences in each others' experiencing and perceiving of events. In this social environment, participants can recognize their mutual responsibility to assist each other's mutual empowerment. Providing each other encouragement and assistance can be in itself an empowering dynamic for participants. To understand their ability to assist each other, members may have to examine ways that they escape the anxiety of responsibility by projecting it onto leaders or systems of thought that will "save" them from themselves. Thus, a dynamic of mutual empowerment tends to be a movement away from concepts determined by religious, political, or in-group authorities. Instead, members learn to be their own authorities for determining directions and values.

Throughout the world, millions of people are crying out for justice in a variety of contexts. Individuals who enter therapy are not different in quality from these millions, and each client brings a unique life and a unique demand for justice. The struggle of those who participate in unstructured therapy groups may not represent an attempt to change the world. This form of therapy, however, does offer the possibility that people can change themselves and can help others change by using human abilities to listen, offer what is needed, and accept what is given.

Individuals who participate in these groups may have observed members confront and sometimes transform their past patterns of relationship. Other members may have realized that it is possible to accept and to be accepted by others. If members have experienced a degree of healing or a rejuvenation of hope, they may extend these changes to other relationships in their lives. The unstructured therapy group can provide a psychological environment wherein faith in the possibilities of human existence and interpersonal interaction can be reaffirmed. If a group is effective, members can take small steps (and even large ones) in the direction of personal and collective integration.

References

Adler, A. (1969). *The practice and theory of individual psychology.* Paterson, NJ: Littlefield.

Adler, A. (1972). *The neurotic constitution.* Freeport, NY: Books for Libraries Press.

Agazarian, Y. M. (1992). Contemporary theories of group therapy: A systems approach to the group-as-a-whole. *International Journal of Group Psychotherapy, 42,* 177–294.

Alexander, F. (1961). *The scope of psychoanalysis.* New York: Basic Books.

American Association for Counseling and Development. (1988). *Ethical standards.* Alexandria, VA: Author.

American Psychological Association. (1990). Ethical principles of psychologists (amended June 2, 1989). *American Psychologist, 45,* 390–395.

Applbaum, R. L., Bodaken, E. M., Sereno, K., & Anatol, K. W. (1974). *The process of group communication.* Chicago: Science Research Associates.

Arieti, S. (1974). *Interpretation of schizophrenia* (rev. ed.). New York: Basic Books.

Arnett, R. C. (1989). What is dialogic communication? *Person-Centered Review, 4,* 42–60.

Association for Specialists in Group Work. (1989). Ethical guidelines for group counselors. *Journal for Specialists in Group Work, 15,* 119–126.

Aubrey, M. & Dougher, M. J. (1990). Ethical issues in outpatient group therapy with sex offenders. *Journal for Specialists in Group Work, 15,* 75–82.

Bacal, H. A. (1985). Object-relations in the group from the perspective of self psychology. *International Journal of Group Psychotherapy, 35,* 483–501.

Bach, G. R. (1957). Observations on transference and object relations in the light of group dynamics. *International Journal of Group Psychotherapy, 7,* 64–76.

Barret-Lennard, G. (1985). The helping relationship: Crisis and advance in theory and research. *Counseling Psychologist, 13,* 279–294.

Bateson, G., Jackson, D. D., Haley, J., & Weakland, J. H. (1956). Toward a theory of schizophrenia. *Behavior Science, 1,* 251–264.

Becker, E. (1973). *The denial of death.* New York: Free Press.

Berne, E. (1961). *Transactional analysis in psychotherapy.* New York: Grove Press.

Berne, E. (1964). *Games people play.* New York: Grove Press.

Berne, E. (1966). *Principles of group treatment.* New York: Oxford University Press.

Berry, C. E. (1991). Self psychology and its relationship to the practice of group psychotherapy. *International Journal of Group Psychotherapy, 41,* 523–532.

Bion, W. R. (1959). *Experiences in groups.* New York: Ballantine Books.

Bonney, W. C. (1974). The maturation of groups. *Small Group Behavior, 5,* 445–461.

Bozarth, J. D. (1981). The person-centered approach in the large community group. In G. M. Gazda (Ed.), *Innovations to group psychotherapy* (2nd ed., pp. 100–133). Springfield, IL: Thomas.

Bozarth, J. D. (1984). Beyond reflection: Emergent modes of empathy. In R. F. Levant & J. M. Schlien (Eds.), *Client-centered therapy and the person-centered approach* (pp. 59–75). New York: Praeger.

Bozarth, J. (1986). The basic encounter group: An alternative view. *Journal for Specialists in Group Work, 11*, 228–232.

Buber, M. (1957). *Pointing the way.* New York: Harper & Row.

Buber, M. (1970). *I and thou* (W. Kaufmann, Trans.). New York: Scribner.

Bugental, J.F.T. (1978). *Psychotherapy and process: The fundamentals of an existential-humanistic approach.* Menlo Park, CA: Addison-Wesley.

Burnand, G. (1990). Group development phases as working through six fundamental human problems. *Small Group Research, 21*, 255–273.

Cain, D. (1989). The paradox of non-directiveness in the person-centered approach. *Person-Centered Review, 4*, 123–131.

Chang, C. (1963). *Creativity and Taoism.* New York: Julian Press.

Cheng, M. & Smith, R. W. (1967). *T'ai Chi.* Rutland, VT: Tuttle.

Cohen, A. M. & Smith, R. D. (1976). *The critical incident in growth groups: Theory and technique.* La Jolla, CA: University Associates.

Combs, A. W. & Snygg, D. (1959). *Individual behavior: A perceptual approach.* New York: Harper & Row.

Corey, G. (1990). *Theory and practice of group counseling* (3rd ed.). Pacific Grove, CA: Brooks/Cole.

Corey, G. (1991). *Theory and practice of counseling and psychotherapy.* Pacific Grove, CA: Brooks/Cole.

Corey, G. & Corey, M. S. (1987). *Groups: Process and practice* (3rd ed.). Pacific Grove, CA: Brooks/Cole.

Cushman, P. (1989). Iron fists/velvet gloves: A study of a mass marathon psychology training. *Psychotherapy, 26*, 23–39.

Daniels, M. (1988). The myth of self-actualization. *Journal of Humanistic Psychology, 28*, 7–38.

Egan, G. (1970). *Encounter: Group processes for interpersonal growth.* Belmont, CA: Brooks/Cole.

Foulkes, S. H. (1948). *Introduction to group-analytic psychotherapy.* London: Heinemann.

Foulkes, S. H. (1951). Concerning leadership in group-analytic psychotherapy. *International Journal of Group Psychotherapy, 1,* 319-329.

Foulkes, S. H. (1953). Some similarities between psychoanalytic principles and group analytic principles. *British Journal of Medical Psychology, 26,* 30-35.

Foulkes, S. H. (1957). Group-analytic dynamics with specific reference to psychoanalytic concepts. *International Journal of Group Psychotherapy, 7,* 40-52.

Foulkes, S. H. (1975). *Group analytic psychotherapy.* Paris: Interfare Books.

Foulkes, S. H. & Lewis, E. (1944). Group analysis: A study in the treatment of groups on psycho-analytic lines. *British Journal of Medical Psychology, 20,* 175-184.

Frank, J. (1963). *Persuasion and healing: A comparative study of psychotherapy.* New York: Schocken Books.

Frankl, V. (1963). *Man's search for meaning.* New York: Washington Square Press.

Frankl, V. (1965). *The doctor and the soul.* New York: Bantam Books.

Frankl, V. (1966). Self-transcendence as a human phenomenon. *Journal of Humanistic Psychology, 6,* 97-107.

Frankl, V. (1969). *The will to meaning: Foundations and applications of logotherapy.* New York: New American Library.

Freud, S. (1948). *Group psychology and the analysis of the ego.* London: Hogarth Press. (Original work published 1921)

Freud, S. (1953a). Inhibitions, symptoms, and anxiety. In J. Strachey (Ed.), *The standard edition of the complete psychological works.* London: Hogarth Press. (Original work published 1926)

Freud, S. (1953b). Instincts and their vicissitudes. In J. Strachey (Ed.), *The standard edition of the complete psychological works.* London: Hogarth Press. (Original work published 1934)

Freud, S. (1955). Beyond the pleasure principle. In J. Strachey (Ed.), *The standard edition of the complete psychological works.* London: Hogarth Press. (Original work published 1920)

Freud, S. (1961). Civilization and its discontents. In J. Strachey (Ed.), *The standard edition of the complete psychological works.* London: Hogarth Press. (Original work published 1930)

Freud, S. (1962). *The ego and the id.* New York: Norton. (Original work published 1923)

Freud, S. (1964). An outline of psychoanalysis. In J. Strachey (Ed.), *The standard edition of the complete psychological works.* London: Hogarth Press. (Original work published 1940)

Frick, W. B. (1990). The symbolic growth experience: A heuristic inquiry and a quest for synthesis. *Journal of Humanistic Psychology, 30,* 64–80.

Friedman, M. (1963). Dialogue and the "essential we"—the basis of values in the philosophy of Martin Buber. In M. Rosenbaum & M. Berger (Eds.), *Group psychotherapy and group function* (pp. 604–613). New York: Basic Books.

Friedman, M. (1986). Carl Rogers and Martin Buber: Self-actualization and dialogue. *Person-Centered Review, 1,* 409–435.

Friedman, M. (1992). *Dialogue and the human image: Beyond humanistic psychology.* Newbury Park, CA: Sage.

Fromm, E. (1956). *The art of loving.* New York: Harper.

Fromm, E. (1964). *Escape from freedom.* New York: Avon Books.

Fromm, E., Suzuki, D. T. & De Martino, R. (1960). *Zen Buddhism and psychoanalysis.* New York: Harper & Row.

Fung, Y. L. (1948). *A short history of Chinese philosophy.* New York: Macmillan.

Gans, J. S. (1989). Hostility in group psychotherapy. *International Journal of Group Psychotherapy, 39,* 499–516.

Ganzarain, R. (1992). Introduction to object relations group psychotherapy. *International Journal of Group Psychotherapy, 42,* 205–223.

Garfield, S. L. & Bergin, A. E. (Eds.). (1986). *Handbook of psychotherapy and behavior change* (3rd ed.). New York: Wiley.

Geller, L. (1984). Another look at self-actualization. *Journal of Humanistic Psychology, 24,* 93–106.

Gemmill, G. (1986). The dynamics of the group shadow in intergroup relations. *Small Group Behavior, 17,* 229–240.

Gemmill, G. (1989). The dynamics of scapegoating in small groups. *Small Group Behavior, 20,* 406–418.

Gemmill, G. & Wynkoop, C. (1991). The psychodynamics of small group transformation. *Small Group Research, 22,* 4–23.

George, R. L. (1990). *Counseling the chemically dependent: Theory and practice.* Englewood Cliffs, NJ: Prentice-Hall.

Girardot, N. J. (1983). *Myth and meaning in early Taoism.* Berkeley: University of California Press.

Goble, F. (1971). *The third force.* New York: Pocket Books.

Greenson, R. R. (1967). *The technique and practice of psychoanalysis.* New York: International Universities Press.

Guidano, V. F. (1987). *Complexity of the self: A developmental approach to psychopathology and therapy.* New York: Guilford.

Hill, W. F. (1965). *HIM: Hill Interaction Matrix.* Los Angeles: University of Southern California.

Hill, W. F. (1969). *Hill Interaction Matrix Supplement.* Pomona: California State Polytechnic Institute.

Hill-Hain, A. & Rogers, C. R. (1988). A dialogue with Carl Rogers: Cross-cultural challenges of facilitating person-centered groups in South Africa. *Journal for Specialists in Group Work, 13,* 62–69.

Iling, H. A. (1963). C. G. Jung on the present trends in group psychotherapy. In M. Rosenbaum & M. Berger (Eds.), *Group psychotherapy and group function* (pp. 180–187). New York: Basic Books.

Janis, I. L. (1982). *Groupthink: Psychological studies of policy decisions and fiascoes.* Boston: Houghton Mifflin.

Johnson, J. A. (1963). *Group therapy: A practical approach.* New York: McGraw-Hill.

Jourard, S. M. (1971). *The transparent self.* New York: Van Nostrand Reinhold.

Jung, C. G. (1916). *Analytical psychology.* New York: Moffat, Yard.

Jung, C. G. (1933). *Modern man in search of a soul.* New York: Harcourt, Brace, and World.

Jung, C. G. (1956). *Two essays on analytical psychology.* New York: Meridian Books.

Jung, C. G. (1958). *Psychology and religion.* In *Collected works* (Vol. 11). Princeton, NJ: Princeton University Press.

Jung, C. G. (1964). *Man and his symbols.* New York: Doubleday.

Jung, C. G. (1968). The archetypes and the collective unconscious. In *Collected works* (Vol. 91). Princeton, NJ: Princeton University Press. (Original work published 1936)

Kaplan, R. E. (1985). Some hidden elements of control in group facilitation: Appreciating the bounded and binding aspects of openness. *Small Group Behavior, 16,* 462-476.

Kapur, R. & Pearce, M. (1987). Group psychotherapy with the elderly. *British Journal of Psychotherapy, 3,* 289-296.

Kitchener, K. S. & Harding, S. D. (1990). Dual role relationships. In B. Herlihy & L. B. Golden (Eds.), *Ethical standards casebook* (pp. 146-154). Alexandria, VA: American Association for Counseling and Development.

Kohut, H. (1971). *The analysis of the self.* New York: International Universities Press.

Kohut, H. (1977). *The restoration of the self.* New York: International Universities Press.

Kohut, H. & Wolf, E. S. (1978). The disorders of the self and their treatment: An outline. *International Journal of Psychoanalysis, 59,* 413-425.

Korb, M., Gorrell, J. & Van De Riet, V. (1989). *Gestalt therapy: An introduction.* New York: Pergamon Press.

Korda, L. J. & Pancrazio, J. L. (1989). Limiting negative outcome in group practice. *Journal for Specialists in Group Work, 14,* 112-120.

Kübler-Ross, E. (1975). *Death: The final stage of growth.* Englewood Cliffs, NJ: Prentice-Hall.

Kwiatkowski, R. M. (1987). The psychotic adolescent in the group. *British Journal of Psychotherapy, 4,* 23-29.

Lao Tzu. (1963). Tao-te Ching. In W. T. Chan (Ed. and Trans.), *A source book in Chinese philosophy* (pp. 139-176). Princeton, NJ: Princeton University Press. (Original work published in 600 B.C.)

Leszcz, M. (1990). Towards an integrated model of group psychotherapy with the elderly. *International Journal of Group Psychotherapy, 40,* 379-399.

Leszcz, M. (1992). The interpersonal approach to group psychotherapy. *International Journal of Group Psychotherapy, 42,* 37-62.

Lethbridge, D. (1986). A Marxist theory of self-actualization. *Journal of Humanistic Psychology, 26,* 84-103.

Lewis, J. A., Dana, R. Q. & Blevins, G. A. (1988). *Substance abuse counseling: An individualized approach.* Pacific Grove, CA: Brooks/Cole.

Lieberman, M. A., Lakin, M. & Whitaker, D. S. (1969). Problems and potential of psychoanalytic and group-dynamic theories for group psychotherapy. *International Journal of Group Psychotherapy, 19,* 131–141.

Maddi, S. R. (1985). Existential psychotherapy. In S. J. Lynn & J. P. Garske (Eds.), *Contemporary Psychotherapies* (pp. 191–220). Columbus, OH: Merrill.

Mahler, M. (1968). *On human symbiosis and the vicissitudes of individuation.* New York: International Universities Press.

Mahoney, M. J. (1990). *Human change processes: The scientific foundations of psychotherapy.* New York: Basic Books.

Maslow, A. H. (1962). *Toward a psychology of being.* New York: Van Nostrand.

Maslow, A. H. (1964). *Religions, values, and peak experiences.* Columbus, OH: Ohio State University Press.

Matano, R. A. & Yalom, I. D. (1991). Approaches to chemical dependency: Chemical dependency and interactive group therapy—a synthesis. *International Journal of Group Psychotherapy, 41,* 269–293.

May, R. (1969). *Love and will.* New York: Norton.

May, R. (1972). *Power and innocence.* New York: Norton.

May, R. (1977). *The meaning of anxiety* (rev. ed.). New York: Norton.

May, R. (1981). *Freedom and destiny.* New York: Norton.

May, R. & Yalom, I. D. (1984). Existential psychotherapy. In R. J. Corsini (Ed.), *Current psychotherapies* (3rd ed., pp. 354–391). Itasca, IL: Peacock.

McClure, B. A. (1987). Metaphoric illumination in groups. *Small Group Behavior, 18,* 179–187.

McClure, B. A. (1990). The group mind: Generative and regressive groups. *Journal for Specialists in Group Work, 15,* 159–170.

McIlduff, E. & Coghlan, D. (1989). Process and facilitation in a cross-cultural communication workshop. *Person-Centered Review, 4,* 77–98.

Meador, B. D. & Rogers, C. R. (1984). Person-centered therapy. In R. J. Corsini (Ed.), *Current psychotherapies* (3rd ed., pp. 142–195). Itasca, IL: Peacock.

Moreno, J. L. (1947). *Theatre of spontaneity: An introduction to psychodrama*. Beacon, NY: Beacon House.

Moreno, J. L. (1964). *Psychodrama: Vol. 1* (3rd ed.). New York: Beacon House.

Moreno, Z. T. (1965). Psychodrama rules, techniques, and adjunctive methods. *Group Psychotherapy, 18*, 73–86.

Morran, D. K., Stockton, R. & Harris, M. (1991). Analysis of group leader and member feedback messages. *Journal of Psychotherapy, Psychodrama, & Sociometry, 44*, 126–135.

Mosak, H. H. (1984). Adlerian psychotherapy. In R. J. Corsini (Ed.), *Current psychotherapies* (3rd ed., pp. 56–107). Itasca, IL: Peacock.

Murayama, S., Nojima, K. & Abe, T. (1988). Person-centered groups in Japan: A selective review of the literature. *Person-Centered Review, 3*, 479–492.

Naisbett, J. & Aburdene, P. (1990). *Megatrends 2000: Ten new directions for the 1990s*. New York: Morrow.

Napier, R. W. & Gershenfeld, M. K. (1987). *Groups: Theory and experience* (4th ed.). Boston: Houghton Mifflin.

O'Hara, M. M. (1984). Person-centered gestalt: Toward a holistic synthesis. In R. F. Levant & J. M. Schlien (Eds.), *Client-centered therapy and the person-centered approach* (pp. 203–221). New York: Praeger.

O'Hara, M. M. & Wood, J. K. (1983). Patterns of awareness: Consciousness and the group mind. *Gestalt Journal, 2*, 103–116.

Page, R. C. (1978). The social learning process of severely disabled group counseling participants. *Psychosocial Rehabilitation Journal, 2*, 28–36.

Page, R. C. (1979). Developmental stages of unstructured groups with prisoners. *Small Group Behavior, 10*, 271–279.

Page, R. C. (1980). Marathon groups: Counseling the imprisoned drug abuser. *International Journal of the Addictions, 15*, 765–770.

Page, R. C. (1981). Client rights and agency demands: The ethical tightrope of the offender counselor. *Counseling and Values, 26*, 55–62.

Page, R. C. (1982). Marathon group therapy with users of illicit drugs: Dimensions of social learning. *International Journal of the Addictions, 17,* 1107-1115.

Page, R. C. (1983a). The cross-cultural implications of unstructured group therapy. *Counsellor, 1,* 20-30.

Page, R. C. (1983b). Marathon group counseling with illicit drug abusers: A study of the effects of two groups for one month. *Journal for Specialists in Group Work, 8,* 114-125.

Page, R. C. (1984). Unstructured group therapy. In Raymond Corsini (Ed.), *Wiley encyclopedia of psychology* (Vol. 3., pp. 451-452). New York: Wiley.

Page, R. C. (1985). The effects of marathon groups on the ways illicit drug users perceive counseling. *International Journal of the Addictions, 20,* 1683-1692.

Page, R. C. & Berkow, D. (1991). Concepts of the self: Western and Eastern perspectives. *Journal of Multicultural Counseling and Development, 19,* 83-93.

Page, R. C. & Bridges, N. (1983). The interpersonal relationship styles of illicit drug users participating in marathon group therapy. *Small Group Behavior, 14,* 253-259.

Page, R. C. & Chang, R. (1989). A comparison of Gestalt therapy and Zen Buddhist concepts of awareness. *Psychologia, 32,* 33-39.

Page, R. C., Davis, K. C., Berkow, D. N. & O'Leary, E. (1989). Analysis of group process in marathon group therapy with users of illicit drugs. *Small Group Behavior, 29,* 220-227.

Page, R. C. & O'Leary, E. (1992). A pilot study on the effects of a training group on Irish counseling students. *Journal of Multicultural Counseling and Development, 20,* 23-34.

Page, R. C., Richmond, B. O. & DeLaSerna, M. (1987). Marathon group counseling with illicit drug abusers: Effects on self perceptions. *Small Group Behavior, 18,* 483-497.

Page, R. C. & Wills, J. (1983). Marathon group counseling with illicit drug users: Analysis of content. *Journal for Specialists in Group Work, 8,* 67-76.

Patterson, C. H. (1980). *Theories of counseling and psychotherapy.* New York: Harper & Row.

Patterson, C. H. (1985). *The therapeutic relationship: Foundations for an eclectic psychotherapy.* Belmont, CA: Brooks/Cole.

Patterson, L. E. & Eisenberg, S. (1975). *The counseling process.* Boston: Houghton Mifflin.

Perls, F. (1969). *Gestalt therapy verbatim.* Lafayette, CA: Real People Press.

Perls, F. (1971). *In and out of the garbage pail.* New York: Bantam Books.

Perls, F. (1973). *The Gestalt approach and eyewitness to therapy.* New York: Bantam Books.

Perls, F., Hefferline, R. & Goodman, P. (1980). *Gestalt therapy: Excitement and growth in the human personality.* New York: Bantam Books. (Original work published 1951)

Perls, L. (1992). Concepts and misconceptions of gestalt therapy. *Journal of Humanistic Psychology, 32,* 50–56.

Polster, E. & Polster, M. (1973). *Gestalt therapy integrated.* New York: Vintage Books.

Rank, O. (1945). *Will therapy and truth and reality.* New York: Knopf.

Reich, W. (1960). *Selected writings.* New York: Farrar, Straus & Giroux.

Roback, H. B., Purdon, S. E., Ochoa, E. & Bloch, F. (1992). Confidentiality dilemmas in group psychotherapy. *Small Group Research, 23,* 169–184.

Rogers, C. R. (1951). *Client-centered therapy.* Boston: Houghton Mifflin.

Rogers, C. R. (1961). *On becoming a person.* Boston: Houghton Mifflin.

Rogers, C. R. (1967a). The interpersonal relationship: The core of guidance. In C. R. Rogers, B. Stevens, T. Gendlin, J. M. Shlein & W. Van Dusen (Eds.), *Person to person: The problem of being human* (pp. 89–103). Lafayette, CA: Real People Press.

Rogers, C. R. (1967b). Some learnings from a study of psychotherapy with schizophrenics. In C. R. Rogers, B. Stevens, T. Gendlin, J. M. Shlein & W. Van Dusen (Eds.), *Person to person: The problem of being human* (pp. 181–192). Lafayette, CA: Real People Press.

Rogers, C. R. (1970). *On encounter groups.* New York: Harper & Row.

Rogers, C. R. (1977). *On personal power.* New York: Delacorte Press.

Rogers, C. R. (1980). *A way of being*. Boston: Houghton Mifflin.

Rogers, C. R. (1983). *Freedom to learn for the 80's*. Columbus, OH: Merrill.

Rogers, C. R. (1987). The underlying theory: Drawn from experience with individuals and groups. *Counseling and Values, 32,* 38–46.

Roller, B. (1989). Having fun in groups. *Small Group Behavior, 20,* 97–100.

Rossel, R. D. (1981). Word play: Metaphor and humor in the small group. *Small Group Behavior, 12,* 116–136.

Rubin, T. I. (1969). *The angry book.* New York: Collier Books.

Rutan, J. S. & Groves, J. E. (1989). Making society's groups more therapeutic. *International Journal of Group Psychotherapy, 39,* 3–16.

Sampson, E. E. (1988). The debate on individualism. *American Psychologist, 43,* 15–22.

Sartre, J. P. (1956). *Being and nothingness.* New York: Philosophical Library.

Scheidlinger, S. (1980a). Current psychoanalytic group theory. In S. Scheidlinger (Ed.), *Psychoanalytic group dynamics: Basic readings* (pp. 285–299). New York: International Universities Press.

Scheidlinger, S. (1980b). Freud's group psychology. In S. Scheidlinger (Ed.), *Psychoanalytic group dynamics: Basic readings* (pp. 5–13). New York: International Universities Press.

Schneider, K. (1990). *The paradoxical self: Toward an understanding of our contradictory nature.* New York: Insight Books/Plenum Press.

Shepard, M. (1975). *Fritz.* New York: Dutton.

Shostrom, E. L. (1976). *Actualizing therapy.* San Diego, CA: Edits.

Simkin, J. S. (1976). *Gestalt therapy mini-lectures.* Millbrae, CA: Celestial Arts.

Slavson, S. R. (1951). The dynamics of analytic group psychotherapy. *International Journal of Group Psychotherapy, 1,* 208–217.

Slavson, S. R. (1953). Common sources of error and confusion in group psychotherapy. *International Journal of Group Psychotherapy, 3,* 3–28.

Slavson, S. R. (1957). Are there group dynamics in therapy groups? *International Journal of Group Psychotherapy, 7,* 131–154.

Smith, B. (1973). On self-actualization: A transambivalent examination of a focal theme in Maslow's psychology. *Journal of Humanistic Psychology, 13,* 17-33.

Snider, M. (1992). *Process family therapy: An eclectic approach to family therapy.* Boston: Allyn & Bacon.

Suler, J. R. (1991). The T'ai Chi images: A Taoist model of psychotherapeutic change. *Psychologia, 34,* 18-27.

Szasz, T. S. (1961). *The myth of mental illness: Foundations of a theory of personal conduct.* New York: Harper & Row.

Tillich, P. (1952). *The courage to be.* New Haven, CT: Yale University Press.

Tillich, P. (1954). *Love, power, and justice.* New York: Oxford University Press.

Tillich, P. (1955). *The new being.* New York: Charles Scribner's Sons.

Travis, C. (1982). *Anger: The misunderstood emotion.* New York: Simon & Schuster.

Unger, R. (1990). Conflict management in group psychotherapy. *Small Group Research, 21,* 349-359.

Van De Riet, V., Korb, M. & Gorrell, J. (1980). *Gestalt therapy: An introduction.* New York: Pergamon Press.

Vander Kolk, C. J. (1985). *Introduction to group counseling and psychotherapy.* Columbus, OH: Merrill.

Vaughan, F. (1986). *The inward arc: Healing and wholeness in psychotherapy and spirituality.* Boston: Shambhala/New Science Library.

Vaughan, F. (1991). Spiritual issues in psychotherapy. *Journal of Transpersonal Psychology, 23,* 105-119.

Watts, A. (1961). *Psychotherapy East and West.* New York: Pantheon Books.

Watzlawick, P. (1990). *Münchausen's pigtail, or psychotherapy and "reality."* New York: Norton.

Wilber, K. (1980). *The atman project.* Wheaton, IL: Quest.

Wilson, S. R. (1988). The "real self" controversy: Toward an integration of humanistic and interactionist theory. *Journal of Humanistic Psychology, 28,* 39-65.

Winnicott, D. W. (1958). *The maturational processes and the facilitating environment.* New York: International Universities Press.

Wolf, A. & Schwartz, E. K. (1962). *Psychoanalysis in groups.* New York: Grune & Stratton.

Wood, J. K. (1982). Person-centered group therapy. In G. M. Gazda (Ed.), *Basic approaches to group psychotherapy and group counseling* (3rd ed., pp. 235–275). Springfield, IL: Thomas.

Yablonsky, L. (1965). *Synanon: The tunnel back.* Baltimore, MD: Pelican Books.

Yalom, I. D. (1975). *The theory and practice of group psychotherapy* (2nd ed.). New York: Basic Books.

Yalom, I. D. (1980). *Existential psychotherapy.* New York: Basic Books.

Zimpfer, D. G. (1992). Group work with adult offenders: An overview. *Journal for Specialists in Group Work, 17,* 54–61.

Index

285; flexible, 151; forms of, 178; in gestalt with love and power, 183–186, 189; interpersonal, and personal boundaries, 175–177; as new organization, 182–183. *See also* Love, power, and justice

K

Kaplan, R. E., 134
Kapur, R., 269
Kitchener, K. S., 256
Knowledge, as goal, 85
Kohut, H., 80, 81, 82, 88, 160, 161, 165, 166, 217
Korb, M., 57–58, 65, 91, 92, 219
Korda, L. J., 34, 211, 213, 240, 254, 257, 265, 267
Kübler-Ross, E., 227, 228
Kwiatkowski, R. M., 269

L

Lakin, M., 262–265
Lao Tzu, 184
Larry, 35–36, 37
Leaders: ambivalence toward, 202–210; applications by, 267–272; aspects of self for, 273–274; and awareness, 125; care and respect by, 256–258; and communication, 4–5; construct of, 13; dual role relationships of, 259–260; ethical guidelines for, 255–258; frames of reference for, 272–274; and freedom, 133; and group atmosphere, 13–15; and group process, 192, 197, 199, 201, 202–210, 221, 224–225, 231; and justice, 183; and love, 163–164; and patterns of relationship, 12; and power, 173; and process goals, 28–29, 31, 33; and relationship dynamics, 23; responsibilities of, 8–9, 233–234, 237, 241–242, 243, 248, 252, 253–254, 259–260; roles of, 235, 263; and self-actualization theories, 74, 75, 76–78, 79, 85, 102, 107, 108; self-revelation

by, 225; supervision for, 266–267; transferring roles of, 238–239
Learning: from differences, 243–245, 278; experiential, 266–267; extension of new, 248–252; generalizing, 265; interpersonal, 55–59; as process goal, 27, 34, 45–46, 48–49, 55–59, 60–61, 63; about responsibility, 141–142
Leszcz, M., 29, 40, 42, 48, 102, 130, 155, 162, 170, 172, 175, 202, 269, 271
Lethbridge, D., 93
Letting go: as ontological process, 101; and responsibility, 142–143; and unfinished business, 162
Lewin, K., 45
Lewis, E., 77
Lewis, J. A., 101, 161
Lieberman, M. A., 262–265
Love: aspects of, 152–167; barriers to, 154–155, 156; construct of, 152; distorted, 162–164; forms of, 155–162; in gestalt with power and justice, 17, 22, 183–186, 189; in group process, 153–155, 203, 222; and healing, 160–161; power related to, 150–151, 165–167, 173, 175, 207–208, 217–218; and present-oriented concerns, 164–165
Love, power, and justice: in disharmony, 6–7; as gestalt, 17, 22, 183–186, 189; as ontological categories, 6–7; as patterns, 12, 25

M

McClure, B. A., 18, 103, 108, 109, 110, 146, 154, 155, 170, 174, 195, 202, 219, 246
McIlduff, E., 277, 278
Maddi, S. R., 120
Mahler, M., 78
Mahoney, M. J., 183, 220
Mary, 121, 156
Maslow, A. H., 10, 16, 65, 67, 82,